AF662267

Code Dependent

Code Dependent

Living in the Shadow of AI

MADHUMITA MURGIA

PICADOR INDIA

First published in the United Kingdom 2024 by Picador
First published in India 2024 by Picador India
an imprint of Pan Macmillan Publishing India Private Limited
707 Kailash Building
26 K. G. Marg, New Delhi 110001
www.panmacmillan.co.in

Pan Macmillan, The Smithson, 6 Briset Street, Farringdon, London EC1M 5NR
Associated companies throughout the world
www.panmacmillan.com

ISBN 978-81-19300-80-8

Copyright © Madhumita Murgia 2024

The views expressed in this book are the author's own and the facts reported by her have been verified by the publisher to the extent possible. The publisher hereby disclaims any liability to any party for loss, damages or disruptions caused by the same.

All rights reserved. No part of this publication may be reproduced, stored in or introduced into a retrieval system, or transmitted, in any form, or by any means (electronic, mechanical, photocopying, recording or otherwise) without the prior written permission of the publisher. Any person who does any unauthorized act in relation to this publication may be liable to criminal prosecution and civil claims for damages.

3 5 7 9 8 6 4 2

This book is sold subject to the condition that it shall not, by way of trade or otherwise, be lent, re-sold, hired out, or otherwise circulated without the publisher's prior consent in any form of binding or cover other than that in which it is published and without a similar condition including this condition being imposed on the subsequent purchaser.

Typeset by Palimpsest Book Production Ltd, Falkirk, Stirlingshire
Printed and bound in India by Gopsons Papers Pvt. Ltd., Noida

FSC www.fsc.org
MIX
Paper | Supporting responsible forestry
FSC® C116313

For Maya & Meera

Contents

Introduction

Just over a decade ago, as I was starting out in journalism, I became curious about a harmless-sounding digital object known as a 'cookie'.

I thought I knew what it was. A piece of code on my device that worked as a tagging mechanism for internet companies to identify me and learn more about my online behaviour. These cookies kept popping up every time I visited any website on my phone or computer, asking for my permission to start a digital trail of crumbs. So I decided to find out where they led.

Reporting that story for *Wired* magazine[1] took me down a dizzying series of rabbit holes that I am yet to emerge from fully. It revealed the murky world of 'data brokers' – shadowy companies that collect data about our online lives and turn them into saleable profiles of who we are today, and who we will one day become. And eventually, it took me beyond the brokers, deep into the business models of the world's most valuable companies, grouped loosely together as Big Tech, who made their money in the same way: by converting our lives into swarming clouds of data for sale.

But before I followed that trail, I wasn't convinced I wanted to spend several months writing about a bunch of statistics. I needed to make the story feel tangible to me. What did all that data actually look like? So I tracked down the profile of someone I was intimately familiar with. Myself.

To do this, I found a small adtech start-up called Eyeota, which walked me step-by-step through how I could pull the information being collected about me from my own web browser and then decoded it for me.

The afternoon that Eyeota sent me the full report of an 'anonymized' version of me, I was on a train to Brighton. It included a report that ran to more than a dozen pages compiled by Experian, a credit-rating agency that doubled as a data broker.

Experian had categorized me as a 'Bright Young Thing', one of sixty-four profiles that it had available at the time – a category of young professionals living in urban flats.

The profile described a twenty-six-year-old British Asian woman working in media and living in a north-west neighbourhood in London. It detailed her TV-watching habits (on-demand rather than cable), food preferences (Thai and Mexican), her evening and weekend plans. It even broke down her spending in detail – on restaurants and travel, rather than on furniture or cars.

The data Eyeota sent listed the number of holidays this woman had taken in the past year and indicated an imminent flight purchase. It suggested that she didn't have any children or a mortgage, and that she usually buys her groceries at Sainsbury's, but only because it's on her way home. It predicted she had a cleaner who let herself in while she was at work.

Beyond her day-to-day activities, a little section at the end outlined her 'liberal opinions' – including her level of ambition, political leanings and personality traits (optimistic, ambitious, not easily swayed by others' views).

I remember the feeling of shock and I spent an hour mulling over this set of characteristics that came pretty close to defining me as a person. Of course, that data cloud wasn't a true representation of reality – it had missed out much of the nuance that made me, me – but through a pattern picked out of my online data, the cookies had created an approximation, a shadow of me that was somehow recognizable.

The story, which was published in *Wired* in 2014, revealed a multi-billion-pound industry of companies that collect, package, and sell detailed profiles like the one I had found, based on our online and offline behaviours. The discovery revealed to me a lucrative business model that profited off all our digital behaviours.

I started to unpick the structure of this flourishing data economy. Every time I interacted with an online product – say Google Maps, Uber, Instagram, or contactless credit cards – with a single click, my behaviour was logged by these little cookies. Combined with public information such as my council tax or voter records, along with my online shopping habits and real-time location information, these benign datasets could reveal a lot about me, from my gender and age, down to nuances about my personality and my future decision-making.

My life – and yours – is being converted into such a data package that is then sold on. Ultimately, we are the products.

This glimpse, ten years ago, into the nascent world of data scraping sowed in me a seed of fascination about all the data we were generating by simply living in the modern world – and what was being done with it.

I've spent the rest of my career chronicling the fortunes, both financial and otherwise, of the companies built on top of these data dumps: corporate giants like Google, Meta and Amazon, who have refined the gushing data reserves pouring into their platforms, generated by billions of people around the world. To make their money, these companies had learned to mine the data, and use it to sell personalized and targeted recommendations, content, and products.

The heir to the big data business is a single technology that I first learned about in 2014: artificial intelligence. The term has morphed and mutated over recent years, but essentially AI is a complex statistical software applied to finding patterns in large sets of real-world data.

The technology's dramatic progress over the last few years has been contingent on three things: the explosion of available data on human behaviour and creativity, the increasingly powerful chips needed to crunch this data, and the consolidated power of a few large technology companies that could dedicate the considerable resources required to supercharge its development.

Tech giants like Google and Meta have applied machine learning to target advertising as narrowly as possible and grow their worth up to $1tn. This lucrative business model that monetizes personal data is what American social psychologist and philosopher Shoshana Zuboff has called 'surveillance capitalism'.

As the artist James Bridle wrote in an essay last year, 'These companies made their money by inserting themselves into every aspect of everyday life, including the most personal and creative areas of our lives: our secret passions, our private conversations, our likenesses and our dreams.'[2]

*

Nowadays, we live daily alongside automated systems built on data, their inner workings dictating our personal bonds, power dynamics at work, and our relationship with the state. We lean on algorithmic technology just as we once did on each other, and our ways of life – globally – are shifting to accommodate them.

When you open Google Maps to plot a route for your holiday run, call out to Alexa, book an Uber or a self-driving Waymo, you are dealing with a form of AI. The content on your social feeds and the ads you are served for golfing holidays or children's clothing are targeted at you using AI. When you try to get a loan from a bank, you are screened by AI. What price you pay for your home, or your car insurance, are decided by AI. When you are interviewing for a job, your face and responses may be analysed by AI. Maybe you even used AI to *write* your job application. And if you ever end up in the criminal justice system, your fate – bail or jail – could be determined by AI.

The outputs of AI software today can help human experts make consequential decisions in areas such as medical diagnoses, public welfare, mortgage and loan requests, hiring and firing, among others. Cutting-edge AI software is even used by researchers, such as chemists, biologists, geneticists and others, to speed up the scientific discovery process.[3]

Over the past year, we have seen the rise of a new subset of AI technology: generative AI, or software that can write, create images, audio or video in a way that is largely indistinguishable from human output. Generative AI is built on the bedrock of human creativity, trained on digitized books, newspapers, blogs, photographs, artworks, music, YouTube videos, Reddit posts, Flickr images and the entire swell of the English-speaking internet. It ingests this knowledge and is able to generate its own bastardized versions of creative products, delighting us with this humanlike ability to remix and regurgitate.

For many of us today, this is embodied in ChatGPT, a website that can respond with detailed answers to conversational queries – our first *direct* interaction with an AI system, made more magical by the fact that it can 'talk' back to us using our own method of communication: written language.

This has marked a profound shift in our relationship with machines. As the new generation of AI can articulate using words and visuals and is trained on our own academic and creative outputs, it can easily manipulate our moods and our emotions, and persuade us what to think and how to behave, in a more powerful way than ever before.

I had already seen AI insidiously enter our lives over the past decade, and when I set out to write this book, I wanted to find real-world encounters with AI that clearly showed the consequences of our dependence on automated systems. Now, the rise of generative AI systems has made this need obvious and urgent. Over the past year, we have begun to see, already, the early human impact of technologies like ChatGPT: on our work, on children's education and on creativity. But AI is simultaneously affecting other, significant areas of our society: healthcare, policing, public welfare and military warfare, creating rippling consequences and lasting social change. It is altering the very experience of being human. That's what this book is about.

*

My job at *Wired* magazine served to turn me into an inveterate techno-optimist. When writing daily about DNA editing, flying cars, 3D-printed Moon bases and brain–machine interfaces, it is impossible *not* to be amazed by the ingenuity of humanity and our high-tech creations. I was also captivated by the innovators themselves: mad-cap inventors, brash entrepreneurs and irrational dreamers.

So, when I began researching this book, I expected to uncover stories of how artificial intelligence had solved gnarly problems, taken on insurmountable challenges and dramatically improved people's lives. This was the promise of *all* new technologies, something I learned to believe in many years ago.

Each of these stories could be yours. AI systems will impact your health, your work, your finances, your kids, your parents, your public services and your human rights, if they haven't already.

I wanted to ask the small, human questions. What does it feel like to 'talk' to a black-box system? Do you get a choice between human or machine? How do you appeal a life-altering decision made by an app? What would you need to know to be able to trust it? How would you know when *not* to trust it?

To find answers, I went on a journey around the world, observing how ubiquitous automated systems are shaping the ways of life for different communities. Each of the lives you will encounter charts the unintended consequences of AI on an individual's self-worth, on families, communities, and our wider cultures. Through their experiences, I hope to answer the question I started out with: how is artificial intelligence changing what it means to be human?

*

Despite my innate optimism about technology, the mosaic of stories I had found told a different, darker tale.

I had made a deliberate choice to focus on people living outside of Silicon Valley, far from the nexus of technological power, yet subject to the consequences of this new group of technologies. But as I uncovered them one by one, it became impossible to avoid the elephant in the room: that the power is concentrated in the hands of a few companies, who hold all the cards.[4]

Exploring this imbalance led me to sociologists Nick Couldry and Ulises Mejias via their book *The Costs of Connection* and their big idea: data colonialism. The land grab they refer to is human lives converted into continuous streams of data. And through this never-ending stream, they see historical continuities with colonialism, where the inequalities of the past keep growing and, ultimately, the datafication of society is nothing but a new form of plunder and oppression.

Couldry points at gig work – app workers for places like Uber, Deliveroo or DoorDash – whose livelihoods and lives are governed by algorithms that determine job allocation, wages and firing, among other things. 'It's a tyranny,' he told me. 'There are moral questions here about what limits we must have to make lives liveable. This is where solidarity between people around the world is important.

There are common struggles between workers in Brazil, in India, in China, in the US – it might not seem urgent in San Francisco right now, but it soon will be.'

For me, this framing was a revelation. Slowly, the connections between the individuals in this book began to crystallize, like a Polaroid photo appearing in bright contrast from a swirl of hazy shapes. It dawned on me that the framework linking the algorithmic encounters I had gathered, spanning seemingly disconnected people, times and places, was actually predictable, and had been conceptualized by a small but growing community of academics around the world. Some names proposing the early roots of these ideas I recognized – Timnit Gebru, Joy Buolamwini, Kate Crawford, Cathy O'Neill, Meredith Whittaker, Virginia Eubanks[5] and Safiya Umoja Noble.[6] They were all, I noted, women, and their areas of expertise were in studying the disproportionate harms of AI experienced by marginalized communities.

As I read their work and followed the trail of academic papers they cited, I discovered a wider pool of authors that were lesser known to the mainstream. These researchers were mostly women of colour from outside the English-speaking West, ranging from Mexico's Paola Ricaurte,[7] to Ethiopian researcher Abeba Birhane, India's Urvashi Aneja, and Latin American researchers Milagros Miceli and Paz Pena. These women had witnessed first-hand what discrimination and social inequity in their communities looked like, and many were inhabitants of the very places highlighted in this book.

Time and again, their work drew the same conclusions that Couldry and Mejias's data colonialism theory had. Scalable systems like machine learning are built to benefit large groups, but tend to work well at the expense of some. The 'some' are usually individuals and communities that are already othered, floating in society's blurry edges, fighting to be seen and heard. In the lives of the people in this book alone, I could see how AI systems had harmful effects on women, black and brown people, migrants and refugees, religious minorities, the poor and the disabled, to name a few.

Human beings, and the endless lines of code we live by, are co-dependent. Our blindness to how AI systems work means we can't properly comprehend when they go wrong or inflict harm – particularly on vulnerable people. And conversely, without knowledge of our nature, ethical preferences, history and humanity, AI systems cannot truly help us all.

*

The power of machine-learning models is that they make statistical connections that are often invisible to humans. Their decisions and methods are not determined by the people who build them, which is why they are described as black boxes. This makes them supposedly far more objective than their human counterparts, but their reasoning can be opaque and non-intuitive – even to their creators.

For instance, researchers developing Covid-19 diagnostic algorithms used a corpus of pneumonia chest X-rays as a control group, which happened to belong to children aged one to five. This resulted in their models erroneously learning to distinguish children from adults, rather than Covid from pneumonia patients.[8] These systems are mysterious entities with unknowable cognitive patterns.

Aside from being technically opaque, people whose lives are impacted by automated systems are rarely aware of it. The way in which algorithms have been introduced into society has caused an erosion of our individual feelings of autonomy, but also a diminishing of the power and agency of those we trust as experts – transfiguring our society.

If individuals are aware of an algorithm making decisions that affect them, they are usually locked out of the system's workings, by institutions and companies. We're all stuck in an endless loop of 'computer says no'.

Losing our sense of autonomy and control means it is harder to take responsibility for our own actions. It becomes harder to legally assign blame or judgement to individuals or corporations, who can place responsibility on AI software. After all, a machine can't yet be put on trial.

In the 1980s, Stanford psychologist Albert Bandura described agency – that feeling of control over our actions and their consequences – as intrinsic to human nature and, ultimately, to our evolution as a species. Humans, he said, were *contributors* to their life circumstances and society, not just a product of them.[9]

Bandura outlined how people exercised their influence in three distinct ways: as individuals, through proxies and as a collective. Proxy agents are generally people with expertise or resources – like doctors, law enforcement officers or elected representatives – that we choose to speak for us, and collectives pool their knowledge and power to shape a better future for everyone.

Philosophers believe that ultimately a person's freedom is threaded inextricably with the quality of their agency – their ability to perceive their actions and desires as their own, and to feel able to create change. In small and large ways, AI systems are impinging on this, creating a feeling of individual disempowerment – even a sense of loss of our free will.

This is our predicament as a society: the ways in which AI, and other statistical algorithms, are governed over the coming years will profoundly impact us all. Yet we lack the tools to interrogate that change. We don't fully comprehend their impacts. We cannot decide what morals we want to encode in these systems. We disagree on the controls we may want to impose on AI software. We are collectively relinquishing our moral authority to machines.

But while people are feeling robbed of their individual ability to direct their own actions and attention, AI systems have led, unexpectedly, to a strengthening of *collective* agency. Ironically, the intrinsic qualities of automated systems – their opaqueness, inflexibility, constantly changing and unregulated nature – are galvanising people to band together and fight back, to reclaim their humanity.

By reflecting on the march of AI, we can start to address the imbalances in power, and move toward redress. My hope is that the experiences of the people in this book will rouse us from our fears, to take back our agency and self-respect. My chosen subjects, on the surface, had nothing in common: a doctor in rural India, a food delivery worker in Pittsburgh, an African American engineer, an Iraqi refugee in Sofia, a British poet, an Argentinian bureaucrat, a single mother in Amsterdam, a Chinese activist in exile and a priest in Rome. But as I tugged on those individual threads, they formed a coherent design. And you are in the centre of it.

CHAPTER 1
Your Livelihood

Going Places

On a September morning, the kind of equatorial summer day where the air is thick with the threat of rain and your clothes stick to your skin by nine o'clock, Ian Koli is waiting for me outside Connie's Coffee Corner, a busy cafe in the Kibera neighbourhood of Nairobi, Kenya. As I introduce myself, we are joined by Ian's friend and former co-worker Benjamin Ngito, who is loping towards us with an arm outstretched in greeting.

Ian and Benja know each other from their time working together at Sama, a US non-profit that outsources digital work to East Africa. Benja, who wears a two-day-old beard and a faded Superdry T-shirt, tells me he started his journey with Sama right here where we are standing, by Connie's. Back in 2008, Sama's local recruitment team promised him a fee if he could sign up twenty young locals for IT training at an internet cafe next to Connie's. He only managed to find nineteen volunteers. 'So I signed up. I had no choice,' he said. 'I needed that cash.' He ended up working at the company for five years.

Ten years later, when Ian heard about a potential job, he thought it might involve admin or cleaning, and was surprised when his friend said it was artificial intelligence. 'I had no idea what AI meant,' he says. He'd never had an office job, let alone one in technology, having spent his teenage years working a series of informal jobs – cleaner, bricklayer, grassroots political organizer. When he couldn't find work, he took small change from local politicians to instigate neighbourhood 'chaos' around election time, things like barricading roads, burning tyres or throwing stones at police. 'In the ghetto here, it's hand-to-mouth, you get paid cash and put it in food,' he says.

Ian knew, from talking to Benja, and other friends, that working for Sama had changed their lives. Maybe, he thought, it could change his too and he would be able to move out of the place he was sharing with six other young men, and perhaps even save for the future. So he signed up to work for Sama and has worked there ever since.

When we'd met virtually during the coronavirus lockdown two years ago to talk about Sama and his work, Ian had been a skinny kid with a shy smile and a scraggly moustache. Today, he is walking us to his new home which he shares with his wife and four-month-old baby in the heart of Kibera. 'Things are different,' he says.

The neighbourhood of Kibera in central Nairobi is an informal settlement, or a slum, one of the largest in Africa that houses some of the country's poorest families. This undercity of a million people is constantly moving, a flowing stream of camaraderie, haggling and humanity. We bob along like paper boats on its currents. Ruts and ditches are paths to be used, not dodged. On these narrow paths, pedestrians must defer to *boda-bodas*, or motorcycle taxis, imperiously honking vans, and kids kicking footballs. Butcheries and barbershops vie for space with women's hair salons and chicken shops. They all advertise M-PESA services, the African digital wallet that is ubiquitous here. A pungent scent of slick garbage, heat and humans sits heavily in the still air.

Kibera is a complex, amorphous organism with its own villages, tribes and social classes. There's an unspoken hierarchy here. Up the hill from where we are, in *Laini Saba*, crime is rife and houses are made of mud or canvas sheets, six or seven people to a single dwelling. But down here in the mini-village of *Gatwikira*, you can have your own shack that you share with maybe one or two others, made of sheet iron or eventually brick walls, and you can walk the streets in daylight without fear.

Kiberans live to survive, Ian tells me, fighting over the meagre amounts of water, electricity and jobs they are forced to share. But what unites them is a fierce loyalty to their neighbours and a collective mistrust of the state. Disputes are settled by local leaders, known as elders. They call the politician who's been in charge here for twenty years 'Baba', Father.

I've never been to Nairobi before, but I grew up in Mumbai. And somehow this place – its entrepreneurialism, its everyday sorrows and big-hearted joys – reminds me of the home I've left behind.

As we arrive at Ian's place, he jerks his thumb upwards at some wooden stairs. 'First floor,' he smiles. The elevation, a rarity in these parts, is a matter of pride. We ascend and duck through a narrow makeshift tunnel flanked by shacks, a boulevard of broken roofs. It smells of fresh soap. The residents outside, all women, are focused on the task of hanging up piles of dripping, clean washing. Some have infants tied to their backs. They nod in greeting.

Ian leads me to the last home on the left. A single naked bulb lights the neat space. Kibera's soundtrack of hip-hop is muffled and faraway in here. A whirring desk fan roars in the sudden quiet. 'My home,' Ian says. 'Karibu sana.' *You're very welcome.*

Every square inch of Ian's home is perfectly utilized. The room comfortably fits a couch, two chairs, an upturned wooden crate that acts as a desk, and a large bed in the corner, curtained in patterned paisley for privacy. Along one wall, a dozen pairs of Ian's trainers are displayed in pigeon-hole shelving, with baseball caps hung neatly underneath. At the foot of the bed, hidden from view, is a stove where the family cooks their meals.

The laptop sits on an elevated shelf next to the large TV, a deity of sorts. Netflix is loaded up, mutely cycling through ads for a series of Hollywood and Bollywood films and series. In late 2020, Sama teamed up with local telecoms providers to lay fibre broadband in large swathes of Kibera and elsewhere in the city to allow its agents to work from their homes during the pandemic. Ian was one of the workers whose homes went online, so he suddenly became popular amongst his neighbours.

'This is my mobile office,' he says. 'I wake up here, work through the day, finish up, then I have time to go to school. I want to learn to code.' Last year, Ian won a scholarship from Sama to attend college, where he is now studying for a bachelor's degree in IT.

Ian's job at Sama is to perform data annotation: he helps to train artificial intelligence software made by global corporations, by creating detailed labels for the datasets used to train them.

Ian works primarily on image-tagging for driverless cars. The computers inside these cars, developed by the likes of Volkswagen, BMW, Tesla, Google, Uber and others, need to know how to read a road – street signs, pedestrians, trees, road markings and traffic lights – so they can control the car's driving functions. Ian usually receives driver's-view clips of cars driving down anonymous roads, a bit like a hazard perception test for learners. The accompanying instructions ask him to tag every single object he can see by drawing bounding boxes around them; he draws little rectangles around all visible objects in the footage – vehicles, people, animals, trees, street lights, zebra crossings, bins, houses, even the sky and clouds.

The tasks remind me of the endless hours of 'I Spy' I play with my toddlers while on the move, with their little voices calling out triumphantly, 'fence', 'gate', 'girl', 'puppy', 'truck', as we drive or walk or ride. An hour of video might take Ian eight solid hours to annotate with labels.

While the work can seem repetitive, mindless even, Ian doesn't mind it. 'I found it interesting because I learned a lot about traffic rules and signs,' he told me, knowledge he tucked away for the day he could drive a car. He'd also labelled the inside of homes, and various joints of the human skeleton. He didn't need to know the names of the joints, he explained – just to mark them visually on an image.

As a kid, Ian loved playing with wires and electronics and had dreamt of being an electrical engineer. When he left high school, he'd had to support his mother and sisters and hadn't had the money to go to college. 'Now I wanna be a developer. When I joined Sama, I was imagining that these things that we are doing here, it is a stepping stone to Tesla, the company, or the Tesla technology itself.'

The mention of Tesla tickles Benja. 'I saw that guy, Elon Musk, on TV. I said hey, that guy, I'm building his car!'

Ian wants to eventually start his own business, a dream of many Nairobi locals I meet both within and outside Kibera. 'You know, causing chaos on the streets, that was the order of the day,' he says. 'You pick it up from your brothers and sisters. But after you have something that keeps you busy, your mindset changes, you cease to think like an ordinary ghetto boy, like an ordinary Kiberan, you think outside the box.'

Benja, too, was a rabble-rouser for hire, paid by local politicians to throw stones at the police. Now, he has just started his own walking tour company. But he also runs a chicken shop, leads a youth political activist organization and is opening a bar. He's dabbled in selling water and electricity, lucrative businesses controlled by powerful cartels in Kibera. In his spare time, he's a youth leader in Lindi, one of Kibera's villages, where he helps prepare kids for formal office-based jobs. 'I have been able to instil the Sama spirit and the culture into people that I meet in my area. And it goes on and on.'

Ian says he's brought friends into formal employment too. 'One guy, my school friend, was into pickpocketing, each and every day he was involved in these crimes,' he says. 'When he got the link from me, he joined Sama, he reformed drastically. If I tell you this was the guy, you won't imagine it, you'll say I'm lying.'

The mention of crime chastens Benja. He looks at Ian. 'I wanna move out of Kibera by next year. And I want you to move too.'

'It is in my plan, in three years coming, I should be out of Kibera,' Ian says.

'But then you have to speed it up.' Benja cautions him. 'You have a responsibility to leave. I always told you, hey, you don't even need to be a team leader at Sama. You can be anything you want in this world. Man, I *know* you're going places.'

*

As you drive down Mombasa Road, you trace the curves of Nairobi National Park, a wild oasis which makes Nairobi one of the only urban centres where you can spot giraffes alongside tall buildings while speeding down the expressway. Sama's primary facility is on this road, four floors of a building in a large commercial business park, housing more than 2,800 people. Outside, a towering sign announces Sama, with its tagline 'The Soul of AI'.

This building is all polished concrete floors and walls accented with corrugated iron. It is furnished in reclaimed wood and tin, with colourful hanging works of local art and potted plants. I'm told it's supposed to be reminiscent of the workers' homes in the informal settlements they come from. The designer, who consulted with early employees, wanted to use these familiar materials so that employees would think of the space as beautiful, and also as theirs.

Sama's building is aesthetic, but it is ultimately an office. Banks of agents, the name Sama gives to its workers, sit at computers, clicking and tracing shapes around images of all kinds. Room after room is filled with twenty-somethings, young women and men, clicking, drawing, tapping. It requires precision and focus, but is repetitive, a game of shape-sorting, word-labelling and button-clicking. For human beings, these tasks are largely easy, obvious even, although for AI systems they are novel and complex. The agents confer sometimes, but mostly focus on their own screens, a few seconds per image and onto the next. Hip-hop streams out of one corner. The mouse-clicks drum along with the beats. A team of agents is tagging cars driving on streets in China and Japan; others are tagging close-ups of maize plants, satellite imagery of European towns, logging trucks lifting wood, and women's clothing. Click, draw, tap.

An average work shift here starts around seven o'clock in the morning, lasting eight hours. Workers join Sama mostly from informal jobs like domestic cleaning, or selling chapatis on the street. Because of how the AI supply chain is broken down into bite-sized chunks, many of these workers have little, if any, visibility of the shape or commercial value of the final product they are helping to build. But they do know they are helping train software for some of the most advanced technological applications in navigation, social media, e-commerce and augmented reality.

For OpenAI, the creator of ChatGPT, Sama's workers were hired to categorize and label tens of thousands of toxic and graphic text snippets – including descriptions of child sexual abuse, murder, suicide and incest. Their work helped ChatGPT to recognize, block and filter questions of this nature.

The agents work in teams of around twenty, annotating data almost continuously through the day, bar two scheduled breaks for food and drink. Outside of these, they are allowed toilet breaks but are otherwise expected to be at their desks. Team leaders are more mobile, milling about between rows, and looking over shoulders. At the end of each line, quality-control analysts spot-check the agents' annotation work.

When it's time for their scheduled lunch break, the agents troop noisily downstairs to the cafeteria hall, past signs saying 'Silence please!' and join a snaking line for their food. Today, there's beef stew, with coriander rice, shredded cabbage in soy sauce, and *mukimo*, a Kenyan dish of mashed potato studded with greens. Slices of watermelon sweat in paper bowls. Everyone eats together.

I sit down to eat at a long table filled with chattering employees, including agents, team leaders and operations managers. Liliosa, a manager in her late thirties who assesses the company's impact on its agents' lives, is chatting about colonialism, the British royal family and Kenyan elections. She's writing a hip-hop musical about a Kenyan freedom fighter who rebelled against the British. 'Politics is our culture. And it's tribal, each tribe wants their own to lead,' she tells me. 'But the youth don't care anymore, they just want internet and jobs and money.'

After lunch, the cafeteria empties out rapidly, and I head back to the labelling floor. A young man is tapping through dozens of images of buildings around the world, Chinese pagodas and French apartments, marking whether they are historical or modern. For each image, he has to also click a series of boxes to describe the picture: moody, saturated, sharp or sepia. Click, click, click. He's currently hovering over an image of an ancient Japanese Buddhist temple in Tokyo, standing behind a telegraph tower. It's both, he decides, clicking on the option, a blend of history and modernity.

Each tap and click, I later discover, helps train algorithms that classify images for Material Bank, a platform for searching and ordering samples of architectural and design materials. The goal is to create an objective tool to pull out the most relevant information. It means when you search for a specific construction material or architectural style, the algorithm can serve you the perfect selection of examples you'll need.

How does he know if he's done it right? 'Sometimes, it's not clear,' he tells me. 'Then you just have to go with how you feel.'

The Ghost in the Machine

The pursuit of building intelligent, superhuman machines is nothing new. One Jewish folktale from the early 1900s describes the creation of a *golem*, an inanimate humanoid, imbued with life by Rabbi Loew in Prague, to protect the local Jews from anti-Semitic attacks. The story's consequences are predictable: the golem runs amok and is ultimately undone by its creator. This tale is resonant of Mary Shelley's *Frankenstein*, the modern-day tale that helped birth the science-fiction genre, and of the AI discourse in recent news cycles, which is growing ever more preoccupied with the dangers of rogue AI.

Today, real-world AI is less autonomous and more an assistive technology. Since about 2009, a boom in technical advancements has been fuelled by the voluminous data generated from our intensive use of connected devices and the internet, as well as the growing power of silicon chips. In particular, this has led to the rise of a subtype of AI known as machine learning, and its descendent deep learning, methods of teaching computer software to spot statistical correlations in enormous pools of data – be they words, images, code or numbers.

One way to spot patterns is to show AI models millions of labelled examples. This method requires humans to painstakingly label all this data so they can be analysed by computers. Without them, the algorithms that underpin self-driving cars or facial recognition remain blind. They cannot learn patterns.

The algorithms built in this way now augment or stand in for human judgement in areas as varied as medicine, criminal justice, social welfare and mortgage and loan decisions. Generative AI, the latest iteration of AI software, can create words, code and images. This has transformed them into creative assistants, helping teachers, financial advisers, lawyers, artists and programmers to co-create original works.

To build AI, Silicon Valley's most illustrious companies are fighting over the limited talent of computer scientists in their backyard, paying hundreds of thousands of dollars to a newly minted Ph.D. But to train and deploy them using real-world data, these same companies have turned to the likes of Sama, and their veritable armies of low-wage workers with basic digital literacy, but no stable employment.

Sama isn't the only service of its kind globally. Start-ups such as Scale AI, Appen, Hive Micro, iMerit and Mighty AI (now owned by Uber), and more traditional IT companies such as Accenture and Wipro are all part of this growing industry estimated to be worth $17bn by 2030.[1]

Because of the sheer volume of data that AI companies need to be labelled, most start-ups outsource their services to lower-income countries where hundreds of workers like Ian and Benja are paid to sift and interpret data that trains AI systems.

Displaced Syrian doctors train medical software that helps diagnose prostate cancer in Britain. Out-of-work college graduates in recession-hit Venezuela categorize fashion products for e-commerce sites.[2] Impoverished women in Kolkata's Metiabruz, a poor Muslim neighbourhood, have labelled voice clips for Amazon's Echo speaker.[3] Their work couches a badly kept secret about so-called artificial intelligence systems – that the technology does not 'learn' independently, and it needs humans, millions of them, to power it. Data workers are the invaluable human links in the global AI supply chain.

This workforce is largely fragmented, and made up of the most precarious workers in society: disadvantaged youth, women with dependents, minorities, migrants and refugees. The stated goal of AI companies and the outsourcers they work with is to include these communities in the digital revolution, giving them stable and ethical employment despite their precarity. Yet, as I came to discover, data workers are as precarious as factory workers, their labour is largely ghost work and they remain an undervalued bedrock of the AI industry.[4]

As this community emerges from the shadows, journalists and academics are beginning to understand how these globally dispersed workers impact our daily lives: the wildly popular content generated by AI chatbots like ChatGPT, the content we scroll through on TikTok, Instagram and YouTube, the items we browse when shopping online, the vehicles we drive, even the food we eat, it's all sorted, labelled and categorized with the help of data workers.

Milagros Miceli, an Argentinian researcher based in Berlin, studies the ethnography of data work in the developing world. When she started out, she couldn't find anything about the lived experience of AI labourers, nothing about who these people actually were and what their work was like. 'As a sociologist, I felt it was a big gap,' she says. 'There are few who are putting a face to those people: who are they and how do they do their jobs, what do their work practices involve? And what are the labour conditions that they are subject to?'

Miceli was right – it was hard to find a company that would allow me access to its data labourers with minimal interference. Secrecy is often written into their contracts in the form of non-disclosure agreements that forbid direct contact with clients and public disclosure of clients' names. This is usually imposed by clients rather than the outsourcing companies. For instance, Facebook-owner Meta, who is a client of Sama, asks workers to sign a non-disclosure agreement. Often, workers may not even know who their client is, what type of algorithmic system they are working on, or what their counterparts in other parts of the world are paid for the same job.

The arrangements of a company like Sama – low wages, secrecy, extraction of labour from vulnerable communities – is veered towards inequality. After all, this is ultimately affordable labour. Providing employment to minorities and slum youth may be empowering and uplifting to a point, but these workers are also comparatively inexpensive, with almost no relative bargaining power, leverage or resources to rebel.

Even the objective of data-labelling work felt extractive: it trains AI systems, which will eventually replace the very humans doing the training. But of the dozens of workers I spoke to over the course of two years, not one was aware of the implications of training their replacements, that they were being paid to hasten their own obsolescence.

'These people are so dependent on these jobs, that they become obedient to whatever the client says. They are prepared not to think about whether what they're doing makes sense, or is ethically questionable, but trained to think simply of what the client may want,' Miceli told me. AI development is a booming business, and companies in the data-labelling industry are competing to be as inexpensive as possible, providing labour to massive corporations and flush start-ups for a few pennies per task.

'It needs to be said – the technology industry is growing and benefiting from this cheap labour.'

Work Not Aid

I decided to put these concerns to Leila Janah, a woman who spent her career nurturing the data-labelling industry from its infancy. In 2018, Leila founded Sama as a non-profit whose goal was to give digital work to vulnerable people. 'The great false hope of Silicon

Valley is automation. But we're only pretending – it's actually humans behind it,' she told me back in 2019. She had recently been diagnosed with a rare form of cancer known as an epithelioid sarcoma, and she was putting all her entrepreneurial skills to work to fight it off.

Leila grew up in suburban Los Angeles, the daughter of Indian immigrants. The summer before her seventeenth birthday, she received a scholarship to teach English in Ghana, and she fell in love with the country, sparking a lifelong passion for the African continent. In 2019 she converted Sama into a for-profit social enterprise, or a B-corp, for which she raised nearly $15m of private funding, including from Meta, formerly known as Facebook. The relationship would later prove to be a complicated one.

Most of Sama's employees – roughly 3,000 of them – are youths from Kenya. It also operates in Uganda and India, where its workers are more educated, but equally impoverished, part of a global precariat. The company serves a who's who of corporate America – from Google, Facebook, Apple and Tesla, to Walmart, Nvidia, Ford and Microsoft. Benja, Ian and their colleagues have worked on Tesla's self-driving cars, Walmart's online product search, Apple's Face ID and Instagram's content filters. They even helped train AI chatbot ChatGPT, launched by OpenAI just over a year ago.

In 2022, the company said it had lifted more than 50,000 people in East Africa out of poverty through digital work – this number includes dependents of their employees and those they trained but didn't employ.[5] It has an office in Uganda's capital Kampala, but its second office in the country is in Gulu, a small town in the north of the country, ravaged for decades by the Lord's Resistance Army – a violent guerrilla group that recruited child soldiers. Sama is the town's largest employer of under-twenty-fives.

When she started her company in San Francisco in 2008, investors were critical of Leila's plans to outsource jobs cheaply in a recession-hit America. But Leila claimed her goal was not just to provide affordable services to clients – she wanted to make the population of ambitious, hungry youth in East Africa digitally literate and economically self-sufficient.

'We have a labour model that employs people as full-time workers with benefits, paid at a living wage,' said Janah, 'which I found equates to a monthly take-home wage of about $300, plus medical insurance. On average, we almost quadruple our workers' incomes when we hire them. We work with a population usually coming from informal settlements, rural villages, so the chance to have a job that pays well, gives you computer skills and exposes you to AI, it means people treat this very seriously.'

Sama says it also funds four scholarships every year for workers who want to continue their studies, and provides some seed funding for those who want to set up their own businesses.[6] The motto Janah constantly espoused was 'give work, not aid'. In Sama's Nairobi offices, employees wear 'Give Work' hoodies and T-shirts and everyone is encouraged to have a 'side hustle', a business idea that could, in turn, create new jobs. In a makeshift factory built in the middle of a field of rubble, a dozen women and girls sew footballs by hand – a business funded with a Sama grant. Employees have launched herbal beauty products, opened M-PESA or digital wallet shops, raised chickens for slaughter and founded girls' football clubs in the settlements they come from.

In early 2020, just before the coronavirus pandemic swept in, Leila died of epithelioid sarcoma, aged thirty-six. Her mission and the visible passion for the community of East African youth she had built up made me curious. Was Leila's idealized view of things close to reality? Did Sama workers like Ian and Benja feel truly empowered by the work? Were they able to demand change? The answers lay in Nairobi.

Flashy Cars and Tuk-Tuks

A few minutes from its data-labelling facility, Sama had a second building on Mombasa Road until 2023 – a squat, unassuming concrete block, purely devoted to its client Meta. The social media giant had contracted Sama to employ a few hundred content moderators to tag, categorize and remove illicit and distressing content from its platforms Facebook and Instagram, and simultaneously train the company's AI systems to do the same. Although I was given a whistle-stop tour of this space, I was not allowed onto the actual working floor due to Meta-mandated non-disclosure agreements that covered the toxic content these employees have to handle.

On the other side of the doors that I was not permitted to enter, young men and women watched bodies dismembered from drone attacks, child pornography, bestiality, necrophilia and suicides, filtering them out so that *we* don't have to. I later discovered that many of them had nightmares for months and years, some were on antidepressants, others had drifted away from their families, unable to bear being near their own children any longer.

A few months after my visit, a group of nearly 200 petitioners sued both Sama and its client Meta for alleged human rights violations and wrongful termination of their contracts.[7]

The case is one of the largest of its kind anywhere in the world, and one of three being pursued against Meta in Kenya. Together, they have potentially global implications for the employment conditions of a hidden army of tens of thousands of workers employed to perform outsourced digital work for large technology companies.

The content-moderation work was distinct from the labelling tasks that Ian, Benja and their colleagues had been doing. Sama's chief executive, Wendy Gonzalez, told me she believed content moderation was 'important work', but 'quite, quite challenging', adding that that type of work had only ever been 2 per cent of

Sama's business.[8] Sama was, at its heart, a data-labelling outfit, she said. In early 2023, as it faced multiple lawsuits, Sama exited the content-moderation business and this entire office was shut down.

The closure of the Meta content hub was sparked by Daniel Motaung, a twenty-seven-year-old employee of Sama who had worked in this very building. In early 2022, Daniel sued the company, as well as Meta, for wrongful dismissal and exploitation. The South African migrant's job was to manually screen Facebook content from across Sub-Saharan Africa, violence and hateful acts that scarred him for years to come.

When he arrived in Kenya from his hometown in the countryside outside Johannesburg, Daniel was optimistic about the new job. He thought it had something to do with marketing content, based on the vague job description. He'd been hired for his Zulu skills. But after working at Sama for a year, he was broken. For work that dealt with imagery of human sacrifice, beheadings, hate speech and child abuse, Daniel and his colleagues at Sama were reportedly paid about $2.20 (£1.80) per hour.[9] 'Public companies going to poor countries, or employing poor people anywhere, under the guise of upliftment and economic empowerment, can still be exploitation,' he said, in a phone conversation from his home. 'These companies are only interested in profit and not in the lives of the people whom they destroy.'

Although his job was to make judgements on graphic or illegal material, rather than label data like Ian and Benja, his work was also used to train algorithms – every decision he made was teaching Facebook's content-moderation AI systems how to distinguish between good and bad content on the platform.

According to Daniel, Facebook had designed its moderation system to time workers per task. All workers and their supervisors at Sama had quotas per day, and were not allowed breaks, except the timed lunch break and bathroom time. Employees would make up excuses to use the toilets just to stretch their legs. Meta and Sama have strenuously denied these claims, and they are currently being challenged by Daniel in Kenyan courts. He is suing them for being fired, allegedly for trying to unionize. Sama says it pays workers on par with teachers and nurses in Kenya, and that it supports unionization.

'When you are poor and hungry,' Daniel told me, 'you basically don't have a choice, and you don't have a voice if you are exploited. The only thing they did was to give people something to eat. That's it.'

The woman representing Daniel in court is Kenyan lawyer Mercy Mutemi, who is also representing the petitioners suing Meta and Sama for alleged workplace violations. Giving people work is not charity, she tells me. It's not enough to simply pay people. You may be lifting them out of poverty, while still disenfranchising them and treating them as 'pawns with no agency'.

'AI jobs, they are flashy cars, and everyone wants them,' she says. 'Replace that car with a tuk-tuk, because at the end of the day, a job is a job,' she tells me, over Nigerian beef stew, fried plantains and strong coffee. 'I see a lot of people willing to close their eyes to a lot of human rights violations and to demeaning people, because they're getting a skill in "AI".'

Mercy has an uncanny ability to peel away extraneous layers and grasp the heart of a matter. In her view, Sama's clients – Meta in particular – are simply going down the path of standard outsourcers. The data-labour industry is reproducing the same yawning chasms, the same inequalities that we have seen play out in traditional outsourcing businesses like fashion and IT. Yet, people see this work as unique, because of what she calls the 'illusion of AI'.

In particular, she points out, algorithm-training work, like teaching software to filter extreme social media content, was nothing new when you looked at the evolution of global capitalism. It was simply the next step along from Bangladeshi clothing factories, or flower farms in the Kenyan town of Naivasha, or even the cotton-picking estates in the United States. It's just that the consequences of AI on people's lives were being obscured by its shiny newness.

'It's the story of Gucci,' she says. 'And it's the story of Louis Vuitton. The factory worker just thinks, all I'm making is a shoe. They don't know their shoe is being sold for $3,000 in some store. This is the exact same thing.'

AI looks like a purely high-tech endeavour on the front-end, but she challenges the assertion that technical talent is sufficient for its development. If you look at the pipeline of AI development, 'you find factories, with people who 90 per cent of the time have no idea that the job they're doing has something to do with AI,' she tells me. 'You know why? Because AI is so disjointed. People can't see what they are building. And as long as you keep it disjointed like that, then these workers don't have a leg to stand on to advocate for themselves.'

The only way to fix the pay structure and to know whether data workers are being fairly remunerated at a global scale is to start to view them as part of the process, as part of the AI industry, she says. To benchmark their pay against workers doing similar jobs *inside* Western companies. To allow them to profit fairly from the sale of the final product. 'All revolutions are built on the backs of slaves. So if AI is the next industrial revolution, then those who are working in AI training and moderation, they are the slaves for this revolution.'

Hiba

In search of more perspectives from workers, I discovered a small Bulgarian start-up that also offered AI data-labelling services to multinationals, known as Humans in the Loop. Its workers were primarily refugees and migrants from the Middle East who had been displaced by political conflict and war.

Hiba Hatem Daoud lives in the thirteenth-floor tenement of a Brutalist apartment block in Sofia, which she shares with her three teenage children and husband Ghazwan. She's waiting for me downstairs, to welcome me to her home. Ghazwan, almost two decades older than Hiba, speaks a smattering of English and smiles a lot. He used to be an English teacher back in their hometown of Fallujah in Iraq, but he has forgotten it all since they left, he tells me apologetically in broken Bulgarian.

Laid out on their coffee table is a small feast that Hiba has spent the morning preparing: plates piled with flaky pistachio-filled baklava and neat rows of homemade *kaak*, a type of Middle Eastern pastry smothered in sesame seeds. To wash it down, there is black *chai*, with a generous spoon of full-cream Iraqi milk powder, to be drunk in colourful Turkish tumblers. A television blares an Arabic soap opera that no one is paying attention to. 'Sit down,' Hiba says. 'Make yourself at home.'

Hiba's day usually starts out this way, cooking for the family – 'Arabs eat a lot!' she says – getting her three kids prepped for the day, and doing household chores, until she receives a notification from work on her phone, as she does now. 'Yes', she taps, clicking through to a special website where the task awaits. The accompanying instructions are in English, as they usually are, which Hiba often uses Google to translate. Like always, the client has sent through some images of simple objects that she has to label. It takes her a few minutes to do and she shuts it down, satisfied.

Sitting in this very room, she has labelled satellite images of fields and oceans and towns, annotated road scenes, tagging pedestrians, traffic lights, zebra crossings and pavements; she's marked up the insides of homes and buildings, drawing polygons around rooms, kitchen, living room, bathroom, labelling each one by its name.

She's never quite figured out why the clients need these seemingly simple things done, like captioning a toddler's picture book, but she is loath to question it. The work is straightforward and flexible – and it sustains her family.

Hiba labels datasets to train AI software, like Ian and his friends in Nairobi. Like them, she is far removed from the final products being developed for billions of dollars by companies in the US and Western Europe, unable even to speak the language that clients send her tasks in. I ask if Hiba has views on artificial intelligence, or the impact of what she's helping to build. 'No, no, no,' she says, laughing at the idea. She just wants steady work, and beyond that, she isn't particularly interested in what it's for.

She has a vague notion that this all has something to do with '*almawarid albasharia*', an Arabic term. Pulling out her trusty Google Translate app, she tells me this means '*human resources*'. Yes, she and Ghazwan nod. That's what they do. They work as human resources.

'There, There Was War; Here, There Was No Work'

Hiba came to Bulgaria about a decade ago, after fleeing her home in Fallujah, a city in central Iraq, with her family. Ghazwan had been a well-paid schoolteacher, while Hiba raised the children in a spacious two-floor villa with a small yard. 'Look,' Hiba says, pulling out her phone. This was the kitchen, the guest room, the prayer room. 'So much space.' Their extended families had moved into their home when they left, but the house had been bombed several times since then. They had pictures of that too. Pockmarked walls and cratered ceilings.

Fallujah had always been a locus of resistance against the US-led forces that invaded Iraq in 2003. Over the next decade, it was torn apart by resistance fighters and local militia battling a parade of extremist and terrorist insurgents, who eventually took control of the city in 2014. 'Our life died,' Hiba tells me. 'We took what we could on our backs and left.' Their journey began on a bus to Turkey, and continued on foot for several hours, their children in their arms, until they finally crossed into Bulgaria on a warm morning in 2015.

Their first home in the new country was in Ovcha Kupel, a refugee camp on the fringes of Sofia. The Daouds spent eleven months there before being allowed to officially enter Europe, sharing a room in the low concrete block housing hundreds like them, drying their clothes like all their neighbours on hanging lines around the camp. Months after fruitlessly searching for employment in the city, Ghazwan entered into early retirement, and Hiba had to become the family's primary breadwinner for the first time in her life. 'There, there was war. But here, there was no work,' Hiba tells me. She began looking desperately for a job.

After two years of doing odd jobs, Hiba was referred by the Red Cross to an English language and IT course run by Humans in the Loop. The start-up's office was a converted two-room apartment in central Sofia, sparsely furnished with a few desks, and enlivened by hanging plants and printed photos of former students. Here, Hiba met others like herself, refugees from Iraq, Iran and Syria, who had ended up in Bulgaria, all trying to find jobs and learn English in these new strange surroundings. It was the first time Hiba had ever used a computer independently, or spent time in an office.

In this office, I met with Iva Gumnishka, the founder of Humans in the Loop. In 2017, she moved back home to Sofia as a twenty-one-year-old, freshly graduated from Columbia University in New York. At the time, Europe was in the throes of a refugee crisis and it was while volunteering at Ovcha Kupel that Iva realized that the best way to help the migrant and refugee families was to train them for digital work that they could do flexibly.

Iva set up Humans in the Loop as a dual entity – a foundation and for-profit company – much like what Leila Janah had done with Sama. The foundation would provide English language and IT classes to displaced families while the company would then employ them as freelance AI data workers. The workers at Iva's start-up are all displaced migrants, but the clients it serves are sophisticated Western technology companies, who usually choose data annotation services on the basis of most favourable costs. 'It's a race to the bottom,' she tells me, referring to the pressure to provide data annotation services as cheaply as possible. 'So it's a struggle to explain why our impact is an important part of the business.'

Since HITL's inception, Iva has built out an expanded network of partner organizations around the world to help match clients who need their algorithm data-labelled, with migrants, refugees and victims of war in need of work. Her company takes on annotators from unlikely hubs ranging from Kabul, Kyiv, and Damascus to Aleppo and Beirut, many of whom perform these jobs in the midst of live war zones. The workers she recruits in Sofia are mostly refugees and displaced people from the Middle East, all fleeing war. Her goal is to provide them steady work and skills they can ultimately put to use elsewhere.

At the end of the twelve-week course, Iva offered Hiba a job. She would require another week of training, but once she had got the hang of the tasks, she could work from home at times that fit her schedule as a working mother. She would be paid per task, and she didn't need fluent English to do it.

Hiba knew from her job search that most employers in Bulgaria required language skills, and that hers weren't good enough. They wanted her to work eight-hour days, but she couldn't leave her home and her children for that long. Ghazwan was supportive, but Hiba still had to cook and keep house and look after the family.

This job would allow her to be with her family and to earn a living. It sounded too good to be true.

That was when she was introduced to the term 'artificial intelligence'. Her job would be to train it. *Almawarid albasharia*, she had thought.

I've Got the Power

Hiba is sitting next to me on her couch, in her black leather jacket with bright lipstick and a matching headscarf, still sipping *chai*, when she hears the familiar chirp of Slack on her phone. She beckons me over to the corner desk and opens up her laptop. Ghazwan pulls up a chair for me next to her. Iva has joined us, acting as my translator.

For the past three years, Hiba has mainly worked for one client – a Canadian petroleum company designing algorithms that can estimate the purity of a crude oil sample. She loves the work, she tells me, in fact she can't live without it. It isn't so much the content, she says, but the fact that it is predictable, repetitive, brings in a monthly income and that the client is nice and easy to communicate with over Slack.

Intermittently throughout the day, the client sends her photos of test tubes filled with oil, and if she is free, she claims the image as hers. The image clicks open, and with a slender pianist's finger, she traces the meniscus – or surface level – of the petroleum in the test tube, later tagging any visible impurities or sediments in it. If she can't see it clearly enough in the photo, she toggles to look at the ultraviolet version which can be clearer. These labelled images are then used to teach the client's algorithms to do what Hiba is doing by eye: evaluate the quality of a sample of oil.

For each image she tags, Hiba is paid the equivalent of sixty cents. Depending on how much work is sent her way, she might get through thirty to fifty of these images in a day, but she makes a minimum of four euros per hour of work.

The structure and flexibility of the job appealed so much that Hiba brought Ghazwan into Humans in the Loop to work evenings, so they could double their income.

Their oldest son Abdullah picked up a few odd projects too. They use a shared laptop, and Hiba trained her family herself, at home. She says she has encouraged her youngest to train on the AI platform so she too can earn some pocket money for her own expenses – make-up, clothes, trips to the cinema. It has turned into a family enterprise, she says, and between them in total they earn anywhere from $600 to $1,200 a month.

They supplement their earnings from a nearby beauty salon that her son Abdullah helps to run. Hiba looks down at my unvarnished nails and invites me to have them done at the salon, for free, while I am in town. Their outgoings are roughly $1,600 a month so they just about make it work with the salon income. Every year, around the time of Eid, Hiba donates part of the income from her job to their local mosque, as a way to acknowledge the blessing and pay it forward.

But no job is perfect. I ask Hiba what she would want to change about this one. Iva wants to leave so she can speak freely, but Hiba asks her to stay. 'Anything I say, I can say in front of you,' she says, looking right at her. Hiba and Ghazwan acted as official witnesses when Iva married her husband, a Moroccan Muslim, in an Islamic ceremony. Iva is like family to them, Hiba tells me.

Overall, Hiba says she prefers the flexibility she has now, compared to a 9–5 job with predictable income. However, the question of power asymmetry *had* come up in recent months. While Hiba had been hired as a daytime worker, the company had previously never prescribed what hours people could work, so often she would clock on after dinner, when the kids were in bed, and label images late into the night when she had more free time.

However, as the start-up grew and took on more workers, the leadership team began to enforce a shift system. As a day-shift worker, Hiba therefore wasn't allowed to take on tasks at night, which were the responsibility of the newly recruited night-shift data labourers who were paid higher wages. The shift system was implemented by Tess Valbuena, the start-up's newly hired chief operations officer, to ensure there was enough work to go around.

Some of the workers were unhappy with these new rules, and two of them, including Hiba, contacted the Canadian petroleum company directly to complain. Hiba says she had brought it up with an employee on HITL's leadership team, but wasn't satisfied by their response. She hadn't wanted to bother Iva, and didn't know that she wasn't supposed to approach the client. Humans in the Loop claimed all their workers had been warned not to take internal matters to clients. As a result of Hiba's actions, the leadership team, with Iva's blessing, made an example out of her, punishing her by suspending her access to the platform for thirty days. I look across at Iva, who looks uncomfortable but acknowledges Hiba's story with an apologetic shrug.

Iva and her team banned Hiba from working for the whole of December, a busy and expensive time of year for the family. Meanwhile, Hiba still received notifications for new tasks on Slack, and she would watch them coming in, one by one, ping ping ping, unable to claim them. She felt powerless, frustrated and angry. She knew the money was there for the taking, but she wasn't allowed to touch it. The incident was a symbol of Hiba's vulnerability, the fragility of data workers like her, and their ultimate powerlessness in an industry driven by the world's richest and most ambitious companies. For Hiba's family, the loss of income turned into a big problem and she had to take out a loan from a friend to pay Abdullah's university fees. 'I really suffered through it,' she tells me.

I ask Iva whether she regrets what she did, and the impact it had on Hiba's family. This is part of the growing pains of a small company, she says, and she struggled with making the decisions to implement shifts and to punish her employees. She admits she hadn't considered the fact that it was December and concluded afterwards that a one-month ban had probably been too harsh in Hiba's case. I look to Hiba and Ghazwan for any rankling unease, but Ghazwan is chiding Hiba in Arabic, reminding her that Iva has already apologized to them. Hiba is unrepentant for bringing it up, but she does tell me the incident is water under the bridge. She has moved on.

So what, then, will Hiba do the next time she has a grievance? I ask.

'I just won't say anything,' she says, shrugging. 'I can't afford it.'

Ala

The next day, I am back at the Humans in the Loop office, and this time I recognize Hiba in a photo on the wall, her smiling face wrapped in a turquoise headscarf, standing with her graduating class. I am here to observe the workers' training session. I sit down next to forty-four-year-old worker Ala Shaker Mahmoud. Today's module includes a section on AI ethics – a new addition to the curriculum. The class is being introduced to concepts such as algorithm bias and transparency around informing end users of the use of AI systems.

Afterwards, as the watery winter sun struggles valiantly to push through a high window, I speak with Ala. Up until 2007, he had been a travelling beekeeper in Mosul, the ancient Assyrian city of northern Iraq, flanked by desert and mountains. In Ala's apiary of 150 beehives, he nurtured millions of bees who feasted on pale cotton blossoms, purple liquorice, thorns and heather that grew wild in the fields fed by the *Dijla*, the Tigris river, that flowed near his home. 'I had a caravan and I would drive around, delivering honey, and sleeping under the stars,' he said. 'When I returned from a trip, even if it was three o'clock in the morning, I would take out my little boat and go fishing.'

Ala brushes off his nostalgia impatiently. It was a good life, to be sure, but it had to end, he says. One night he fled Mosul, leaving his parents behind, as bombs rained down on his home. He ended up in Istanbul, where he paid a man to show him the way to the Bulgarian border, a nearly nine-hour overnight journey on foot. When he arrived at dawn, he was sent to Banya, a Bulgarian refugee camp, for just over four months, while he waited for his papers to come through. Eleven years later, he tells me he will never go home.

'Without peace, no human can live,' he says. 'I know I have lost many things in my country – my home, my job, my family, but here in Bulgaria I am safe. Here, I have found peace.'

Ala was one of the first employees at Humans in the Loop. The data labour he has done has been varied and he seems to find the tasks mildly amusing, rather than laborious or repetitive. He has labelled road scenes for self-driving car systems – a few minutes of video used to take him a whole day to label at first, he tells me – and different types of garbage on a conveyor belt for a waste-sorting algorithmic system. This involved drawing polygons around each object and labelling it – plastic, cardboard, paper, glass, metal.

He has worked on projects for car insurers, sugarcane producers and architects, all looking to use machine-learning algorithms to improve and augment their work. The sugarcane project involved tagging individual fibres of raw sugarcane fibre, or bagasse, as healthy or diseased, based on colour. During the Covid-19 pandemic, Ala labelled masks across a series of videos, to indicate who was wearing them correctly and who wasn't. He didn't know who the customer was, but 'that was an easy one', he said about the task, with a grin.

Ala is more aware of his part in the AI supply chain than Hiba was. Since he started working as a data labourer, Ala has been reading about artificial intelligence, and the role that data-labelling plays in its development. 'I see this technology as the foundation, the future for all the world,' he tells me. 'And . . . we need to be a part of this future.'

I ask if he has plans to move onto other jobs. No, he shakes his head vehemently, he will continue to work for Iva, and for Humans in the Loop, as long as they need him. He lives on his own and makes enough money from the work to get by. Plus he likes the flexibility; it allows him to pursue other hobbies.

Recently, he has returned to bee-rearing, buying a few hives from a farmer in the Vitosha mountains which gird the city of Sofia. He scrolls through his phone, through dozens of photos of bees, in search of something specific to show me. Finally, he holds the screen up to me. He has found what he was looking for, a picture of his queen with her delicate, elongated abdomen. 'Look,' he says. 'She is beautiful.'

I have never seen a queen bee up close before. Will he be able to get honey from these bees soon? He laughs, as if I have made a joke. Then, realising I am serious, he shakes his head. 'No, the bees here, they are not honeybees,' he says. 'They cannot make honey, because there are no trees, no flowers. Here, they can live, but they cannot make anything.'

'Just Close Enough, But Not Too Much'

Milagros Miceli, the Berlin-based researcher whom I'd been speaking to, had been studying the empowerment of workers and its impact on the products they trained. In 2021, she published a study alongside a collaborator, Julian Posada, analysing 200 different AI data-related tasks, such as image-labelling and facial recognition, performed by Venezuelan and Argentinian freelance workers for a range of Western companies.[10] They were curious about how working conditions impacted the quality of the algorithms themselves. Their hypothesis was that curtailing the agency of workers was not purely a human rights issue – it could also hamper the accuracy of the technology they were helping to build.

'For instance, all the instructions are given in English, even in Latin America where people rarely speak it,' Miceli told me. Like Hiba, most workers used Google Translate to approximate instructions in Spanish, their mother tongue. They used this method to describe and tag images. 'You can imagine the impact on a dataset labelled like that,' Miceli said.

She also found that workers were not empowered to speak up if instructions didn't make sense in their geographic context, or if they had ideas to improve an annotation task. 'You need to give them room to think. They are being threatened or removed from the task or banned from the platform if they don't obey, or dare to question. They have no direct channel to communicate with the task master if there is a problem . . . or [if] something doesn't make sense for Latinos, for example,' she said.

She was right – many workers I met were unaware of the industry they were a part of, and rarely had contact with the client whose algorithms they were training. The stark difference was brought home to me when I met a team of four data workers at Arbusta, an Argentinian company, who work primarily with Latin American clients such as e-commerce giant Mercado Libre. These workers, whom I met in their warehouse-turned-office in Buenos Aires on a sunny October afternoon, communicated directly with their client and shared a common language. They were invited to sit in on client meetings. They told me they felt valued and in control, which spurred them to participate actively in shaping Mercado Libre's AI systems. They experienced the AI supply chain much more personally compared to their peers at Sama or HITL.

But for most of the workers I met, cracks began to appear in the facade of their jobs over time. They all certainly felt a sense of independence and control in being able to choose how they worked, but they simultaneously admitted that freedom came at a financial cost. In Sofia and in Buenos Aires, the labourers I interviewed concurred that their income was not sufficient to support a family or household of more than one person. At least four workers I spoke to said they had to supplement their income through additional jobs or borrow money from family members just to keep up with their regular expenses, month after month.

I asked Iva Gumnishka how she had calculated wages and she told me that indexing payments for a global workforce in very different markets turned out to be one of her most challenging tasks as a young founder. She had started off planning to pay workers in Sofia higher wages than her freelancers in Syria or Afghanistan due to different local standards of living in those markets. But then she read some of the works of Eduardo Galeano, a Uruguayan poet and journalist who argued that wage differentials were at the core of global inequality. His writings chimed with her, and she felt it was unfair that data workers in poorer countries should receive less compensation for doing the same jobs. 'After all, the goal of digital work is to gain access to higher-paying markets and to be able to earn more money than what you would be able to earn locally,' she said. So, she pivoted to offering all her global workers the same rate of €4/hour, which is half of what her company charges the client, in an effort to be equitable. 'We decided that would be the fair thing to do, but what is fairness? It's all relative,' she said.

Meanwhile in Nairobi, the wages did go a lot further toward supporting individuals' basic needs, and also their wider family networks, such as parents and siblings. It helped alleviate daily pressures and provide financial stability. Many Sama data workers I spoke to said they were able to build up savings and pay for their child or siblings' schooling or their parents' healthcare. But despite working office jobs for clients as well-resourced as OpenAI, Tesla and Meta, the labourers remained precarious, merely one unlucky relationship or bout of illness away from being homeless again, or from being unable to pay for basic needs. One worker I spoke to, Susan, had earned enough to rent a house and support her child, but her ex-husband paid the school fees. When he suddenly stopped, Susan had to give up her house and move back into her parents' home, where we met.

Sama's late founder Leila told the BBC that she did not pay the same wages to her Kenyan employees as their US-based equivalents, because it could distort the local labour market in East Africa. Higher wages in Nairobi 'would throw everything off' with a potentially negative impact on the 'cost of housing, the cost of food in the communities in which our workers thrive.'[11]

Some sociologists and economists contradict this perspective, adding that a moderate rise in wages can change workers' lives but is unlikely to significantly distort local economies. 'The reason these workers in the global South are being paid so little is because of the legacies of violent imperialism that have structured the last two centuries,' said Callum Cant, a researcher of AI in the workplace at the Oxford Internet Institute. 'So now we have a duty as citizens of the global North to undo that relationship . . . we need to supersede what we've been able to achieve in the twentieth century, in terms of the fair distribution of the fruits of this technology.'

The obvious comparison – the one Mercy Mutemi had made – is to sweatshops and factories in the developing world, where workers make the West's garments, toys and electronics in difficult and often dangerous conditions, ranging from excessive hours and low pay to repetitive strain injuries, exposure to toxins and a general lack of safety.

I didn't agree unequivocally with the criticism, partially because the working conditions for data labellers I met weren't observably exploitative or unsafe – many I had spoken with worked from home. I had also seen first-hand how data-labelling jobs had transformed lives of families, helping individuals like Ian, Susan, Hiba and Ala and their communities emerge from poverty and precarity.

However, I had come to see that the existence of the jobs alone was not good enough. Data production and labelling were essential steps in the production of AI systems. Without clean datasets, there could be no artificial intelligence. Yet, I saw the emerging parallels of data labour with other outsourcers. All the data workers I met with were vulnerable: either transitory and unsettled, or struggling to make ends meet – they had essentially no bargaining power at all. When I asked how they felt about their work, most said they were grateful, particularly for the pay, the flexibility and access to basic digital skills. They talked about what the money could buy, but less about the impact of the work itself. When I asked them if they felt the terms of their employment were fair, they didn't even want to speculate. They were unwilling to analyse how it impacted their autonomy, or their sense of equality compared to other workers around the world. This in itself was a problem. I knew their reticence wasn't necessarily because they hadn't considered these questions, but perhaps because they knew that the cost of advocating for themselves might prove too high – like it had for their more outspoken colleagues.

If data workers exercised any agency or resistance – like Hiba, Daniel Motaung and the petitioners in Kenya had attempted to do in their workplaces – they were quickly and ruthlessly struck down. Facebook contractors all over the world, including Daniel, were bound to draconian NDAs, which muzzled and isolated them even from their loved ones. Data annotation jobs in the developing world provided new opportunities and a measure of stability, yet they treated workers as replaceable automatons, inferior to their peers in other countries around the world.

The companies I met with – Sama in Nairobi, HITL in Sofia and Arbusta in Buenos Aires – all claimed to want to help people out of poverty or difficult circumstances, and allow them to progress beyond one particular job. But ultimately they remained answerable to their clients. Sama and HITL had primarily Western customers, based outside of the countries in which data workers lived and worked, who were looking for the cheapest contractor rather than human cognitive input. Iva said she had to position HITL as a premium company in her marketing, emphasising its social mission, in order to push up the rates clients were willing to pay. Arbusta's clients tended to be from their local region and were far more open to communication with its workers, who consequently felt a much deeper sense of empowerment in their day-to-day work.

It became clear to me that improvement of the industry was necessary and urgent. Rules around more equitable pay and working conditions, and better middle management to give workers autonomy and voice, have to be strengthened before the AI industry entrenches itself into the mainstream consumer tech market, and the practices solidify.

As Miceli said, 'It's giving people a little bit of a chance, but not too much that they might revolt. Getting them just close enough, but not too much. You can see the colonialist roots in that.'

'Because I Can'

Back at Hiba's apartment in Sofia, we are finishing our baklava and talking about the future. She tells me that in Iraq, she had chosen to stay at home because they didn't need the money. Now that she's been forced to work, the experience has been eye-opening for her. She has felt alternately empowered and frustrated by the job, sometimes angered by her lack of control over it, but also grateful for the opportunities it has brought.

Hiba isn't content to simply continue doing what she is doing today, over and over, like a robot or a drone. At thirty-eight, she is financially independent and technologically literate for the first time in her life. Hiba has new dreams.

The previous September, she enrolled in a local university, she and her older son both beginning their undergraduate degrees together. It's expensive, about 10,000 Bulgarian leva, or over £4,000, a year. Hiba's face lights up as she talks about how much she loves her classes.

What made her choose to spend her hard-earned money on college fees, rather than on living more comfortably, or saving for a tangible asset like a home or a car? I ask. She thinks about it for a beat, and then says it is really down to human beings' desire for progress and evolution. 'I want to learn more, to know more.'

She has chosen to study biology. Why biology? She raises her eyebrows at me, as if it were obvious. 'Because I can.'

CHAPTER 2
Your Body

Helen

Helen Mort is intrigued by women like Hiba Hatem Daoud – she writes about their frailties and their strength, their power and powerlessness, their bodies and what they embody.

A poet, novelist and memoirist, Helen lives in Sheffield, a town bordered by the rocky hills and crags of the Peak District that she has loved to climb since she was a girl. She writes with dark humour and empathy about women, from radical mountaineer-mothers, to herself, as a child, an anxious adolescent, a climber and a new parent – and the efforts of balancing myriad identities. She dwells, too, on the physicality of female bodies, and how women are scrutinized.

'That word scrutiny, the feeling of being watched, is very interesting. Especially because those who identify as women tend to already have an element of internal surveillance that accompanies them,' she said when we first spoke on a spring afternoon in 2021.

Alongside her empathy for other women, Helen has always felt anxious about how she is perceived. In 2015 she deleted her Facebook account because it triggered her anxiety. 'It was the publicness of it,' she said. 'If I get too into social media, I get other people's comments and voices in my head. It's not particularly good for me, and I didn't like feeling like that.'

One morning in November 2020, in the midst of the Covid-19 pandemic, an acquaintance knocked on her door and asked if he might speak with her about something important. Helen panicked. 'I thought something terrible must have happened to my son at nursery,' she said.

That morning, thirty-six-year-old Helen had walked her toddler to nursery, and then fed the kitten Pippin. Her husband, an English professor, was working in their basement. She had made a cup of coffee and cleared away their toddler's toys. Then, finally, she'd sat down at her work table in the quiet, tidy living room and started a Zoom supervision call with one of her creative writing students at Manchester Metropolitan University.

The man at the door interrupted the call and asked to come inside, 'for the sake of privacy'. She was annoyed at the intrusion. Wrapping up the call, she asked him what he wanted. What he told her was completely unexpected. He had been browsing a pornography site and had come across disturbing and graphic photos of Helen.

Her first reaction was relief – no one was hurt or dead – and then that there must have been some mistake. She had never sent an intimate picture of herself to anybody. Those kinds of pictures of her just didn't exist. The acquaintance, visibly uncomfortable, explained that he was quite sure it was her and handed her a scrap of paper where he and his wife had written down the website and some information as to how Helen could access 'revenge porn' support – a helpline for those who had intimate images of themselves leaked online. He was embarrassed and couldn't look at her, but he was, Helen told me, obviously really trying to help in as human and humane a way as possible.

After he left she made herself go through the motions of the rest of the day. When she went to pick her son up from nursery, she felt a hot flush of shame redden her face. It was that same scrutiny she felt as a young woman, but this time heightened, burning. It felt as if all the parents at the gate were looking at her sideways, and everybody *knew*. She coiled up into herself. A year later, she wrote in an essay addressed to herself, 'Since the pictures, you have learned to retreat without moving a muscle.'

In the evening, Helen asked her husband to look at the website. She couldn't face it herself. When he found the image gallery, he gently told her it was her face, but he was quite sure it wasn't her body.

The perpetrator had used photos of Helen, scraped from her now-defunct Facebook and private Instagram accounts, including pictures of her as a teenager and during her pregnancy. They had then used digital editing tools to depict her as a victim of violent gang-rape. In a post under the photos, they had written: 'this is my girlfriend Helen, I want to see her humiliated, used and abused, and here are some ideas.'

It wasn't clear to Helen how her photos had been manipulated. She later learned these types of images were known as 'deepfakes', realistic pictures and videos generated using artificial intelligence technologies. 'They were all scenarios that made sex look like it might be non-consensual,' she told me. 'A lot of it was the person, with my face, being held down, restrained, or strangled in some way, by multiple men. The strangling one *I* could have believed was me, if I didn't know better.'

Beneath one image, in which the woman's legs were forced open by a tangle of male arms, a viewer had commented: 'this is wild.' It's the image Helen keeps returning to, the one she can't unsee.

The Rise of the Deepfake

The term 'deepfake' is relatively recent, coined in 2017 by a Reddit user referring to a newly developed AI technique for creating hyper-real fake images and videos, like a new-age Photoshop.[1] With this software, he announced, anyone could seamlessly merge porn actors' bodies with the faces of well-known celebrities. The results were completely falsified 'pornography', featuring women who had no knowledge or control over the creation of the images or their distribution.

The 'deepfake' creator was an unnamed software programmer with an interest in artificial intelligence, working on what he described as a 'research project'. He didn't see any ethical issues with the technology, he told a journalist from *Vice News*. If he hadn't demonstrated this, someone else would have. And there were no legal issues with it either. At the time, creating deepfake images wasn't illegal in most parts of the world, and neither was posting and distributing them, so there was no one to police use of the software.

Deepfakes are generated using 'deep' learning: a subset of artificial intelligence where algorithms perform tasks, such as image generation, by learning patterns in millions of training samples. The models learn to generate faces in a hierarchical way – they start by mapping individual image pixels, and then recognize higher-order structures, like the shape of a specific face or figure.

One of the algorithms that create deepfakes are Generative Adversarial Networks, or GANs. GANs work in pairs; one algorithm trains on images of the faces you want to replicate, and generates its own versions of them, while the other tries to tell if that image is real or synthetic. The algorithms lob images back and forth between them, with the false images being continuously fine-tuned to become ever more convincing, until the detective algorithm can no longer spot a fake. The technique can doctor faces or entire bodies into realistic-looking photos and videos – like the eerily lifelike deepfake Tom Cruise videos that went viral on TikTok in 2020.

GANs can generate high-quality images and videos exponentially faster and more cheaply than professional visual-effects studios, making it an attractive alternative in the entertainment industry. Film studios like Disney's Industrial Light and Magic, and VFX companies like Framestore are already exploring the use of deepfake algorithms to create hyper-real CGI content and synthetic versions of celebrities, alive and dead, for advertisements and films.

GANs are not the only tool available to make deepfakes, as new AI techniques have grown in sophistication. In the past two years, a new technology known as the transformer has spurred on advances in generative AI, software that can create entirely new images, text and videos simply from a typed description in plain English. AI art tools like Midjourney, Dall-E and ChatGPT that are built on these systems are now part of our everyday lexicon. They allow the glimmer of an idea, articulated in a few choice words, to take detailed visual form in a visceral way via simple apps and websites.

AI image tools are also being co-opted as weapons of misogyny. According to Sensity AI, one of the few research firms tracking deepfakes, in 2019, roughly 95 per cent of online deepfake videos were non-consensual pornography, almost *all* of which featured women.[2] The study's author, Henry Ajder told me that deepfakes had become so ubiquitous in the years since his study that writing a report like that now would be a near-impossible task. However, he said that indications from more recent research continue to show that the majority of deepfake targets are still women, who are hypersexualized by the technology.

Today, several years after the term deepfake was introduced, there is still little recourse for victims. In most parts of the world, AI-generated intimate imagery remains legal to create and to distribute. A handful of countries – the United Kingdom (whose law comes into effect in mid-2024), Singapore, South Korea, Australia and individual US states like California, New York and Virginia – have recently criminalized the non-consensual distribution of all intimate imagery, including deepfakes, but the creation of AI-generated images still falls outside the purview of most international laws. The only other option for victims is to request platforms to take down the content, using copyright claims. Social media platforms, and even some pornogaphy sites, promise to remove deepfakes and non-consensual imagery from their platforms under their terms of service, but in reality, they often don't.[3,4] Either they aren't proactively detecting this material, and if they are aware of it, they don't prioritize its removal. New legislation in the European Union that came into effect in 2023 obliges social platforms to demonstrate how people can request takedowns of illegal material and to action these requests, but this doesn't work if the material in question – such as deepfakes – isn't illegal in the first place.

AI is hardly the first digital technology adapted to harass and abuse marginalized groups on the internet. Like so many simpler image-based technologies before it, from hidden webcams to Photoshop and social media, deepfakes have been co-opted by armies of perverts and cowards to invade that most intimate of spaces, our bodies.

What makes AI image-manipulation so powerful is that the tools are easy and inexpensive to distribute widely, and can be wielded by amateurs. The results are hyper-realistic, compared to previous generations of technology, and spread quickly through under-policed social media channels that act as megaphones. And, of course, they can be used against victims without their knowledge, much less consent. The technology scales up the mass-scale production of harassment and abuse.

I did a quick Google search and discovered dozens of websites offering deepfake pornography, assuring me that all the videos were fully fake. Hundreds of videos abused the likenesses of real women, depicting them in realistic performances of sexual acts.

These videos featured mainstream celebrities from Hollywood, Bollywood and Korean pop, as well as non-public figures like Helen. On the site where Helen herself was featured, she was shocked to find an entire section devoted to those with no public persona, a market for female bodies, engendered by technology.

Deepfakes aren't unintended consequences of AI. They are tools *knowingly* twisted by individuals trying to cause harm. But their effects are magnified and entrenched by the technology's ease of use, and institutional callousness: a lack of state regulation and the unwillingness of large online platforms to be accountable for their spread. The stories of Helen Mort and the other women that I spoke to are symbolic of this; our collective indifference to their pain.

This Is Wild

In early 2022, I read a proof of *A Line Above the Sky*, Helen's forthcoming book about motherhood and mountaineering. Part memoir, part ode to nature, the book portrayed lucidly the core of Helen. In it, she exposed her own brittleness, her fragility, but also her ironclad sense of self. In the short passages she wrote about deepfakes, she reflected on that experience, of how it changed her sense of identity.

In the three years since that day in 2020, Helen has written a few pieces that have tried to recollect the intensity of the experience.

In an essay titled 'This Is Wild', Helen juxtaposed snippets of her deepfake encounter with an account of a transformative glacier expedition she undertook near Kulusuk, in south-eastern Greenland. In it, she drew parallels between the two experiences, the climb and the fall. She wrote to herself, 'These times you remember how a glacier deports itself. That it is upright, even as it shelves, even as it falls.'[5]

The first thing that she wrote in the immediate aftermath of the incident was a poem, 'Deepfake: A Pornographic Ekphrastic'. Writing it felt like the only thing she knew how to do in those months, liberating her from her intrusive thoughts, allowing her to reclaim her own mind, and to heal. It articulates the psychological impact in a way Helen still could not do in conversation:

These are the warped pixels of my face,
the features I'd learned to find commonplace,
I want to see her filled in every hole!
The eyes, which we call windows to the soul.

'There's no right thing to say in these situations,' she told me. 'My husband tried to make a joke of it. He said, "You'll laugh some of this off – it's so obvious that it's not you or your body." But it did matter to me. I remember thinking, I don't know how to be normal.'

Almost immediately, she'd asked the website to take the photos down, but they hadn't responded. They didn't bear any liability for the images, so had no reason to assist her. She also reported the images to the police, but they told her there was nothing they could do to help. It was illegal to share intimate photos of someone without their consent, they explained, but not if they were fake. Even if she could get the website to identify the perpetrator, he hadn't done anything illegal. She'd been shocked, baffled even, that something so violating, so *unfair*, was perfectly legitimate in the eyes of the law.

With nowhere else to turn, she spent weeks obsessing over which men in her life might have been responsible – they had used her name and had access to her private photos, so she suspected they were known to her. But she never found out. 'There was a time when I was suspecting everyone and thinking, could it be you? You start questioning, there were a couple of people who downplayed it . . . and I'd think, you don't understand, or . . . did *you* do it? I don't even know if it was a man, it's a big assumption, but I was assuming because they presented themselves as a man on the website. That, too, might be a fiction.'

Then she began to look at the men around her – neighbours, acquaintances, strangers – thinking how many might have done the same to other women. 'You think about all the people you know who might use these sites, look at men walking down the streets, and it makes you think about what you don't know about people and what they do in private.'

The encounter poisoned Helen's relationships with men in general, and dimmed her outlook on the world for a long while. She began to dread sleep, whose comfort had been pierced by nightmares featuring her deepfake self, and she re-started anti-anxiety medications that she had taken in the past. She dropped old friends who she felt weren't empathetic enough, and retreated from new ones. She was grateful for her husband's support, but resented his other responsibilities, needing him desperately.

To begin to heal, the first step she made was a conscious choice to stop wondering who was responsible for the deepfakes. Then, to repair her relationship with her body, she began adding to her collection of tattoos. 'I've never had great body confidence, and one of my fears was if these deepfakes get more realistic, someone might do it again and make it exactly like me with all my tattoos,' she said. 'I realized that my tattoos would be proof that it wasn't really me, no one knows about all of them except me. So, it's been a comfort to me, they're like a shield, they're marks that I know someone else couldn't possibly know about if they were making a fake image.'

Yet although the tattoos may paper over it, her identity feels irreversibly cracked. 'I've not been able to dissociate from it, even now. Even now, talking about it, I talk about it as me – that's how it felt,' she says.

Familiar Girls

Today, snips of the original 'deepfake' code have budded off into offshoot algorithms that have propagated around the world. In 2019, an app called DeepNude tantalized users by asking them to upload pictures of partially clothed women for $50, and used AI models to strip them naked, replacing their bodies with algorithmically generated versions. The app only generated breasts and vulvas, and therefore didn't work as intended on images of men.

Although DeepNude was shut down temporarily in 2020, its creator, an anonymous programmer who went by the alias 'Alberto', later programmed more sophisticated features into the code, mutating it like a virus, now allowing users to upload photos of all types – women fully clothed, viewed from one side, shrouded in shadow – to generate nude photos, and even videos, with the click of a button.[6]

Now, hundreds of nudes-for-hire services have bloomed, as easy to use as applying an Instagram filter. Estimates show one such website was visited by fifty million viewers in a ten-month period in 2020.[7] Some months later, its owner claimed their deepfake algorithms were becoming more advanced, and would soon allow users to 'manipulate the attribute[s] of target[s] such as breast size, pubic hair.' Deepfakes, he promised, would move from passive entertainment into a participative sport: choose a woman, any woman, strip her down, transmute her, and put her on display. Rinse and repeat.

A business model has mushroomed around deepfake pornography. Websites often share their deep-nude code with 'partners', or knock-off websites that pay them in return for offering the photo-stripping service, resulting in a thriving ecosystem of sexual harassment sites and apps that cannot be killed off. The platforms themselves can be accessed through a simple online search and require no expertise to use. You simply upload a photo as you would to any other website. Most of these businesses provide deepfakes as a paid service.

One of these partner apps, known as DreamTime, is run by a developer calling himself Ivan Bravo. He describes DreamTime as 'an application that allows you to easily create fake nudes from photos or videos using artificial intelligence.' In an interview with *Wired*, Bravo claimed he had more than 3,000 paying users and made more than enough money 'to support a family in a decent house here in México.'[8] This was, he added, probably an immoral way to make money, but he had no intention of stopping.

2020 was the year when making 'deepnudes' became as straightforward as sending someone an instant message. A bot on the messaging app Telegram popped up, offering a simple deepfaking service to users. You could text the bot a photo of your clothed victim on Telegram, and it would text back a realistic naked image using the person's face, within *minutes*. According to research firm Sensity AI, which conducted a study on this bot, a premium version cost around $8 for 112 images. By July 2020, more than 100,000 unsuspecting girls and women had been abused via this app alone.[9]

In an anonymous poll of the users posted to the channel, and seen by Sensity AI, 63 per cent said they used photos of 'familiar girls, whom I know in real life'.[10] That statistic sent chills down my spine. There was that creeping feeling Helen had described: the sense of inescapable scrutiny.

*

In the spring of 2022, I began to notice constant snippets of news stories addressing the impacts of AI tools on image and identity. One was the story of American software engineer Cher Scarlett, who had discovered explicit and intimate photos of herself on a facial recognition search site known as PimEyes – images that were taken coercively nearly two decades ago, when she was nineteen years old.[11] She had blanked out her memories of the traumatic incident; so discovering the images unexpectedly felt to her like experiencing the trauma for the first time.

I was curious about PimEyes. The site asks you to upload a picture of yourself, and uses AI systems to learn the contours of your face and pull photos featuring you from around the web. So I added a picture of myself to the site to see what it would dig up. It worked fine, unearthing mostly public photos that I had already seen, as well as a handful of stills, close-ups of my face from events I had attended, where I hadn't realized I was being photographed. I wondered if they had been pulled from videos.

A few of these close-ups had been labelled 'explicit' – which led me to discover that they had been published on pornography sites. I couldn't click through to the sites themselves without paying PimEyes, which I chose not to do. But it did leave me with a nagging fear of what might exist out there unbeknownst to me, my scattered digital twins over whom I had no control or ownership.

When I spoke to Cher, she said the idea that someone could take a photo of her face and find out everything there was to know about her felt like an impossible thing: 'Star Trek stuff', she called it. Yet, this technology had made the leap, turning her from an anonymous face in the crowd into a person whose secrets could be forcibly revealed.

Hundreds of thousands of women like Cher Scarlett and Helen Mort, sometimes girls, have no place to go when they stumble across sexually intimate photos and videos of themselves shared without permission online – real, fake, consensual or coerced. Until recently, there was no button on Google, YouTube or Facebook that you could click to have these intimate media removed and erased permanently. And even now, trying to get non-consensual images and videos – let alone deepfakes – removed from the internet permanently is futile because of the lack of legal protections, and the decentralized nature of the internet. Once downloaded onto private computers, these images persist indefinitely, digital ghouls that roam the nether regions of the web, popping up when least expected.

In most parts of the world, creating and distributing deepfakes of intimate and sexual images are not illegal, so there is no obvious path to justice. The issue has been taken on by legal academics, charities, campaigners and women's rights groups, such as My Image My Choice and Not Your Porn, who focus on all types of non-consensual image-sharing, including revenge porn. These organizations offer emotional support helplines, information resources, even free legal advice. But it's hard to find lawyers who will take these cases, as they are tough fights to win in court. Victims who want legal recourse often find their way to Carrie Goldberg, a lawyer in Brooklyn, New York, specialising, as she puts it, in 'clients under attack by pervs, assholes, psychos, and trolls'.[12]

Carrie is the type of woman you don't forget easily – she favours power suits, stilettos and crimson lips. Her oversized dark-rimmed glasses give her an air of studious naivety, softening the killer instincts she wears like a badge of honour. She is unapologetically feminine, foul-mouthed and fierce.

The acts of violence her clients come to her with range from livestreaming sexual assaults of minors to revenge porn posted online, sex-driven blackmail and cyberstalking. Usually, this work boils down to defending women or those who identify as female, often hurt by men using various forms of technology. Most of these acts weren't even classified as crimes when she started her practice in 2014. This is partly why she set up shop in the first place – she wanted to be the lawyer she never had when she needed it most. Her story involved an ex-boyfriend who threatened to post intimate pictures of her online, messaging her family and friends on Facebook that she was a drug addict with sexually transmitted infections.

Goldberg's clients, many of whom are teenage schoolgirls, tend to be socially isolated from their peers and family, following the brutal and senseless acts they have experienced. She sees a little of herself in each of them, often messing with the lines between lawyer and client, acting as an older sister, a therapist and a fairy godmother, whisking them off to manicures and buying them Nikes for their birthdays.

In a *New Yorker* profile of Carrie, a law professor in Miami described receiving a gift from her in the post, a symbol of Carrie's support during a period of online abuse hurled at the professor for her advocacy of revenge porn laws. The package contained a Mac lipstick in the fiery shade Lady Danger. In the card accompanying it, Carrie had written, 'This is what I wear when I want to feel like a warrior.'[13]

During our conversation, I asked her how online abuse should be treated in the eyes of the law. Immediately, Carrie rejected my framing, refusing to be drawn into the false dichotomy of online versus offline. 'In my opinion, all crimes are happening offline, because everyone they are happening to is a human being, and not a computer,' she said. 'The online component is just the weapon that's being used, not the crime itself. Anytime someone talks to me about their cyberstalking or online harassment, I say no, it's just harassment, it's just stalking.'

Goldberg has handled a spectrum of technology-mediated crimes, so I was curious if she had seen a rise in deepfake cases. 'One of my first cases in 2014 was a woman whose pictures were on a revenge porn website, and it was a picture of her at the beach with her friends in a bikini, but somebody had Photoshopped off the bikini, and added big double-G boobs and a hairy . . . in some ways that was the early cousin of deepfakes,' she told me. 'Deepfakes are certainly a more sophisticated use of technology but the fix isn't really that different. For my clients, it's get that the fuck off the internet, confirm who did that to me, make it stop, and go away forever. And arrest that motherfucker, if possible. So much of what I do boils down to that.'

While her priority has been fighting for her clients by pursuing their harassers and abusers, and sometimes the platforms that distribute the content, part of her job has evolved into lobbying for recognition of these acts as punishable crimes. Currently, her strongest weapon to get intimate content taken down is to use copyright law, she explained. In other cases, she might file restraining orders and other protections if stalking is involved, and she generally goes to criminal court if the orders are violated.

But her biggest problem, she said, is that there are no legal incentives for the web's largest platforms, such as Google, YouTube, Facebook, Instagram, and others – let alone specialist pornography websites – to curtail the distribution of non-consensual and AI-generated pornography, and keep users safe.

She has become obsessed with holding internet platforms accountable for the abuse that occurs online. In particular, Goldberg is going after Section 230, a part of the Communications Decency Act in the United States which protects online platforms from liability for any third-party content posted on them. 'This is one of the biggest problems evolving on the Internet. The fact that the most powerful companies in the history of the universe, in terms of wealth but also the information they have about us, the idea that they are immune from liability, when no other industry is,' she said. 'They've monetized everybody's private data, and yet we have no rights against them. It's absolutely intolerable.'

That the law was written in 1996, before the web as we know it today existed, is 'bonkers', she said. Lobbyists fighting to keep online platforms free of responsibility for their content, claim that changing the law would destroy the internet industry. Even digital activists like Electronic Frontier Foundation claim that shifting liability onto internet companies would lead to more proactive censorship of the internet, that it would slow down the real-time nature of social media and would transform the web into a sanitized, closed-off and less 'free' version of itself.[14]

Goldberg scoffs at this. 'Every other industry is liable for the harms they cause, and it hasn't shut down the auto industry or the airplane industry,' she says. 'Tech is such an intensely profit-driven industry that has never budgeted for legal liabilities.'

Although she treats the abuse of her clients online just the same as in the real world, she admits that the weaponization of AI is uniquely damaging. The technology is a more sophisticated, large-scale and sustained way to hurt vulnerable people.

She said, 'It's never before been so convenient to remotely injure somebody and because of the remote access to the internet, and also the global reach of it, the multiplying effect of it, the damages to somebody's privacy, reputation, career, are so much more profound and permanent also.'

Noelle

In Perth, Western Australia, twenty-five-year-old Noelle Martin is living proof of Goldberg's words. Noelle is the second of five girls in a family of middle-class Indian Catholics originally from Goa. 'I'm a brown girl, the daughter of immigrants, ordinary, hardworking folk who go about their lives,' she told me. Her childhood she remembers as largely uneventful, other than the chaos of growing up with four sisters, and some instances of casual racism as one of the few dark-skinned students at her school.

Noelle's family is relatively conservative. She was never in a serious relationship as a teenager, and had always been studious. She knew from a young age that she wanted to be a lawyer, like her father, and was admitted to study law and the arts at Macquarie University in Sydney in 2014. It was during her first year when her life stopped being ordinary, in ways both profound and permanent.

It happened when she was doing a casual Google Reverse Image Search during which she discovered dozens of images of her that had been scraped and posted onto pornographic sites, from her social media, and the accounts of her friends. Confused, she started clicking through to the websites, until she stumbled across naked images of herself, which had clearly been edited from the fully clothed originals.

'I saw many, many doctored images of me, depicting me having sexual intercourse, in fellatio positions, being ejaculated on,' she said during a Skype call from her parents' home in Perth, in an almost clinically detached tone that I had noticed in Helen too.

'I think what happened is that someone somewhere stumbled upon an image of me and I represented someone they sexually fetishized, because they lifted those images and posted them to sites about bustier women. Eventually they ended up on mainstream porn sites, and got shared and shared and shared.' Because of the bottom-up nature of social media, and the web at large, content is impossible to police; the photos had been downloaded by thousands of people onto private servers. By the time Noelle uncovered them, the images had seeded like pernicious weeds, too far and wide to contain.

The photos themselves were crude edits by today's standards – this was before the era of deepfakes – but that was hardly a solace to Noelle. 'How do you explain that to a layperson?' she asked. As an eighteen-year-old living away from home, without any family to lean on, she felt isolated and increasingly despondent.

'For a long period of time, I actually internalized my own objectification. I started smoking, I started drinking, I started spreading myself too thin, because I had increasingly low self-esteem, low self-worth,' she told me. 'I just felt so hypersexualized, so objectified, like I wasn't human in the eyes of people. It rips your dignity and it rips your humanity.'

*

When Noelle and I first talked, she turned on her camera to say hello, her long dark hair cascading down into the lens, her face alive with expression. But as our conversation progressed, she requested to keep the camera off, to avoid what she described as the weariness of having to be constantly 'presentable'. Even as a disembodied voice, she was bright, articulate and raw, though I could feel her struggling with the conflicting emotions of wanting to be bold, while also wanting to crawl away and hide from it all.

Growing up, Noelle said she always felt physically distinct from the rest of her family. Her sisters were all 'skinny and very petite', able to wear anything they liked, while she was 'very curvaceous'. Throughout her teen years, Noelle battled her parents, who would ask her to dress more conservatively than her sisters. 'This is just the way society is, especially when you have a certain kind of body . . . no matter what you wear, you're going to look slutty in the eyes of others. All these assumptions are gonna be made by virtue of your existence in the body you were given.'

As a teenager still figuring herself out, Noelle fought back the only way she knew how – through asserting her individuality. She dressed relatively staidly – rarely showing her legs or arms – but had her own sense of style. 'Maybe to certain people there was too much cleavage,' she says, 'but it was the part of my body I was trying to work through. And I thought to myself, why *can't* I show it? I didn't always like my arms, or bare my stomach, so why can't I fit into my body and work through my own path, without people shaming me for my very existence? Why am I ashamed? There was a lot of defiance and anger there.'

When she discovered the doctored photos in college, Noelle wrote to all the website owners, asking them to take down the images, but she was largely ignored or, in one case, blackmailed by the site's owner, who asked her for real nudes in return for taking down her fake images. Even if a website did agree to take it down, the images had been downloaded and were often later re-posted to other sites quicker than she could stamp them out. She realized she was fighting a losing battle.

That's when she decided to speak out about the experience publicly, an involuntary activist who had to fight for her own dignity and rights.

Image-manipulation technology was still in its infancy, so most people didn't even know crimes like those existed. Noelle decided that for her own sake, if not for others, she had to raise awareness that this could happen to anyone, without provocation. It was the start of her campaign to change the local laws so this type of fake imagery was criminalized.[15]

But using her voice to stand up for herself seemed to draw the attention of even more abusers online. More manipulated images appeared, and they were getting increasingly graphic. 'They were literally taking images of me from media articles and doing the very thing I was advocating against in those articles,' she said. 'They were taking photos of me holding a certificate I had won for my advocacy, and they would edit the certificate to an adult movie cover, as if I was at a porn event.'

The porn website owners were the only ones who could help her track down the culprits, and since the acts were legal in Australia, they either didn't bother to respond at all, or did so too slowly to contain the spread of the graphic fake images.

Noelle's relentless campaigning and advocacy ultimately helped pass a number of state and national laws in Australia, including a 2018 law that criminalized the non-consensual sharing of intimate images, including those altered using technology, and a 2022 law that would fine social media companies up to A$555,000 ($383,000) per day if they didn't comply with orders from online safety regulators to take down image-based abuse.[16]

But the original act turned out to be just the start of years of abuse and bullying for Noelle, punishments for her audacity to speak out. 'They're the cowards hiding behind their keyboards and I'm the one that has to go through the lifelong implications because of their failure to see me as a human,' she told me.

In 2018, after graduating, Noelle received an email: 'There is a deepfake video of you on some porn site, it looks real,' it read. She asked the anonymous sender for a link, which led her to an eleven-second deepfake video of her, fully naked and having sex with a stranger – an act fully fabricated using AI tools. On the same website, she unearthed another video, this one of her performing oral sex on a man.

'The literal freaking title of this video was my full name, the tags on the videos were "Noelle", "feminist in Australia", they were completely stealing my identity,' she tells me. 'What they were doing represented a whole other fucking persona of me, that was extremely violating. They were purposely out to misappropriate and misrepresent me,' she said.

Those videos were far more immersive and visceral than any of the previously doctored images, but Noelle had become inured to the pain. 'It has been normalized in my life to discover such violating content of me, in increasingly worse forms over almost a decade,' she said. 'It strips away your identity. The only thing I can do is own the fuck out of it, because if I don't, I'm screwed.'

Since then, the videos have appeared on multiple pornographic sites, discoverable by Google searches. Once they had been downloaded and re-posted, containing them became impossible. Noelle had the videos analysed by deepfake experts who found that the video depicting sexual intercourse was a true AI-generated deepfake. She'd experienced intimately the increasing sophistication of editing tools, and seen how AI had made it so much easier to create realistic-looking pornography. 'That video had a body that resembled my own, my face was moving in it, and I am having active sexual intercourse with another person, with the title of the video being my name,' she said. 'I was so fucking angry at the audacity of continuing to target me in this way.'

The trauma began to change the core of Noelle's personality, she tells me, and she felt she was constantly flip-flopping between high and low moods. 'There were times where I turned everything private on social media, times where I was very open, times where I may have changed what I wore, there were times where I was like fuck that though, I'm going to wear what I want, or why should I be private, or why should I change my behaviour? It was very up and down all the time. I would try and forget everything that happened to me, almost dissociate from myself, pretend it wasn't happening.' But then at night, just as she was going to sleep, the imagery would pop into her head and she would spend hours worrying about how they might show up again the next day.

She believes that the perpetrators were not in Australia, because they are unafraid of being caught or prosecuted under the local laws that criminalize the sharing of intimate images, including deepfakes, without consent – something that remains legal in other parts of the world, including parts of the United States and the European Union. 'They're continuing to do it because they can, and they want to have power over you,' she said.

The Fight for Change

Last February, I spoke with Olivia Snow, a researcher at the University of California, Los Angeles who also works as a professional dominatrix and is an expert on sex work, technology and policy. When she is working as a dominatrix, she doesn't use her real name. Recently, Olivia and other friends in her line of work started using Lensa, an app which uses AI to turn photos of people's faces into animated versions of themselves, in styles such as anime and fantasy. 'We used it as a safe way to show our faces on our profiles,' she told me. But as she uploaded more photos of herself, she found that the animated images were being hypersexualized by the app's algorithms.

She was curious, so she put in all sorts of photos, including selfies from conferences and eventually, childhood photos, to see how Lensa's AI edited them. She was horrified to discover these, too, were sexualized, even producing partial nudes. 'Apps like Lensa will be used against women very soon. Over the past few weeks I've seen an uptick of women being shown deepfake porn of themselves,' she said.

The lack of responsibility taken on by global regulators to outright criminalize this type of abuse was much too slow, she said. 'We don't regulate technologies like AI until it is too late.'

Olivia is right – change has been slow to come. Victims like Helen and Noelle who are courageous enough – and feel safe enough – to speak about their experiences are fighting for legal recourse, demanding that their governments recognize deepfake imagery is on the rise, and that creating and distributing pornographic AI-generated content without consent is a criminal act.

Their fight is to show how the consequences of AI-image abuse can be just as crippling as sharing images of actual events, which is part of the reason they share their stories widely. In recent years, as more women share stories of their own experiences of being deepfaked, and AI image-creation software becomes better than ever, there has been a rise in lobbying by digital and women's rights campaigners for governments to ban this type of abuse.

Helen, for instance, started an online petition, demanding that the government change the laws to protect victims like herself. 'My ordeal left me feeling frightened, ashamed, paranoid and devastated. But I won't let it silence me,' she wrote.

Her petition, which received more than 6,000 signatures, fought to make deepfakes illegal, 'creating one clear law to ban the taking, making and faking of these harmful images.'[17]

As a result of the advocacy of Helen and others like Sensity AI's Henry Ajder, alongside dozens of other campaigners, the UK has recently criminalized the non-consensual distribution of deepfake intimate images in its new Online Safety Bill, a draft law that has been in the works since 2019. The bill, despite widespread criticism, is in the final stages of debate at the time of writing, and continues to move glacially through the British legislative process. It is expected to come into force in mid-2024.

Clare McGlynn, a law professor at Durham University, who has specialized in legal study of this area for a decade, says despite the UK's move to address this issue, there are currently only scattered national and state-level laws globally that pertain to image abuse, and even fewer that criminalize the creation and distribution of deepfakes. Even the laws that exist aren't being strictly enforced, according to survivors that Clare has spoken to, making it extremely hard for women, who make up the greatest proportion of victims, to be protected from harassment that can stretch over several years, like in Noelle's case.

The resistance to regulatory change, Clare said, is not because fake image-based abuse is controversial or hotly debated, but the opposite: lawmakers don't deem it important enough. AI, like social media and other internet-based technologies, is a complex area to regulate. The technology evolves extremely quickly and doesn't respect borders – AI software may be invented in one country, co-opted and implemented as an app in another, then hacked and used to create non-consensual deepfakes of victims in a third nation.

While AI technology has become a global regulatory priority in the past year, the issues being discussed are primarily around security risks of sophisticated AI systems, including their ability to assist in the design of bio-weapons, the spread of AI-generated misinformation in the political areas, and impact on democracy. Other areas of the law being examined include issues of copyright violation by generative AI software, since the systems require the use of copyrighted words, images, voices and likenesses of creative professionals for their training. At an inaugural summit held in the UK's Bletchley Park mansion last November, state leaders spoke of the need to legislate on AI safety: the practice of designing algorithmic systems that aren't discriminatory and unethical, that can't be co-opted to commit crimes, and in the far future, superhuman technologies that don't harm humanity.

Against this backdrop of complexity, global political leaders, who are overwhelmingly male,[18] simply haven't prioritized the rising prevalence of deepfakes, Clare said. Perhaps, it's because the practice is disproportionately hurting women and those identifying as female, she suggested. In other words, these victims just don't matter enough.

*

The telltale mark of data 'colonialism', the exploitation of vulnerable communities by powerful tech companies, is in how the impacts of an algorithmic system are distributed. Advantages conferred by the technology, because of its statistical nature, are often enjoyed by the majority – whether through race, geography or sex. For instance, poorly designed AI recruitment systems have been found to favour male candidates over female ones, because of the former group's previous success in job-seeking at that specific company.[19] On the flipside, toxic consequences of these systems are suffered most keenly by those who are already victimized and marginalized in societies today. Take facial recognition AI, which systematically misidentifies women and people of colour more frequently than males and Caucasians.

As I began to track the onset of deepfake pornography, I found that this technology had spread far afield of the West and that similar algorithms were being used against women in Egypt, China, Yemen and India, among others. The technology was already targeting female journalists and activists in these countries, exploiting their vulnerable positions in their cultures, to cause disproportionately greater harm to them than those in, say, Western countries.

In 2020, my colleagues and I at the *Financial Times* began reporting a story about how AI was being weaponized to harass women and other minorities on the internet, and we came across a young Chinese programmer called Scsky, living in Germany. Scsky had assembled a team of seven volunteer programmers, who spent more than five months writing an app called 'Can You Forgive Me' in their spare time. The app asked you to upload a photo of your girlfriend's face, and its AI technology would identify if the woman had ever appeared in amateur, revenge or professional porn.

Later, he claimed the app could also be used by the women themselves – to find and remove nudes uploaded without their permission. But my colleague Yuan Yang found when she interviewed him that the core of his idea was to identify 'sexually permissive' Chinese women, so that programmers and engineers, mostly male and perceived to be naive and inexperienced with women, could stop what they saw as being taken advantage of.

The app caused an uproar amongst Chinese feminists online, who viewed this as deliberate harassment of women who voiced an opinion – usually a rejection. The behaviours are part of a larger body of research publicized at the time of the Johnny Depp–Amber Heard trial in 2022, which showed that women who speak out and behave with authority can be seen as 'unlikeable'.[20]

The potential dangers to women outside of Western countries is what keeps Raquel Vazquez Llorente, a human rights lawyer, up at night. Llorente had been contemplating how to defend rights and freedom of expression in a world of AI-made synthetic media, including deepfakes. She is concerned that AI tools could become a part of authoritarian governments' arsenal – deepfaked videos or pictures as a way to discredit individuals at a personal level.

The human rights community that Llorente works with was acutely aware that activists in developing and autocratic states would be hurt disproportionately, as emerging technologies such as AI are more prone to abuse by these governments.[21]

Llorente works at WITNESS, a non-profit that helps people use video-based technology to defend human rights around the world. The organization has hosted a series of workshops across four continents since 2019, including in Nairobi, Pretoria, Kuala Lumpur and São Paolo, that has brought together journalists, policy advocates and human rights defenders from across these regions.[22] Their goal has been to discuss the threats and opportunities that deepfakes and other generative AI technologies could bring to human rights work, including identifying the most pressing concerns and recommendations for future policy work in this area.

During these workshops, it became clear that one of the greatest fears of those in the African, Southeast Asian and Latin American regions was the use of synthetic media to 'poison the well' or break trust in their work. They were worried about the use of deepfakes and other AI technologies to launch targeted, gender-based attacks and create false narratives about individuals fighting against those in power.

'This is already being used to discredit the work of female activists and women's rights defenders,' Llorente told me. 'Put your face on a porn video and circulate it around, all your work is discredited at best, and at worst, you get killed. I'm identifying human rights defenders in Yemen and the Middle East targeted through deepfake imagery. I'm trying to figure out how to defend them. It gets dangerous for activists where something like this can really get you killed.'

*

As digital technologies evolve, the harms resulting from image-producing AI can move from the real to the virtual world – something Noelle has been studying as a legal researcher at the University of Western Australia. Artificial intelligence is also at the heart of the so-called metaverse, a three-dimensional online universe made popular by Facebook, which has renamed itself Meta. In the metaverse, you can roam in the form of an avatar in realistic worlds populated by other avatars of real users, and objects that you can interact with. Anyone can access these virtual platforms such as Roblox, Fortnite and Decentraland, or even Meta's Horizon Worlds, to play games.

Horizon Worlds, for instance, is accessed using Meta's Oculus Quest 2 virtual reality headset. The platform uses generative AI to build avatars that can provide instantaneous speech translation across languages, to power chatbots in this ecosystem, and even to allow the generation of detailed virtual environments by using voice commands.

In 2021, in an undercover investigation for a Channel 4 documentary, British television journalist Yinka Bokinni used Meta's Oculus Quest headset to enter the metaverse through two apps that the Oculus app store offered.[23] She found rampant sexual aggression, harassment, racism and even child endangerment issues in these virtual spaces. Immediately after entering one of these environments that plug into Facebook's Oculus platform, she overheard sexual conversations about children, experienced extreme racial abuse and hate speech, and virtual assault.

In a *Guardian* article about this experience, she wrote, 'At one point, seven users surrounded me and tried to force me to remove my safety shield so they could do things to my body . . . It was the virtual equivalent of sexual assault.'[24]

Bokinni articulated the odd sense of feeling violated, even though the experience was entirely virtual. 'I know it's not real, but when you've got that headset on, it really feels like you're there,' she wrote. 'It tricks your brain into thinking you're really experiencing it. You forget it's not real. It's just so intimidating.'

The Before and After

Ultimately, the human effects of generative AI, or any type of AI-mediated image manipulation, are no different to those engendered by older technologies like Photoshop or even by revenge porn.

Clare McGlynn, the law professor, spoke to over seventy-five survivors in the UK, Australia and New Zealand, who had experienced a range of image-based harassment from revenge porn to deepfakes and studied the human costs of this type of abuse. All of them talked about the constant fear of being recognized, or the images being shared widely. 'Their lives rupture into a "before" and an "after",' Clare told me. 'They move schools, move homes, change jobs. One woman talked about putting on weight, changing her hair colour, because she feared walking down the street and being recognized, entirely transforming her body image so she couldn't be recognized.'

Today, Noelle is a lawyer and researcher at the University of Western Australia, where she is studying technology and policy, particularly focused on immersive technologies like deepfakes and the metaverse, and their impact on individuals.

Over the years, her closest friends have fielded dozens of phone calls from Noelle, as she spent hours re-hashing and working through the torrent of harassment. This was particularly acute when it was still early on in her battle for legal rights, and Noelle was navigating new and more graphic instances of abuse, month after month. 'I could never show up for my friends in the way I wanted to,' she said. 'It was always all about me.'

Noelle felt like people didn't understand how this type of harassment rippled into your everyday life – among the people you meet, every job interview, in any and all romantic relationships and with your friends. And because most people don't understand AI technology, she finds herself having to explain it constantly, which she says, on top of the abuse itself, is triggering and emotionally draining.

She felt as though anyone she met couldn't see past her story, which in turn made her feel as if they had made assumptions about her and could never know her as just *her*. Recently, she had been on a first date with someone she'd met online. 'I was not planning to talk about it or mention it on my profile. I don't think I owe anyone the story of this horrific pain in my life before I meet them,' she said. But during their date, the man told her he had looked her up, and suddenly she went from feeling pretty good about him, to feeling small and humiliated.

Yet, she continues to speak up, in the hope of being a beacon for others muddling through the disjointed and scarring experience of being 'deepfaked', and to help them find closure. She, like so many other victims, just wants the offending imagery to be taken down and the harassment to stop – something she feels should be straightforward to regulate. Over the years, she's committed herself to public talks, events and government campaigns, tireless efforts to speak out against image-based sexual abuse and push to change the laws across Australia, and at the Commonwealth level. While she has had some success, she knows it isn't enough. As deepfake technology becomes better, cheaper and more easily accessible to the average person, she has observed that the number of deepfake porn victims continues to rise.

The internet, she has come to realize, can't be policed by individual countries through a patchwork of regulations that are individually enforced (or often not). As AI technologies become ubiquitous and ever more sophisticated, Noelle believes there must be globally agreed rules and standards so perpetrators cannot evade justice as they have done with her. And so, her fight continues.

'There's absolute truth when I say sometimes it's been the best thing for me,' she says, describing how the experience has given her purpose, and pushed her to be a role model. But most days, she tells me, it feels the opposite way. 'It's a very contradictory thing, a paradox. It is simultaneously the worst and best thing that could have ever happened to me.'

Helen captured this same feeling in her essay, 'This Is Wild', the rupture and the cleavage of the encounter – much like the formation of a glacier. These majestic slabs of ice metamorphose from soft snow over centuries, into complex, evolving things. But only when a glacier melts does it expose its inner skeleton, what scientists describe as a 'profoundly eroded landscape' scarred by its history.

To Helen, John Grant's song 'Glacier' became a healing mantra. She writes in the essay about the song's paradox of pain morphing into beauty.

She continues, 'You put it on repeat.'

CHAPTER 3

Your Identity

The first time Karl Ricanek was stopped by police for 'driving while black' was in the summer of 1995. He was twenty-five, just qualified as an engineer and had started work at the US Department of Defense's Naval Undersea Warfare Center in Newport, Rhode Island, a wealthy town known for its spectacular cliff walks and millionaires' mansions. That summer he had bought his first nice car – a two-year-old dark green Infiniti J30T that cost him roughly $30,000.

One evening, on his way back to the place he rented in First Beach, a police car pulled him over. Karl was polite, distant, knowing not to seem combative or aggressive. He knew, too, to keep his hands in visible places, and what could happen if he didn't. It was something he'd been trained to do from a young age.

The cop asked Karl his name, which he told him, even though he didn't have to. He was well aware that if he wanted to get out of this thing, he had to cooperate. He felt at that moment he had been stripped of any rights, but he knew this is what he – and thousands of others like him – had to live with. The cop pointed to his car. This is a nice car, he told Karl. How do you afford a fancy car like this?

What do you mean? Karl thought furiously. *None of your business how I afford this car.* Instead, he said, 'Well, I'm an engineer. I work over at the research center. I bought the car with my wages.'

That wasn't the last time Karl was pulled over by a cop. In fact, it wasn't even the last time in Newport. And when friends and colleagues shrugged, telling him that getting stopped and being asked some questions didn't sound like a big deal, he let it lie. But they had never been stopped simply for 'driving while white', they hadn't been subject to the humiliation of being questioned as a law-abiding adult, purely based on your visual identity, to have to justify your presence and your choices to strangers, and be afraid for your life if you resisted.

Karl had never broken the law. He'd worked as hard as anybody else, doing all the things that bright young people were supposed to do in America. 'So why,' he thought, 'can't I just be left alone?'

Can Computers Recognize Faces?

Karl grew up with four older siblings in Deanwood, a primarily black neighbourhood in the north-eastern corner of Washington, DC, with a white German father and a black mother. When he left Washington, DC at eighteen for college, he had a scholarship to study at North Carolina A&T State University, which graduates the largest numbers of black engineers in the US. It was where Karl learned to address problems with technical solutions, rather than social ones. He taught himself to emphasize his academic credentials and underplay his background so he would be taken more seriously amongst peers.

After working in Newport, Karl went into academia, at the University of North Carolina, Wilmington. In particular, he was interested in teaching computers to identify faces even better than humans do. His goal seemed simple: first, unpick how humans see faces, and then teach computers how to do it more efficiently than we do.

When he started out back in the eighties and nineties, Karl was developing AI technology to help the US Navy's submarine fleet navigate autonomously. At the time, computer vision was a slow-moving field, in which machines were taught to merely recognize objects, rather than people's identities. The technology was nascent – and pretty terrible. The algorithms he designed were trying to get the machine to say that's a bottle, these are glasses, this is a table, these are humans. Each year, they made incremental, single-digit improvements in precision.

Then, a new type of AI known as deep learning emerged – the same discipline that allowed miscreants to generate sexually deviant deepfakes of Helen Mort and Noelle Martin, and the model that underpins ChatGPT. The cutting-edge technology was helped along by an embarrassment of data riches, in this case, millions of photos uploaded to the web that could be used to train new image-recognition algorithms.

Deep learning catapulted the small gains Karl was seeing into real progress. All of a sudden, what used to be a 1 per cent improvement was now 10 per cent each year. It meant software could now be used not just to classify objects, but to recognize unique faces.

When Karl first started working on the problem of facial recognition, it wasn't supposed to be used live on protesters or pedestrians or ordinary people. It was supposed to be a photo analysis tool. From its inception in the nineties, researchers knew there were biases and inaccuracies in how the algorithms worked. But they hadn't quite figured out why.

The biometrics community viewed the problems as academic, an interesting computer vision challenge affecting a prototype still in its infancy. They broadly agreed that the technology wasn't ready for primetime use and they had no plans to profit from it.

As the technology steadily improved, Karl began to develop experimental AI analytics models to spot physical signs of illnesses like cardiovascular disease, Alzheimer's or Parkinson's from a person's face. For instance, a common symptom of Parkinson's is frozen or stiff facial expressions, brought on by changes in the face's muscles. AI technology could be used to analyse these micro-muscular changes and detect the onset of disease early. He told me he imagined inventing a mirror that you could look at each morning that would tell you (or notify a trusted person) if you were developing symptoms of degenerative neurological disease. He founded a for-profit company, Lapetus Solutions, which predicted life expectancy through facial analytics, for the insurance market.

His systems were used by law enforcement to identify trafficked children and notorious criminal gangsters such as Whitey Bulger. He even looked into identifying faces of those who had changed genders, by testing his systems on videos of transsexual people undergoing hormonal transitions, an extremely controversial use of the technology. He became fixated on the mysteries locked up in the human face, regardless of any harms or negative consequences.

In the US, it was 9/11 that, quite literally overnight, ramped up the administration's urgent need for surveillance technologies like face recognition, supercharging investment and development of these systems. The issue was no longer merely academic and within a few years the US government had built vast databases containing the faces and other biometric data of millions of Iraqis, Afghans and US tourists from around the world.[1] They had invested heavily in commercializing biometric research like Karl's, who had received military funding to improve facial recognition algorithms, working on systems to recognize obscured and masked faces, young faces, and faces as they aged. American domestic law enforcement adapted counterterrorism technology, including facial recognition, to police street crime, gang violence and even civil rights protests.

It became harder for Karl to ignore what AI facial analytics was now being developed for. Yet, during these years, he resisted critique of the social impacts of the powerful technology he was helping to create. He rarely sat on ethics or standards boards at his university, because he thought they were bureaucratic and time-consuming. He described critics of facial recognition as 'social justice warriors' who didn't have practical experience of building this technology themselves. As far as he was concerned, he was creating tools to help save children and find terrorists, and everything else was just noise.

But it wasn't that straightforward. Technology companies, both large and small, had access to far more face data, and a commercial imperative to push forward facial recognition. Corporate giants such as Meta and Chinese-owned TikTok, and start-ups like New York-based Clearview AI and Russia's NTech Labs, own even larger databases of faces than many governments, and certainly more than researchers like Karl. And they're all driven by the same incentive: making money. These private actors soon uprooted systems from academic institutions like Karl's and started selling immature facial recognition solutions to law enforcement, intelligence agencies, governments and private entities around the world. In January 2020, *The New York Times* published a story about how Clearview AI had taken billions of photos from the web, including sites like LinkedIn and Instagram, to build powerful facial recognition capabilities bought by several police forces around the world.[2]

The technology was being unleashed from Argentina to Alabama, via Ayrshire, with a life of its own, blowing wild like gleeful dandelion seeds taking root at will. In Uganda, Hong Kong and India, it has been used to stifle political opposition and civil protest.[3] In the US it was used to track Black Lives Matter protests and Capitol rioters during the uprising in January 2021, and in London to monitor revellers at the annual Afro-Caribbean carnival in Notting Hill.[4]

And it's not just a law enforcement tool: facial recognition is being used to catch pickpockets and petty thieves. It is deployed at the famous Gordon's Wine Bar in London, scanning for known troublemakers.[5] It's even been used to identify dead Russian soldiers in Ukraine.[6] The question of whether it was ready for primetime use has taken on an urgency, as it impacts the lives of billions around the world.

Facial Recognition's Race Problem

Karl knew that the technology was not ready for widespread rollout in this way. Indeed, in 2018, Joy Buolamwini, Timnit Gebru and Deborah Raji – three black female researchers at Microsoft – had published a study, alongside collaborators, comparing the accuracy of face recognition systems built by IBM, Face++ and Microsoft.[7] They found the error rates for light-skinned men hovered at less than 1 per cent, while that figure touched 35 per cent for darker-skinned women. Karl knew that New Jersey resident Nijer Parks spent ten days in jail in 2019 and paid several thousand dollars to defend himself against accusations of shoplifting and assault of a police officer in Woodbridge, New Jersey.[8] The thirty-three-year-old black man had been misidentified by a facial-recognition system used by the Woodbridge police. The case was dismissed a year later for lack of evidence and Parks later sued the police for violation of his civil rights. A year after that, Robert Julian-Borchak Williams, Detroit resident and father of two, was arrested for a shoplifting crime he did not commit, due to another faulty facial recognition match.[9] The arrest took place in his front garden, in front of his family.

Facial-recognition technology also led to the incorrect identification of American-born Amara Majeed as a terrorist involved in Sri Lanka's Easter Day bombings in 2019.[10] Majeed, a college student at the time, said the misidentification caused her and her family humiliation and pain after her relatives in Sri Lanka saw her face, unexpectedly, amongst a line-up of accused terrorists on the evening news.

As his worlds started to collide, Karl was forced to reckon with the implications of AI-enabled surveillance – and to question his own role in it, acknowledging it could curtail the freedom of individuals and communities going about their normal lives. 'I think I used to believe that I create technology,' he told me, 'and other smart people deal with policy issues. Now I have to ponder and think much deeper about what it is that I'm doing.'

And what he had thought of as technical glitches, such as algorithms working much better on Caucasian and male faces, while struggling to correctly identify darker skin tones and female faces, he came to see are much more than that.

'It's a complicated feeling. As an engineer, as a scientist, I want to build technology to do good,' he told me. 'But as a human being and as a black man, I know people are going to use technology inappropriately. I know my technology might be used against me in some manner or fashion.'

In my decade of covering the technology industry, Karl was one of the only computer scientists to have ever expressed their moral doubts out loud to me. Through him, I glimpsed the fraught relationship that engineers can have with their own creations, and the ethical ambiguities they grapple with when their personal and professional instincts collide.

He was also one of the few technologists who comprehended the implicit threats of facial recognition, particularly in policing, in a visceral way.

'The problem that we have is not the algorithms, but the humans,' he insisted. When you hear about facial recognition in law enforcement going terribly wrong, it's because of human errors, he said, referring to the over-policing of African American males and other minorities, and the use of unprovoked violence by police officers against black people like Philando Castile, George Floyd and Breonna Taylor.

He knew the technology was rife with false positives, and that humans suffered from confirmation bias. So, if a police officer believed someone to be guilty of a crime, and the AI system confirmed it, they were likely to target innocents. 'And if that person is black, who cares?' he said.

He admitted to worrying that the inevitable false matches would result in unnecessary gun violence. He was afraid that these problems would compound the social malaise of racial or other types of profiling. Together, humans and AI could end up creating a policing system far more malignant than the one citizens have today.

'It's the same problem that came out of the Jim Crow era of the sixties, it was supposed to be separate but equal, which it never was, it was just separate . . . fundamentally, people don't treat everybody the same. People make laws, and people use algorithms. At the end of the day, the computer doesn't care.'

Super-Recognizers on the Streets

The face is a gateway between our internal and external selves, the part that represents us most publicly, yet defines us most intimately. It's what we learn at the start of our lives, as babies, to recognize when we look in a mirror, and what strangers use as shorthand to make assumptions about who we are. Our face is an outward marker of our personhood.

So when Helen Mort and Noelle Martin found violent sexual images and videos of themselves on the internet, it was their faces that invaded their dreams and ruptured their lives, sending them spiralling into anxiety and fear. When the Newport policeman saw

Karl's car in an upscale neighbourhood at night, it wasn't his driving, but his face that made the officer pull Karl over.

My curiosity about faces – and what makes them recognizable – was sparked in 2015, when I was reporting on a story about so-called super-recognizers in London's Metropolitan Police force. These were human officers handpicked for their extraordinary natural ability to identify faces accurately. I spoke to beat cops and detention officers who had viewed thousands of hours of grainy CCTV footage of masked or hooded people in a crowd, or glanced at an individual in custody, and instantly recognized where they'd seen them before, or who they were and what crimes they were wanted for.

After the London riots in 2011, twenty Met police super-recognizers trawled through approximately 5,000 images of suspects. They identified more than 600 of them, 65 per cent of whom ended up in court.[11] When I was writing my story, the force was trying to cultivate and recreate their powers, using AI technology, driven by two questions: what makes these super-recognizers so good at spotting faces in large crowds, and can we capture that essence and distil it into code that computers can read?

It turns out we can and, increasingly, our faces, unique identifiers in a sea of humanity, are being captured without our knowledge or consent by ubiquitous lenses. They are then being used to train machines to become super-recognizers, just like those Met Police officers I encountered nearly a decade ago.

In London, some 900,000 CCTV cameras are surveilling us.[12] Many of the city's surveillance cameras were put in place in the early 1990s in response to IRA bombings in the city, followed by waves of installations after the September 11 and London Underground terrorist attacks in 2001 and 2005, and, later, for the 2012 Olympics. For years, these cameras were unseeing, merely digital peepholes that were naive to who or what they were looking at. But now, many are being upgraded with face recognition capabilities. In parts of the city, AI-enabled cameras already scan the public, searching for citizens on a special police watchlist.

On a chilly February day, I walked out of Stratford underground train station with my scarf pulled tightly around my neck to see a large blue van parked in the street with two large cameras mounted on its roof. The London Metropolitan police were identifying people using facial recognition software as they walked past.

Most passers-by paused to read one of the four signs around the van. Some stopped to speak to the uniformed officers, asking questions and expressing their approval. Others shook their heads in disbelief as they took out their phones to photograph the signs or covered their faces with scarves to prevent identification. A protester stood apart, teeth chattering, with a placard that read 'STOP FACIAL RECOGNITION'.

I struck up a conversation with a bystander named Blem, who lived locally. The Ghanaian-British entrepreneur ran a record label and music production house from inside the St John's Church round the corner, he told me. He mentored youth from local gangs, encouraging them to make music – free studio time in return for staying off the street. The studio has helped support artists like J Hus, Blem told me proudly. It was a community hub, and a safe place for lost kids.

Today, Blem was furious. 'It is appalling. This is the ultimate invasion of privacy. You can't walk the streets with machines looking at your face. What if I've committed no crime, but now my face is on your database?' he said.

I also met Pete Fussey, a criminologist who has been studying crime and surveillance in urban spaces for the past twenty years and is a long-time resident of Stratford. For decades, this area of London had been largely derelict, lined with bombed-out homes from the war, open marshlands and foul-smelling waterways.

Newham, the borough in which Stratford sits, was consistently one of the most deprived in England, with high levels of crime and unemployment; but it was also the most diverse in the country, with over 250 languages spoken within a few square miles, he told me.

'I remember when this shopping centre was just open piles of garbage and refrigerator mountains,' Fussey said, waving his hands at the shiny consumer mecca around us.

When London hosted the Olympics in 2012 right in Stratford's backyard, the neighbourhood got a rapid and expensive facelift. The Westfield shopping mall opened, with luxury branding plastered across it. In its shadow across the street stood its grimy low-rise cousin, the Stratford shopping centre, with small local businesses such as Grandma Mary's Jollof Hut. It offered pedestrians a through road at night, and homeless locals a sheltered place to sleep. Today, it is hidden by a giant sculpture of a shoal of shimmering fish. And the refrigerator mountain that Fussey had recalled was replaced by a Zaha Hadid-designed Aquatic Centre.

It was at this time that CCTV cameras began sprouting in dark bunches along the streets, and by the train station. A yawning steel bridge arched across the railway tracks. At its mouth, two flagpoles stood tall. Perched on top were cameras, watching, logging, saving a feed of those who were crossing back and forth, a way to reassure people they were safe and protected.

Fussey showed me a small equipment room overlooking the bridge, with a door marked 'Private'. For a period in 2019, he had spent several hours here embedded with Metropolitan police officers, who were trialling facial-recognition technology on pedestrians.

Fussey was given unfettered police access during the trials to study their methodology. He had sat with the officers in this make-shift stakeout for several hours over many weeks, while they attempted to identify criminals from amongst the passers-by.

He concluded that the use of the software weakened individual police discretion, while also dulling officers' observational powers and intuition. He had watched them chase down many unknowing and innocent pedestrians after an incorrect face-match from the software, made by Japanese corporation NEC. Rather than an assistive tool, it looked to Fussey like the human officers were often mindlessly carrying out the orders of the machine.

Surveillance technologies like facial recognition also caused a deepening divide between the communities who had lived in Stratford, and those moving in to take their place. While cameras had been installed for the latter group to feel safer, it made the local youth feel like they were under surveillance. As Blem, the music producer, said to me, 'How do they define "criminal"? It's a matter of perspective. These are troubling times.'

The Camofleurs

Just a few miles from Stratford, in a small copse of conifers outside the Francis Crick Institute in London's King's Cross, a dozen young Londoners were preparing to walk the streets in defiance of the city's surveillance cameras. It was a bright September day, and they were using each other's faces instead of protest signs. Their tools: pots of face paint and brushes.

One of the group, Emily Roderick, had painted a thick black line across her face and part of her mouth, with asymmetric orange triangles on one cheek that matched her hair, a slash covering one eyebrow, and white stripes just off her chin. The make-up had turned her face into a misshapen bundle of random shapes and jarring contours. Others had painted on multi-coloured stripes, triangles and thick black-and-white spokes jaggedly crisscrossing their faces.

When they were finished, Emily and her painted companions

gathered and followed their leader for the day, artist Anna Hart. They walked past the St Pancras International train station, through Goods Way, over the canal to Granary Square, a recently re-designed public square with ebullient fountains and a row of restaurants with al fresco diners. There, the group stood, watching the students coming in and out of Central St Martins art college, families splashing in the rainbow sprays, lovers and friends sprawled on the canalside green steps, and then at the tiny cameras positioned around the square, watching, watching, watching.

A few days earlier, I had revealed in a news story in the *Financial Times* that Argent, the property developers who owned this land, had been secretly surveilling passers-by using facial-recognition cameras over the past year.[13] They had been doing so without the permission or knowledge of locals, and working in conjunction with the Met Police.

Emily and three fellow artists studying and working at Central St Martins, located right by the Granary Square cameras, had stumbled across my story, and felt violated. They'd assembled the walking collective, known as the Dazzle Club, in the days afterwards.

The students and faculty at Central St Martins already clashed frequently with Argent, because of the restrictions the company applied to the use of common spaces in the King's Cross area. Two students that Emily knew had been stopped on the square by Red Caps, security guards employed by Argent, who demanded to know why they were pushing a sofa into their studio. 'It's just totally unnecessary,' Emily told me, as we sat together in the same spot in Granary Square. They were artists after all, so they wanted to articulate their protest. As spatial practitioners with an interest in landscape and environment, they also wanted to meditate on how public surveillance changes urban places and citizens.

Before the Dazzle Walks were conceived, Emily and her artistic partner Georgina had been experimenting with CV Dazzle, a make-up technique developed by Berlin-based artist and computer scientist Adam Harvey, to hide from facial recognition software. Based on the 'dazzle camouflage' techniques used on naval warships in the first World War, Harvey's technique involved painting faces in a way that would confound and disrupt face recognition algorithms.

Facial recognition models tend to use facial landmarks – the eyes, and region around them, eyebrows, forehead, nose – and facial symmetry to map, and eventually match, faces. By painting jagged lines and haphazard shapes onto a face, covering up a single eyebrow, or part of the mouth, a simple artist's brush can break the face's symmetry and obscure its landmarks, rendering it invisible to many commercial facial-recognition systems.

'I'm from Leamington Spa, where there was a whole collective of artists called the Camofleurs, and they'd paint buildings to hide them from fighter planes and submarines during the Second World War,' Emily said. 'Time and time again, it's artists that are finding an alternative way to make these conversations more accessible to the public.'

Under today's laws, we don't always get to choose to participate in AI surveillance – even by the private sector. We have no agency as individual citizens when cameras scan our faces, and our images are used to train AI surveillance software. After my story about the King's Cross cameras broke, the UK's data privacy watchdog opened an investigation into it, which remains unresolved as of the time of writing.

Studies done by the UK's Information Commissioner's Office showed that facial recognition changes how people express themselves in public – from displaying their political and religious affiliations, to what they wear and how they act.[14] As it proliferates, it will render the most vulnerable among us – overpoliced groups, activists, journalists – relentlessly and totally visible when outside of our homes, driving those who crave anonymity underground, or into the shadows, or locked away in our homes. At the most intimate level, widespread facial recognition will make it harder for anyone to keep secrets and have private lives.

In Emily's view, the presence of smart cameras dissolves the collective trust we rely on as a society, particularly as women in public spaces. 'That's what Dazzle Club was about, we need to be in public spaces, physically, and look out for one another,' she said. 'We shouldn't have to hide from technology, shrink from being watched.'

That first procession, starting in the Crick trees and ending in Granary Square, turned into twenty-four walks that dozens of artists, activists and other citizens participated in. It spread from King's Cross to other parts of London, and further afield to Manchester, Leeds, Plymouth, Bristol, Birmingham and Margate. The walks were carefully planned so they snaked through housing estates and streets patrolled by smart cameras. No phones or speaking were permitted, the walks purely an hour devoted to reflecting on the experience of being watched.

After two years, the Dazzle Club wound down, its demise brought on by the Covid-19 pandemic, and the founding artists all moving on to different jobs. Emily and her friends still bring out their face paints at heavily surveilled events like the Glastonbury Festival, but they are now considering what the Dazzle Club should evolve into as facial recognition continues to be mostly unregulated.

The last walk Emily led was in her own neighbourhood of Stratford in East London, where the London Metropolitan Police first trialled – and later deployed – live facial-recognition systems to identify pedestrians. The Dazzle group started and finished at the Stratford Centre, the run-down shopping mall across from Westfield. 'It felt like the place to end the walks,' Emily said, 'and talk about how visible certain types of people become when these spaces are being surveilled by facial-recognition cameras.'

Exporting AI Surveillance

The impact of facial recognition starts with the individual, changing the course of a single life like that of Nijer Parks or Amara Majeed or the many unnamed pedestrians across the world who have been caught on camera. But it's increasingly clear that the outcomes of these systems have ripple effects on entire communities, curtailing the freedom and agency of those in cities, across countries.

In Nairobi and Kampala, spherical Huawei cameras perch like glossy black lollipops on lamp-posts lining busy roads. Unblinking eyes observe train commuters in Berlin's Südkreuz terminal, and Buenos Aires's Retiro station. Cameras watch children in public schools in Delhi and Hong Kong. They stand guard on Johannesburg's Vilakazi Street, where Nelson Mandela and Desmond Tutu grew up. In China, the police force holds the world's biggest national database of over a billion faces, and citizens are subject to mass identification.[15]

On 26 January 2021, the day India celebrated its seventieth Republic Day, a ragtag bunch of patriots came riding in trickles and bursts from the edges of New Delhi into the heart of the city. From little towns and villages, Singhu, Tikri and Ghazipur, tens of thousands of farmers rode in on tractors and horses, flying the Indian tricolour flag, the tiranga. They were there to protest restrictive new farm laws enacted by the central government and to fight for their livelihoods – and their families' survival.

Meanwhile, thousands of decorated soldiers were marching on bedecked camels down Rajpath, the grand boulevard at the heart of the capital city, amongst a pride of military tanks and swooping jets.

The farmers broke through the police barricades, shattering the peace. They drove their tractors into flagpoles and destroyed public property. As they did, hundreds of CCTV cameras watched them, analysing their faces.

The police were brutal and swift: they unleashed tear gas and charged with sticks and batons. In the days following, they made it clear there would be consequences for the disruption. 'We are using the facial-recognition system and taking the help of CCTV and video footage to identify the accused,' said the Delhi police commissioner at the time. 'No culprit will be spared.'[16]

Nearly 200 people were eventually identified and arrested for their participation in protests that day.[17]

The Chinese government is one of the heaviest users of facial recognition, and the technology is employed by local governments, private landlords and businesses, and most extensively by law enforcement, to identify individuals of interest across the country. Facial recognition was used to identify protesters and arrest them in their homes during the recent anti-lockdown demonstrations across the country.[18] The software forms part of an extensive technological system used to restrict the Muslim Uyghur community in the province of Xinjiang – a portrait of a province caged by tech-enabled authoritarianism. Chinese academics and military research organizations are adapting the same training data scraped off the internet and used in the West, to inform the architecture of regional surveillance systems.

The government is also exporting its surveillance infrastructure abroad. In the months leading up to Uganda's presidential election in January 2021, Dorothy Mukasa, a long-time civil and digital rights activist based in Kampala, discovered that the Chinese telecommunications giant Huawei was rolling out a massive surveillance system using facial recognition and other artificial intelligence software, with the stated intention to fight crime in her country.

The AI software, which the Ugandan government bought for about \$126m, was part of a wider surveillance of public spaces that Dorothy had been tracking for many years.[19] Facial-recognition technology was a particular problem: it was unregulated, unaccountable and opaque, all things that made her nervous, as Uganda's longtime leader President Yoweri Museveni geared up to run for his sixth term in office since 1986.

In Dorothy's view, this sort of technology, a black box with no technical or ethical standards around it, would bring with it an abuse of rights. Her fear was that AI surveillance would be used by the government to clamp down on free expression of citizens, and on their freedom of assembly and association in public spaces, especially when it came to expressing opposition. She worried that public identification would drive activists into hiding.

This is what Dorothy saw all the time through her work: the notion of surveillance dressed up as national security by those in power. At the end of the day, it was ordinary people's agency being curtailed, and whose rights were being trampled upon. 'Given the history of Chinese surveillance,' she told me, 'it should be concerning to every Ugandan. We all know how the Chinese government is conducting surveillance operations back home. We can't trust them with the provision of surveillance in Uganda.' She worried, too, that black, Ugandan faces would be used to further improve Chinese surveillance systems, in a new and twisted form of colonial resource extraction.

A few months before the election, in November 2020, opposition leader Bobi Wine, whose real name is Robert Kyagulanyi Ssentamu, was arrested on the pretext of Covid-19 violations. The arrest sparked a wave of riots and protests across the country. At least forty-five young people died during the clashes with police.[20] A police spokesperson confirmed that the Huawei-supplied CCTV technology, as well as licence plate readers and facial recognition, was used to identify protestors, and to track down hundreds of suspects who were eventually arrested.

The following January, Yoweri Museveni was re-elected, although

Wine and his team alleged electoral fraud. Dorothy continues to advocate for Ugandan citizens' right to privacy, raising the alarm on surveillance without accountability.

Collective Action

There are currently no clear laws regulating the use of facial recognition by the state, and few that provide protection against private surveillance. The European Union's draft Artificial Intelligence Act is the first to address this gap, proposing to ban facial recognition in public places, although it will likely include exceptions for reasons such as searching for missing children, dangerous criminals and terrorists.[21] Scattered US cities have issued moratoriums on police use. But clear federal laws limiting the use of facial recognition don't yet exist. Meanwhile, citizens all over the world are slowly beginning to challenge the use of the AI technology in courts, creating early legal precedents.

In Hyderabad, S. Q. Masood was locked down with his family, like most of the country during India's second wave of Covid-19 in May 2021. One afternoon, outside of curfew hours, he took his father-in-law out on his scooter to a nearby market to run a couple of quick errands. As they rode home through the narrow streets of Shahran, a majority Muslim neighbourhood, Masood saw a group of two dozen police officers randomly stopping cyclists and riders and snapping photos of them using tablets.

They stopped Masood and asked him to remove his facemask. 'So, I said why? I didn't want to remove mine. I said I'm not going to remove it,' he said. The officers discussed it and stepped back and took Masood's picture with his mask still on, alongside his scooter licence plate.

A few days later, he read that the Hyderabad police were using an app on their tablets to monitor citizens via facial recognition.

The app, called TS-Cop, logged images taken by police into a database of ex-criminals, suspected criminals and other minor offenders, among other categories, to further train the facial-recognition system.[22] Masood's photo, once added to this database, was also accessible to other government and law enforcement agencies. 'I realized the police were building a 360-degree profile of citizens,' he said. 'This was very concerning to me, they had taken my photograph, and I wanted to know which database they will store it in, will they delete it, who else will they give access to? I didn't know anything.'

The Hyderabad police had picked the wrong man to photograph that day. In 2007, when Masood was twenty-three, a pipe bomb triggered by a mobile phone exploded at the nearby mosque where Masood's friends and family worshipped, killing at least a dozen people and igniting religious riots in his neighbourhood. In the weeks that followed, the local police began to illegally detain and arrest Muslim youth.[23] The attack transformed Masood into a civic organizer.

In the aftermath of the bombings, he empowered his community by arming them with information. Over the next decade and a half, he worked with hundreds of Muslim women and youth, informing them about their government entitlements, benefits and rights, teaching them how to claim and assert them, eventually becoming a civil rights activist and a policy advocate for minority groups like his own.

So, when he was photographed by police, Masood spoke to a fellow civic activist who explained facial-recognition technology to him. He began to observe cameras in poor, mostly Muslim populated neighbourhoods around him and wondered how they were being used. That same year, a cluster of campaign groups including Amnesty International recruited local volunteers to map the locations of visible surveillance cameras in two neighbourhoods, including Kala Pathar, where Masood lives with his family.

They found that about 54 per cent of the total area was being watched by CCTV cameras.[24] These cameras were going to be connected up with hundreds of thousands across the city, their footage processed in a 'command and control' centre in the upscale neighbourhood of Banjara Hills, about six miles north of Masood's home. The idea was to identify individuals by applying facial recognition software across all the images.

Masood stopped attending political protests and religious gatherings, and even stopped praying at the Mecca Masjid near his home. But he wanted to fight back. So, he became the first person to sue the Indian government, in his case the state of Telangana in which Hyderabad sits, for building a face database of citizens and violating his fundamental right to privacy.

To prepare for the case, Masood began reading about the technology more widely. He found reports of the same type of surveillance being used in the state of Palestine by the Israeli military and government. He read about how they were linking CCTV to facial recognition algorithms, how all the data was accessible to cops on mobile phones.

He dug further and discovered reports on how AI surveillance has been misused or mistakenly used against black people in the US, and against Uyghur Muslims in China – profiling, targeting and identifying them in public places. The same model, he felt, was being imitated here, in Hyderabad: minorities, in this case religious, being identified at scale, like criminals, with no legitimate underlying rationale. It made people like him feel like criminals without even committing any crime. It took away their ability to roam freely, and gather in groups, without scrutiny. It forced them to continuously justify their very existence.

'They won't stop a car and ask them to remove their mask – then why only stop poor people on scooters?' Masood asked.

Masood's case is still making its way through the courts, where the police have claimed they have the legal right to use facial recognition on citizens, in order to prevent suspicious activities and maintain law and order.

'They can't do this exercise in Banjara Hills or in Jubilee Hills,' he said, referring to Hyderabad's wealthy neighbourhoods. 'They're doing this in the slum areas and South Hyderabad largely, where minorities and Dalit [marginalized castes] tend to live. Why us?'

*

In 2020, Welsh campaigner Ed Bridges won a landmark victory in what was the world's first legal challenge of the police use of facial recognition. The judge ruled that there were 'fundamental deficiencies' in the legal rules governing deployment by the South Wales Police, whom Bridges was suing, and that too broad a discretion was given to officers.[25]

Despite the ruling, UK police forces have continued to deploy and expand their use of live facial-recognition technology across the country, claiming that they are exempt due to their duty to protect citizens.

According to Karl Ricanek, a safer use would be for police detectives to apply facial-recognition tools to photos of suspects on police databases during investigations, rather than in person, where emotions run high and the chance of mistakes is elevated.

Part of the problem is the lack of global laws and standards around facial recognition. Whether that's technical standards for corporations to follow, or ethical and social rules put in place by governments, there has been a torrent of public discourse, but very little action.

Because of the absence of standards and audit requirements for AI algorithms, different parts of a country – even the world – could have completely different AI software. London might have a facial-recognition system designed to minimize racial bias, but

Manchester could have huge error rates on darker-skinned populations. Moscow might have a system with a gender skew, Hong Kong's might struggle with Caucasian faces. No one subject to these systems could know what rules are being applied to them, or why they have been flagged or identified. We would have no choice but to submit to Kafkaesque black boxes.

As I was trying to imagine what that world would look like, I found a fictional vignette on facial recognition written by Indian novelist Rana Dasgupta. It spoke right to my fears about living in a world where private actions, and perhaps even thoughts, cease to exist.

'When every single truth was known – fully and simultaneously to everyone, everywhere – the lie disappeared from society,' he wrote. 'The consequence was that society also disappeared.'

CHAPTER 4
Your Health

Ashita

It was a sunny December afternoon in Chinchpada, a small village about a hundred miles or so inland from the western coast of India, and Dr Ashita Singh was the only physician at the village hospital that day. She was puzzling over fourteen-year-old Parvati, who had been brought in that morning from a village three hours away on the back of a motorcycle. Parvati's symptoms were debilitating: she had a gaping wound in her chest, was the weight of a five-year-old and unable to turn in her bed. Ashita took a chest X-ray to look for tuberculosis, which is rampant in the area. But the scan failed to show the obvious signs of clouded, TB-infected lungs. Still, she suspected the wretched bacteria that killed so many of her patients here. At that moment, Ashita wished for something she often missed in this little hospital: a trusted second opinion.

Outside Chinchpada Christian Hospital, pink bougainvillaea branches hang low over a red-brick wall, framing the neat compound like a picture. Inside, painted wooden benches are crowded with patients who have travelled many hours – some on foot, others on the backs of motorcycles, bullock carts or buses – to see a doctor. Other than Ashita, the hospital has seven junior doctors and no trained radiologists.

Ashita and her husband Deepak, the hospital's only surgeon, had moved to this tiny, blue-painted mission hospital, having spent nearly twenty years working in rural parts of India as part of the Emmanuel Trust, a Catholic charity. The hospital is in the district of Nandurbar, a cluster of remote tribal villages in a fertile valley in Western India. Because of the Satpura hills to its north, Nandurbar's villages are mostly disconnected from the country's rail network, with only a few access roads and highways, cutting it off from expert medical care in other parts of the country.

The majority of Ashita's patients – including Parvati – are *adivasis*, or indigenous people, belonging to the Bhil tribe, one of South Asia's oldest tribal communities. The Bhils are mostly farmers, skilled at growing crops like maize, millet, sugarcane, onion and garlic. They use indigenous seeds and homemade pesticides to nurture fields of wild rice, lentils and barley. They respect and worship the elements that sustain them, 'jal, jameen, jangal', *water, earth, forest.*

In Nandurbar, the majority live in poverty – they work as seasonal labourers for the landowners. In April, the start of the agricultural season, migrant families like Parvati's leave their homes in the villages and pitch temporary tent shelters in sugarcane fields, or build windowless single-room mud huts, so they can live and work there all day.

To treat nearly two million people, the district of Nandurbar had roughly fifty-eight primary healthcare centres as of 2014, units of the public healthcare system which are essentially single-physician clinics providing basic medical care.[1] Many of these centres are unstaffed by doctors, their buildings and staff quarters fallen into disrepair. The very poorest patients are brought to these decrepit shacks on what locals call 'bamb-ulances' – makeshift stretchers, in the place of ambulances, made from bamboo and bedsheets – on the shoulders of healthy relatives.

The Bhils are besieged by specific medical problems, often worsened by overcrowding and poverty, such as malnutrition, alcoholism and tuberculosis, a highly infectious illness that thrives in airless spaces and starving bodies.

In Nandurbar's inhabitants, tuberculosis bacteria fester freely, facilitated by the lack of timely medical care, making it one of the worst-hit areas in a country riddled with the deadly infection. Left unchecked, the disease often spreads beyond the lungs, and into their victims' every organ, from their spines to their brains.

Despite their extreme need, Ashita found that most of the indigenous communities mistrusted the hospital's methods of Western medicine. They preferred their local ayurvedic or indigenous medical practitioner, who administered herbal treatments and was cheaper and more accessible. When she arrived, Ashita's first big challenge was getting the Bhils to place their faith in her expertise. She was also aware that she needed to learn from them if this was to be a true partnership in trust.

At first, Ashita saw her patients primarily in the hospital. This was where they wore their best clothes, put on their best faces and came in utter desperation from hundreds of kilometres away. Hospital was usually a last resort. She would diagnose them with, say, advanced tuberculosis, write prescriptions for drugs and send them home. She knew there was an access problem: it pained her to see her patients dying from a curable disease, one that could be treated if it were just caught early in primary health centres. But she didn't, at first, consider what they ate for dinner nor where they'd left their children when they came into the hospital.

She knew, of course, they were poor. That's why she and her husband had chosen to move here in the first place. The private hospital prided itself on being inexpensive: tuberculosis antibiotics and outpatient consultations cost about Rs.50 (50p), with a further

Rs.20 (20p) cost for follow-up appointments. It cost between Rs.3,000 and Rs.5,000 (£30–£50) all in for a hospital admission, which included all the tests, drugs and treatments needed until the patient was discharged. But even that was too expensive for some of the locals. The public hospital in town was free.

A few months into her new job, Ashita started a palliative home-care programme. Along with her medical staff, Ashita went to schools, marketplaces, *anganwadi* or rural childcare centres, and community health workers' meetings. She was invited into people's homes to teach them how to dress wounds and draw blood for their sick loved ones, so they wouldn't have to come into the hospital. It was during these visits that Ashita realized that eating rice was a luxury for the Bhils, that the mud houses had no windows, that the men drank home-brewed liquor made from the flowers of the *Mahua* tree, that the children didn't go to school in the agricultural season.

She learned to ask about her patients' social and psychological needs – not just their medical ones – when they came in to see her. *Where are you coming from? What time did you leave home? How much did it cost you to get here?* About half her patients had borrowed money just to come into the hospital. That helped her adapt the hospital's caregiving to them. She couldn't order extra tests for her own comfort or prescribe alternative drugs that cost slightly more than what she had estimated, because many patients came with exact change in their pockets.

She used to tell the newly diagnosed TB patients to eat protein when she discharged them with prescriptions, but soon realized they couldn't afford to. So she put her own money aside to provide a monthly supply of eggs as a nutritional supplement to all patients on TB drugs.

Aside from her clinical practice, Ashita also began to study bioethics. She wanted her patients to have dignity, not just drugs.

She respected that physical autonomy – the ability to make decisions about our own bodies – mattered to everyone. Our bodies are sacred spaces, rarely given over to anyone for safekeeping. We choose who to trust with them. We feel violated if even *virtual* versions of them are watched, distorted or interfered with, without our consent – as in the case of deepfake manipulation or face recognition. The Bhils were no different.

Doctors are one of the few classes of experts to whom we do give over our agency. We expect them to make informed, ethical decisions to keep us safe and alive. They are an example of what Albert Bandura describes as our 'proxy' agents.[2] Ashita took that responsibility seriously and she understood that without her patients' acceptance, diagnostic tools and technologies would be no use to her.

The App Will See You Now

On the day Parvati came in, her condition critical, Ashita was in a race against time. If this had been a few months earlier, she might have sent a sputum sample for testing at the larger district hospital. They would have returned the results in a few days. But Parvati didn't have days left, she was barely alive, so Ashita decided to try an app that she had been testing for a few weeks already. It was easy to use and she figured that she didn't have anything to lose in the context of such urgency.

The qTrack app was powered by a set of machine-learning algorithms trained on past X-rays and sputum test data, that could perform the task which it had taken Ashita years to perfect: spotting potential tuberculosis from an X-ray, as accurately as a radiologist might. Its benefit was that it could act as an additional screening tool, a second opinion for Ashita. And in hospitals where doctors like Ashita simply weren't available, the app could act as a diagnostic screen on its own.

Since the early days of her training, Ashita had found herself gravitating towards doctors who put patient relationships at the centre of their teaching methods. 'Yes,' she told me with her customary twinkly smile, 'medicine is a science, but being a physician is an art. Practising medicine, it's very human. It takes a high emotional IQ, a lot of heart to actually apply the science to be effective.'

And what makes the best doctors effective, according to her, is how they relate to patients and win their confidences. Sometimes, that means 'sacrificing your academic knowledge at the altar of a patient's wellbeing.' Her goal was to practise with intuition and empathy and that, she said, 'takes a different kind of intelligence.'

The best doctors, Ashita suggested, didn't impose an objective view; they were acutely aware of their own fallibility, the fact that they can *never* be 100 per cent sure. This perspective is what allows them to operate – thrive, even – within the constraints of having to heal a multitude of complex and unique human bodies.

So in 2019, when a friend from medical school mentioned an AI program, designed by a Mumbai-based company called Qure.ai, that could help to diagnose tuberculosis, Ashita was sceptical. The Bhils needed the basics: better nutrition and housing, access to more qualified doctors and early diagnoses, and common life-saving drugs like antibiotics. She felt that technology such as digital medical devices often failed her patients because the systems were not designed for remote and under-resourced settings like Chinchpada.

But then, her curiosity was piqued, and she began reading about Qure's AI system, known as qXR. She learned that the software was trained to pick up visual patterns suggesting tuberculosis in X-rays and output a patient's potential risk for tuberculosis. The way she understood it, these so-called diagnostic algorithms were not automated versions of human doctors. They were simply investigative tools. The underlying AI software was trained using a narrow set of data, such as doctors' labels or gold-standard tests like X-rays, to estimate risk of tuberculosis. Other trials had shown it performed on par with the best radiologists.

A suspected TB patient would still need medical infrastructure. Their app score had to be confirmed by a microbiological diagnosis – re-growing the bacteria from a sample of their phlegm in a lab. And a human was needed to deliver a diagnosis and prescribe treatment. Plus, she didn't even know if the tech really worked.

But if they could read X-rays accurately, Ashita believed AI systems could be transformational for rural folk. The technology was relatively cheap to scale, and it could be deployed out in the field *without trained doctors*. This was crucial because in remote government clinics and even mobile X-ray vans that drove into the heartlands of rural districts like Nandurbar, there were often no qualified human specialists. A clinically validated AI app could act as a screen, and instantly flag the highest-risk patients for follow-up. It would close the lag time, usually days or weeks, between conducting and analysing an X-ray, during which these patients could either disappear, spread the infection, or be killed by it. 'We have people travelling to us five or six hours each way for a straightforward diagnosis of TB, simply because of the many months they spent going to quack after quack, getting IV fluids and cough syrups,' she tells me. In the previous week alone, she'd had five patients admitted on a single day with advanced TB. Two had died.

This was the key. 'We aren't talking about improving quality of life here, we are talking about preventing death,' Ashita said. 'Imagine what a gift it would be.'

Keen to see the algorithms in action, she didn't mind being a guinea pig. No money exchanged hands. She agreed to try it out alongside her regular clinical methods. 'If it's going to make a difference to our communities, I'm happy to help train the AI. And if it isn't, it will simply be disproved. It wasn't going to increase our patients' load,' she said.

The experiment at Chinchpada Christian Hospital has been mutually beneficial for Qure.ai and the hospital. Ashita uses the qTrack app at least once a day, and gives feedback to the company, although her patients' data isn't used to train the system. When she first started using the mobile app, she found there were too many steps: it had to be uploaded and read in the cloud, making it impractical for use on the wards. 'We kept telling them, unless it's handy and quick, we aren't going to use it. If I've seen the X-ray and the patient and made a decision, I'm not going to go back to the app in five hours,' she shrugged. The company worked on making the app more seamless. Now, X-rays are instantaneously uploaded into the app and analysed. 'The decision is on our phone within minutes,' Ashita said.

On the day Parvati's uncle brought her in, curled up in a ball, she was a perfect candidate to test qTrack on, a diagnostic grey area. Ashita knew that antibacterial drugs, like those used to treat tuberculosis, could be toxic for children – particularly if they are prescribed based on a mistaken diagnosis. Nevertheless, when the app warned that Parvati – who was also a Type 1 juvenile diabetic – was a presumptive, or suspected, tuberculosis case, Ashita decided to start treatment immediately. Without the app, she might have waited for confirmation of her diagnosis from the lab at the district hospital, sixty kilometres away. But since time was of the essence, and the app had backed her up, she chose to treat quickly. 'It really helps to confirm your thoughts, it is reassuring, like a colleague,' she told me.

Within days, Parvati's wound had healed, and she began to put on weight, speaking again, smiling and painting pictures in the ward. Under the tender care of the nurses, she blossomed. They discovered she could read and write in multiple languages, including English. Because she was literate, Ashita was able to teach her how to use a glucometer to record her own sugar levels in order to manage her diabetes – and gave her one to keep. Three weeks later, she was sent home to recuperate. Today, she is healthy enough to be back at school.

When the app flashed Parvati's TB risk as 'presumptive', Ashita felt a sense of disbelief. 'Imagine a non-human making such detailed conclusions from something that's not just mathematical or objective,' she said. 'I would have said, how can you teach a machine to do that? It is impossible. But here it was. You can.'

A Plague and a Blessing

At the start of 2020, Chinchpada saw a rise in cases of a new, virulent virus that had hitched its way nearly 3,000 miles from Wuhan, China. At Qure.ai's headquarters in Mumbai, computer scientists used hundreds of lung X-rays of thousands of Covid-19 patients to train a new set of algorithms that could produce a diagnosis of coronavirus infection, which they built into an app. The Mumbai city government deployed frontline health workers with the app to drive into heavily infected areas such as the Dharavi slum settlement where they could conduct spot tests and quarantine families, before PCR tests became widely available.

In those early days of the pandemic, Ashita also began using qTrack to help diagnose the novel coronavirus, as Qure.ai had assured her it could. However, pretty early on, she found it was making a crucial error: it often confused the X-rays of her tuberculosis patients with Covid-19.

The confusion was understandable to an infectious disease expert – the ravage of TB-infected lungs is strikingly similar to that of lungs colonized by the coronavirus. Many physicians struggled to distinguish the two – and as the AI software was trained on human physicians' diagnoses, it did too.

But Ashita was attuned to tuberculosis – she saw the bacteria walk through her doors every single day in all its grisly forms. So she reported the problem to the company, who worked to add a tuberculosis filter into the app – if a patient came in with fluffy, clouded lungs, the app first screened for their TB risk, before looking for unique signs of Covid. It learned statistically to tell the two diseases apart.

In this case, the AI model wasn't able to assist her, as it had been designed to do. Instead *she* had helped improve the software, which was then deployed more widely.

Qure.ai can now help diagnose diseases including Covid-19, tuberculosis, head trauma and lung cancer. They operate at more than 600 sites in sixty countries across the world, from slums in the Philippines, to cities in Malawi, Peru and Mexico.[3] In Mumbai's state hospitals, the diagnosis of tuberculosis went up 35 per cent because of the AI screen.[4] The company has raised more than $60m in funding from foreign investors like blue-chip Silicon Valley venture firm Sequoia Capital and pharmaceutical giant Merck.[5]

In the spring of 2021, Chinchpada was hit by a fresh tsunami of cases of a new variant of Covid-19. This second wave of the pandemic in India killed 100,000 people in weeks, bringing the healthcare system to its knees and forcing people to dispose of their dead in the streets.[6] Having escaped the first wave relatively unscathed, the country – my country – became the epicentre of the global pandemic.

For Ashita, life quickly became overwhelming and in our subsequent exchange of messages, I could see how traumatic this time was for her. 'We have increased the bed capacity of our fifty-bed little rural hospital to eighty-four beds . . . all full the whole time,' she WhatsApped me. 'Forty to fifty patients on oxygen, four on a ventilator and two to five deaths daily. Plus many dying at home in the villages because they don't want to be isolated in a hospital. People with other illnesses are going without any care: heart attacks, snake bites, tuberculosis. This month we have so far only diagnosed two tuberculosis patients. The government machinery for free tuberculosis testing has ground to a halt. The pandemic has just revealed the broken healthcare system of our country. I just don't know when all this will end. It is too painful.'

It was on one of those distressing mornings in 2021, a day that merged into all the others for Ashita, that Jainabai, a Bhil farm labourer and severe diabetic in her forties, came in with a raging fever. She was from a nearby village and one of the hospital's regular patients. When she was brought in on the back of a bullock cart, Ashita immediately noted her symptoms with dread. Her X-ray didn't look particularly like Covid-19 to Ashita, but her oxygen saturation was a dangerous 92 per cent and Jainabai was on the borderline for needing urgent intervention.

When faced with coronavirus at that point, there were a few key decisions a doctor could take to save a life. They could treat with steroids, for instance, or put the patient on a ventilator. Jainabai was the kind of patient who would benefit from steroids, *if* she had Covid-19. But Ashita was hesitant, because in Jainabai's case, the treatment could also kill her. The steroids would cause her blood sugar to shoot up from already life-threatening levels, caused by Jainabai not taking her diabetes medication in recent weeks. So Ashita reached for the qTrack app, which she saw as an objective filter.

When the software flagged Jainabai as being at high risk for Covid-19, it helped make up Ashita's mind. 'I knew if I delayed the steroids, she might deteriorate badly. So we aggressively controlled the sugars with a lot of insulin and we did give her steroids, because of what the app said. Thankfully, she did well, and she recovered.'

And so it was, that through the roiling waves of the pandemic, the technology became a consistent presence in Chinchpada. It improved with each case it was fed, and offered a steady risk indicator in the midst of so many uncertainties. It was a time when even doctors were constantly re-evaluating what they had learned. 'The app became something we could fall back on, something to add to our clinical suspicions,' Ashita told me. 'It was a great blessing.'

Now, Ashita believes, is the right time to roll out X-ray screening algorithms to entire communities like the Bhils. This would help catch diseases like tuberculosis which were neglected during the pandemic before they become full-blown problems, allowing the *adivasi* community a quality of life and access to healthcare they need and deserve.

*

Ashita's first job as a newly qualified doctor back in 2005 was in a hospital on the outskirts of Tezpur, a small city in the eastern state of Assam known for its lush tea plantations and its unparalleled view of the Himalayas. Tribal populations who made their home in the hills would often come down to the city, the first urban settlement they could get to on foot, for urgent medical attention.

Not only was Ashita the sole doctor, but the hospital also lacked much of the basic equipment modern physicians rely on: X-rays, blood-gas machines, CT scanners, ventilators. There were no nearby labs to confirm diagnoses and no functioning public health infrastructure to embed patients into. She realized it was going to be impossible to practise the type of medicine that her medical textbooks had taught and she was going to have to accept her limitations as a doctor.

The year after she and her husband arrived, a malaria epidemic swept Tezpur in the humid, mosquito-filled summer of 2006. The small hospital had nearly 300 deaths within weeks.[7] Ashita, pregnant with her first child at the time, was present at the bedside of almost all of these patients. 'I was really torn, I couldn't sleep at night,' she said. 'That was really hard for me, watching children come in, gasping and dying. We couldn't do anything.'

She grieved each death, replaying her decisions late at night while she lay awake. Had she overlooked a solution? Made a diagnosis too late? Was there a way to save them staring her in the face? It took her many months to come to a place of peace, to accept that her elite medical training was insufficient to save lives here and that she needed to learn how to make do and trust her instincts.

Practising medicine through a crisis with minimal resources is what shaped Ashita and it's why, after years being forced to practise medicine with the most basic technological aids, she has never allowed technology, including AI, to usurp her agency as a physician. Artificial intelligence is designed to provide an answer in black or white. It lacks nuance. If her experience disagrees with its output, she knows she cannot place blind trust in it.

'It's not a magical tool, I cannot let it become a master over my decisions, to let it rule over me,' she says. She is aware of its limits, and that it can make errors, as human doctors do. 'Doctors are also uncertain, but we are still responsible for our patients. I'm making nuanced decisions, moral choices as a doctor. AI can't do that.'

As the use of AI becomes widespread, its users must become wary of automation bias, a widely studied phenomenon in which people start to become over-reliant on automation to do their jobs. It's the case with everything from self-driving cars to security cameras. Does Ashita worry, I wonder, that doctors too will become less vigilant and more complacent about second-guessing diagnostic AI's assumptions? Will it ultimately leave their own skills and agency diminished?

Ashita has thought about this, and she says using Qure's app hasn't changed how she makes decisions – but only because she is hyper-aware of its presence and views it as experimental. But it may not stay that way for long. 'In a new generation of medical students looking for quick fixes and early gratification, it's hard to help them to see the value of engaging deeply with patients, with histories and [physical] exams,' she says. 'I see a risk of it becoming your master only if you're not grounded in good medicine.'

Widespread effects of automation bias amongst doctors would be crippling, but in the context of her patients, she believes the gains from medical AI would far outweigh this risk.

'Of all the resources that are being poured into TB prevention, treatment and care, this should be invested in, it's an affordable option,' she says. But Ashita knows it's only affordable for patients like hers if it's subsidized by the government, leapfrogging the need for existing healthcare infrastructure. If it remains an expensive perk, it will never reach those who need it, she said. 'I've told [Qure.ai], if you tell me it's going to cost extra for my patients, I'm out,' she told me. 'The moment you do that, I'm out. I'd rather buy them eggs.'

Ziad

More than 8,000 miles away, in the heart of Silicon Valley, Ziad Obermeyer, a Harvard-trained emergency physician and artificial intelligence researcher at the University of California, Berkeley, is trying to redress inequities in his own small way.

In 2012, as a medical resident working in Boston's most prestigious hospitals, resources were no obstacle for Ziad. But as a self-described 'somewhat-bumbling' resident in the emergency room at Mass General Brigham, Ziad discovered that even the world's best-resourced doctors routinely make fatal errors. He was dismayed by just how hard and often medical professionals fail every day.

'Particularly in the emergency room,' he told me, 'you just make a lot of mistakes and those are very painful. You're working for about ten to twelve hours at a time. So you see twenty, thirty, sometimes forty patients in that span of time and you're constantly making decisions. Decisions like, is this person having a heart attack, should I do a test, what will happen to this person if I send them home?'

All human beings struggle with multivariate questions. In emergency rooms, doctors' brains stitch together enormous numbers of possibilities, using often incomplete, messy and difficult-to-access data.[8] Then, they have to make highly accurate risk estimates about a person's survival. The quality of these estimates can depend on the individual physician, influenced by their background and experience, even their moods. The process is neither precise, nor objective.

Ziad spent a decade pondering the errors made by his professional peers, publishing a study exploring how physicians make decisions, specifically when diagnosing heart attacks.[9] Using data from the hospital where he worked – 246,265 emergency visits from 2010–15 that tracked tests, treatments and health outcomes – he showed that doctors over-test low-risk people for heart attacks, who do not benefit from them; but they also tend to under-test patients at high risk, who go on to have adverse outcomes such as heart attacks or even death, at unacceptably high rates. The results pointed to 'systematic errors of judgements' amongst physicians, partly due to their mental model of risk being too simple.

Ziad had also seen how hospitals operated *without* trained specialists. After completing his residency in Boston, a friend had asked if he'd be willing to do a short stint at the emergency department of the Tséhootsoí Medical Center at Fort Defiance, Arizona. The hospital had an unusual catchment area, sitting on the border of New Mexico and Arizona, in the vast plains of the Navajo Nation, serving the indigenous Navajo community in its emergency room. Ziad spent a year working as the only emergency doctor at Tséhootsoí.

The beauty of the North American desert, riven with deep canyons and rocky buttes, was marred by severe societal strains: the region had sky-high rates of crime, alcohol abuse, traffic accidents, depression and suicides, particularly among young people.[10] Being in Tséhootsoí, Ziad decided, was like being marooned on a beautiful but bleak island. 'The kinds of choices you have to make there, you just don't in Boston,' he said. 'Because it's so isolated and the landscape is harsh, you have agonising decisions to make.'

Like Chinchpada, this was the sort of place that desperately needed the basics: more trained doctors, life-saving equipment, and social care. The Navajo hospital had a small intensive care unit, for instance, but no specialist surgeons or catheterization labs which are required to treat heart attacks. So if a patient's symptoms suggested a heart attack, the doctors would need to get an air ambulance on standby to Albuquerque or Flagstaff, three hours away. But, as Ziad explained, if they were going to be OK, you didn't want to send someone several hours away without their family, and with no way of coming home.

Each decision could be life-or-death. Ziad often felt there had to be a more objective and consistent way to make these calls than relying on individual doctors. The answer, he felt, could be artificial intelligence.

People Like Us

During his time at Tséhootsoí, and in the Boston emergency rooms, Ziad had felt that Western medicine was failing those at the margins of the system – people of colour, all those who identify as female, or are poor, unemployed, and uneducated. He had seen first-hand how the Navajo community suffered from a lack of sophisticated healthcare.

This wasn't, he told me, just a social issue. Inequality is widespread in the *design* of health technologies too. Take the ubiquitous pulse oximeter – a device that clips to the end of your finger to measure the level of oxygen in your blood. This tool is a familiar sight in local family physician offices and in the homes of the sick and elderly, acting as a quick, efficient way to monitor potentially fatal changes in your body chemistry. It works by detecting changes in the amount of light absorbed by your skin, a measure that can detect the percentage of oxygen in the blood.

The device doesn't, Ziad told me, account for differing levels of melanin in the skin though, and studies have shown that the pulse oximeter doesn't work as accurately on darker-skinned patients, whose skin absorbs more light than their light-skinned counterparts.[11] The device is biased by design. In a 2020 study, researchers at the University of Michigan found the device reassured 12 per cent of black patients who had dangerously low levels of oxygen in their blood that their levels were safe.[12] The oximeter, still widely used around the world in its current form, shows how technology design can be discriminatory and result in avoidable deaths, particularly of people of colour.

It was the widespread inequities in medicine that led Ziad to study AI as a potential solution, and he developed a fascination with how data-driven tools like machine-learning models could help doctors improve their decision-making – and serve all patients better. The more he understood it, the more confident he became that these pattern-spotting systems would bring to the emergency room skills that human physicians lacked: better understanding of minority population health, the ability to correct cognitive biases, and to make more informed predictions about life and death. He believed not only that AI could deliver better medical care, but also that it could close existing disparities, rather than widen them.

Ziad was aware, though, that AI systems weren't infallible. After all, the AI models were designed by humans, and the data they ingested reflected the society they came from. *We* choose which data points to take into account, what the AI's gold standard 'objective' is, say, in a radiologist's diagnosis – and we influence how these variables are weighed, such as indicating that doctors' insights are more valuable than patient experiences.

Deep-rooted biases – like how racial minorities and women are treated by the medical establishment, for instance – are baked into these choices. I had learned that to believe that AI intrinsically provides objectivity or skills that human beings cannot is pure fantasy. Unless we are able to visualize those biases plainly, and then design AI systems to avoid their pitfalls, they will pockmark algorithmic decisions, just like they do our own.

Back in 2019, Ziad decided to audit medical algorithms already in use by healthcare institutions to assess their accuracy. The first program he got access to was an AI system designed by Optum, a large American healthcare provider, whose algorithms were used to recommend extra medical support for roughly seventy million people in the United States each year.[13] The healthcare system relied on this algorithm to refer primary-care patients with complex health problems for additional care, such as dedicated nurses or extra GP appointments. The goal was to prevent their deterioration, such as ending up in hospital. The models produced risk scores for each patient, which were used by medical providers across the country to decide which patients should be referred for 'high-risk management'.

While plotting the algorithm's risk scores for individual patients, Ziad noticed an oddity in the data: black patients seemed to have lower scores than he would have expected, given how sick they ended up being. When he dug further, he discovered why. The algorithm's designers had made a design choice that on its surface seemed innocuous – they had trained their system to estimate a person's health based on their total healthcare costs in a year. In other words, the model was using healthcare *costs* as a proxy for healthcare *needs*.[14]

At a glance, that seems reasonable, because when people get sicker, they are generally more expensive to their healthcare system. But the problem with this assumption, which was reflected in the model's underlying design, is that not everyone generates costs in the same way. Minorities, and other under-served populations lacking access to healthcare, may be less able to get time off work for doctors' visits, or experience discrimination within the system that puts them off, resulting in fewer treatments or tests, which can lead to them being classed as less costly. But their healthcare needs were, on average, higher than white patients with equivalent health costs.

This particular design error resulted in widespread racial bias in the AI system: the model was systematically prioritising healthier white patients over sicker black patients who needed the extra attention and care. The researchers calculated that the algorithm's bias more than halved the number of black patients that should have been referred for special care. 'Your costs are going to be lower even though your needs are the same. And that was the root of the bias that we found,' Ziad said. He offered to help Optum redesign its AI using data that was more reflective of a patient's actual health – which they did – and the redesign reduced the racial bias significantly.

Unlike the biases or mistakes of individual doctors, this AI-initiated error affected black patients at a staggering scale. Cost was used as a proxy variable for healthcare needs in several other similar AI systems, a decision that Ziad estimated affected the lives of around 200 million Americans. And it reached beyond the United States.

'It was a systematic error in how we were all thinking about this problem – the problem of predicting whose health was going to deteriorate,' said Ziad. 'That error propagated through the entire sector, through government healthcare insurance in the US and in healthcare systems run by governments in Europe. All of us were making the same error.'

Doctor vs Data

Despite uncovering widespread AI errors in healthcare, Ziad remained optimistic about how algorithms might help to care better for all patients. He felt they could be particularly useful in improving diagnostics that doctors tended to get wrong, but also in improving our current medical knowledge by discovering new patterns in medical data. Most modern healthcare AI is trained on doctors' diagnoses, which Ziad felt wasn't enough. 'If we want AI algorithms to teach us new things,' he said, 'that means we can't train them to learn just from doctors, because then it sets a very low ceiling – they can only teach us what we already know, possibly more cheaply and more efficiently.' Rather than use AI as an alternative to human doctors – who weren't as scarce as in rural India – he wanted to use the technology to *augment* what the best doctors could do.

He decided to take on a medical puzzle that has thwarted doctors for decades: why African Americans experience more pain than those of the same age and condition from other ancestries. He wanted to solve this not just for his patients' benefit, but to answer a more philosophical question for himself: could an AI model surpass the limitations of human beings and add to existing medical knowledge?

It had long been observed that African American patients report higher levels of pain compared to others, for what physicians perceive as the very same traumas. If you take two arthritis patients of different ancestries and control for biological factors like age, African American patients on average will report more pain from knees that look the same on an X-ray to a trained radiologist.[15] Researchers have tried to explain this with a range of hypotheses including stress and poverty, among others. However, all those explanations have one thing in common: that the problem is not in their bodies. Ziad's hypothesis was that doctors were missing some biological differences in how pain is experienced differently amongst ethnically diverse patients.

We have all felt pain – dull, throbbing, searing, visceral, earthy, indescribable. Pain is a human inevitability, an evolutionary shield. Estimating someone else's pain is subjective, and influenced by everything from your culture, gender and language to your individual neurophysiology – the chemical signals pinging in your brain. Quantifying pain is a task racked with individual biases. Yet it has been attempted by scientists for decades. Take the epidemiologist John Lawrence, who in 1952 decided to classify pain by turning the city of Leigh into his laboratory.

Leigh, part of Manchester, was at the heart of England's mining country, dissected by low bridges and colliery railways that in the 1950s carried millions of tonnes of coal to factories around the nation. Lawrence spent two years studying osteoarthritis in local coal miners, and comparing and contrasting their bone structure and blood chemistry with that of the town's office workers. The X-rays he collected and painstakingly annotated by hand form the foundation of the global system that radiologists use to rate the physiological extent of osteoarthritis today, known as the 'Kellgren & Lawrence' classification system.

Lawrence glossed over one important feature of his dataset: the miners and office workers of 1950s Leigh were mostly all male and of European ancestry, like Lawrence himself. 'All of our grading systems and knowledge about arthritis that we use in medical practice today come from the studies from this very specific time and place and population,' Ziad told me. It means the classification system didn't reflect the biological reality of people Lawrence didn't include in his study – largely women and people of other ancestries. That narrow dataset being used to make broad medical diagnoses led Ziad to suspect there was more to the story of human pain than we think.

To solve the mystery, Ziad had to return to first principles. He wanted to build a software that could predict a patient's pain levels based on their X-ray scans. But rather than training the machine-learning algorithms to learn from doctors with their own intrinsic biases and blind spots, he trained them on patients' self-reports. To do this, he acquired a training dataset from the US National Institutes of Health, a set of knee X-rays annotated with patients' own descriptions of their pain levels, rather than simply a radiologist's classification. The arthritis pain model he built found correlations between X-ray images and pain descriptions. He then used it to predict how severe a new patient's knee pain was, from their X-ray. His goal wasn't to build a commercial app, but to carry out a scientific experiment.

It turned out that the algorithms trained on patients' own reported pain did a far better job than a human radiologist in predicting which knees were more painful.

The most striking outcome was that Ziad's pain model outperformed human radiologists at predicting pain in African American patients. 'The algorithms were seeing signals in the knee X-ray that the radiologist was missing, and those signals were disproportionately present in black patients and not white patients,' he said. The research was published in 2021, and concluded: 'Because algorithmic severity measures better capture underserved patients' pain, and severity measures influence treatment decisions, algorithmic predictions could potentially redress disparities in access to treatments like arthroplasty.'[16]

Meanwhile, Ziad plans to dig deeper to decode what those signals are. He is using machine-learning techniques to investigate what is causing excess pain using MRIs and samples of cartilage or bone in the lab. If he finds explanations, AI may have helped to discover something new about human physiology and neuroscience that would have otherwise been ignored.

'The AI method opens the door to so many interesting possibilities of medical discovery,' he said. 'That's the really exciting part.'

The New, New Colonialism

The conversations I had with Ziad and Ashita over two years always left me feeling optimistic. Through my journey reporting on the effects of AI on human beings, healthcare was the one area where the technology felt like it had genuinely life-changing potential. Clinically tested AI software can now read scans as well as human radiologists, helping to diagnose deadly diseases early, and to find new cures. In the circumstances that both Ziad and Ashita envisioned – tools that could bridge existing societal inequalities, for patients being failed by the current system – the algorithms became a symbol of certitude, and of hope.

Urvashi Aneja, a political scientist who lives just a few hours away from Chinchpada, has spent the past six years studying applications of AI in healthcare in India, trying to weigh up the benefits and the risks for the most vulnerable pockets of the population. But she's not as optimistic as I am.

As she surveyed the various AI prototypes and projects being trialled across the country, she found the landscape littered with what she calls a 'graveyard of pilots'. While Qure's small-scale pilot at the 50-bed Chinchpada Christian Hospital may have shown promise, it hasn't been scaled up meaningfully in the area as yet. Aneja had seen dozens of others like it, trials that remained nothing but successful experiments. To benefit the rural patients that were falling through the cracks, the technology would have to be integrated into the public healthcare system, not just private hospitals. And Aneja couldn't see any sustainable ways to do this without a *lot* more state investment.

The irony hit home on a sultry September afternoon in 2020, when she was visiting a family member in a large private hospital in Delhi. A big sign by the reception desk asked visitors: 'Do you want to be diagnosed by AI for tuberculosis? This way → for a VIP service.'

'AI-enabled diagnostics were being offered as a premium service, an added package if you want to pay for it. *That's* the market today,' she said. 'It doesn't make sense for companies to invest in the poorest and most remote regions, because this section of the population can't afford AI-based healthcare, just as they can't afford non-AI healthcare. That basic tension still remains.'

The development of AI diagnostics has been turbocharged mainly by investment from private Western corporations like Google and Amazon, rather than governments. The prize, according to estimates, ranges from anywhere between four and seven billion dollars by 2028.[17]

Data collection through local partnerships is key to the development of AI technologies, because access to sensitive medical information is highly regulated and extremely hard to come by. And without that data, there can be no AI.

For instance, Google has teamed up with India's best-known, low-cost chain of hospitals, Aravind Eye Hospital, to test an AI software that could diagnose diabetic retinopathy, a serious condition that can cause blindness if left untreated.[18] Google trained the AI models on anonymized medical datasets donated by Aravind. The Silicon Valley giant has now expanded and rolled out this tool in other countries such as Thailand and the United States too.

Meanwhile, Qure.ai has expanded into lucrative Western markets, including the UK's National Health Service and hospitals in the US and European Union. Aneja fears that the data collected by these companies from poor and rural Indians will result in expensive technology that will benefit those customers, including governments, who can afford to pay, and exclude the marginalized patients that helped build them.

Her most pressing concern was about shifting power dynamics, led by data ownership. 'What we are seeing playing out in India, and the Global South more broadly,' she told me, 'is a form of digital colonialism, where a lot of data is being collected from citizens, with little value-add on the ground, and maximum value extraction by tech corporations.'

*

Across India, the distribution of healthcare in the rural backwaters of the country like Chinchpada is done in the most human of ways: door to door, by frontline workers known as Accredited Social Health Activists, or ASHAs. In Hindi, *Asha* means hope. These workers are primarily local women, empowered by the village *panchayat* or council to work within their communities – the connective membrane of trust between households and the government health system. They are recruited to drive immunization, to provide prenatal and postnatal care, facilitate hospital births, give nutritional guidance, and to monitor the health of children in their region.

In practice, Asha workers care for mothers and babies, informally give out medical advice and medication, function as an early warning system for outbreaks, and act as a valuable ear to the ground from the innards of a vast and populous country, with a creaking healthcare infrastructure. If a doctor like Ashita is the pinnacle of care that rural communities can receive, Asha workers are the rockface of India's public health network.

But as artificial intelligence companies enter the healthcare market, Asha workers have also become data collectors, increasingly logging digitized medical information into iPads provided by the government, about everything from household vaccinations to women's health, children's nutrition and sexually transmitted infections. The women are paid a small fee by the state but are often co-opted and paid by private organizations who need oceans of clean, reliable data to build AI systems. They are trusted by local families, who consent to sharing their information, making the Ashas valuable data syphons.

Wadhwani AI, an Indian non-profit funded by a $2m grant from Google among others,[19] worked with Ashas across four states and fifty locations to create a dataset of videos of newborn babies.[20] The dataset is now described as the 'bedrock' of the company's work on anthropometry, the science of human measurement, for the development of an AI-enabled tool to detect the weight of infants in rural locations.

Aneja had conversations with dozens of Asha workers and rural physicians to map out how these local data gatherers helped to improve AI algorithms for multinational companies. She found that Indian start-ups who build the models are often regional talent-bases for Western companies who leverage their data and expertise through partnerships and develop specialized algorithms for other markets. Qure.ai, for instance, has teamed up with the UK's National Health Service and AstraZeneca to provide its lung cancer screening algorithms across the world.

If the communities themselves saw clear utility from sharing their data, this could be seen as a positive way to advance scientific understanding and provide better healthcare for all. However, those who Aneja spoke to felt excluded from the benefits of these new technologies that they had contributed to building.

In an ethnographic study on the role of Ashas, Meena, a worker living in a southern Delhi slum, asked, 'Where does the data go?' No one seemed to have clear answers for her. Many of the women complained that they rarely got to see the products built with the data they supplied. Often, they never heard from the companies again.

'It's not just a question of data, it's also about the dependence of the state on Big Tech actors,' Aneja said. The reliance on American companies was too high, she felt. 'Most government [health] systems run on Amazon Web Services. A lot of infrastructure and expertise that shapes how the government thinks about AI is coming from Big Tech. They are filling a gap in state capacity.'

Ashita, too, has a measured outlook. She likes the Qure.ai product and believes it has huge potential, but to improve real-world access the technology has to move from private hospitals like hers into free government-run healthcare centres and mobile vans. At her hospital, it had worked well as a quick second opinion but it was a nice-to-have, rather than an essential. Ashita was a qualified and experienced physician, who would likely have made those diagnoses with or without the app. 'We tell the company, having your tool in our hospital isn't going to make a life-and-death difference,' Ashita said.

In 2022, Ashita introduced the Qure.ai team to the government's district tuberculosis office and World Health Organization's representatives in Nandurbar. To deploy the qTrack app to the crumbling corners of the country required a sizable initial investment of time and money, she told them. The Qure team presented their technology at the district headquarters and impressed the representatives. But despite agreeing to deploy the technology in principle, things have stalled due to bureaucracy, as Ashita feared. Galvanising the state to roll out qTrack at scale has been a tortuous process; conversations between Qure and the district authorities are still ongoing.

Ashita could see clearly the chasm between her dream of implementing an AI screen for tuberculosis around the nation, and the reality on the ground. The root of the issue is that profit-driven corporations and marginalized communities, like the ones her patients are from, often exist at cross-purposes.

I spoke to Paola Ricaurte, a Mexican academic and civil rights activist who works on understanding this tension. Her research helps clarify what Aneja called 'data colonialism' – the extractive act of profiteering off the data of marginalized and vulnerable people to build AI systems.

'Big Tech companies concentrate money, they concentrate value generated through data collection, but they also concentrate knowledge, and for me that is most important,' Ricaurte told me. During the pandemic in 2020 for instance, it became clear that the Mexican government needed Google's help to craft its own internal health policy, she said.

That knowledge comes from data, which Ricaurte argues is a mirror to society, reflecting back our experiences, our behaviours, the core of who we are. 'Because we don't have access to that knowledge they are collecting from us, we are left behind. So this is an unequal relationship, it's an asymmetry of power.'

Ashita understands societal asymmetries deeply, being embedded in them every day as part of her work and life. But that's why she also knows that communities like the Bhils will never have enough human doctors or resources accessible to them. I too believe that

AI, if designed and deployed appropriately, can help save the lives of those that have the greatest need. If it can reach the right places, I am optimistic that this technological advancement will improve all our lives and augment the work of human doctors.

'When . . . human beings are absent . . . I think technology comes a close second,' Ashita said. 'It would just revolutionize the care we are able to give.'

CHAPTER 5
Your Freedom

Diana

At seven o'clock on a weekday morning in 2015, Diana Sardjoe was woken by fists banging on her door in IJburg, the east Amsterdam neighbourhood to which she and her family had recently moved. Her seven-year-old daughter was asleep in her bedroom, and her two teenage sons in their rooms. When she looked out of the window she could see police swarming the garden and when she opened the door they surged in, searching the house room by room, until they found who they were looking for: fourteen-year-old Damien. They arrested him for threatening a boy his age with a knife.

As the police took him away, Diana shattered into a million pieces.

*

For the next year, Diana put all her effort into getting Damien's life back on track. She accepted he'd done something terrible, but she believed no child was beyond redemption. She lobbied successfully for house arrest, rather than prison, where she was afraid it would change Damien and push him deeper into criminality. She took on the role of his round-the-clock police guard to keep him out of trouble. 'I expected my mom to turn her back on me because, you know, I felt like I was the black sheep. What I did was the worst and could not be forgiven. But she actually stood beside me,' Damien recalled in an interview some years later. 'My mother,' he said. 'She's a warrior.'

But despite her efforts to stay his course, police came often to interrogate Damien about other crimes – a stolen iPad, a robbery on the other side of town – that Diana and Damien claimed had nothing to do with him. After weeks of this, Damien lashed out at being constantly monitored and when his house arrest came to an end, Damien committed another street crime during his probation, which lengthened his monitoring period, and he started hanging around with the same kids who got him into trouble in the first place.

Then the police started knocking at all times of the day and night, sometimes taking Damien, and his older brother Nafayo, to the station for questioning. Other times, they'd stop and ID him for simply walking down the street or gathering with friends. It became a vicious cycle of constant surveillance and teenage rebellion. Each incident was logged in the boys' records as a 'police contact', data that would become a part of their profiles for years to come. Diana was trying to keep them all together, a family held together with duct tape and a prayer.

A few months later, in the summer of 2016, a letter arrived from the then-mayor's office informing Diana that Damien had been included on the 'Top600', a list of violent criminal youths. Nafayo, sixteen years old at the time, had been registered on the 'Top400', a second list that included several of the brothers of those 600 'criminals' and was made up of children, aged between twelve and eighteen, who were supposedly at high risk of *becoming* criminals in the future – like those in Philip K. Dick's *Minority Report*. Many boys on the 400 list had no criminal record at the time, according to reports from mothers.

Amsterdam's current mayor, Femke Halsema, has said in a letter in Dutch that the predictive scores were 'aimed at stopping crime, improving the opportunities and quality of life of these persons, [and] preventing the negative influence of these persons on their minor brothers and sisters . . . and their minor children.'

Families could neither choose to take themselves off the lists, nor could they refuse the social help offered.

Diana had not been consulted. She alone was responsible for her children, but she wasn't told why her children had been identified, nor how – or even if – they could ever remove the targets on their backs. For the next three years, her family would be trapped in a tangle of more than two dozen government agencies, including the police, social work, public health, judiciary and city officials, each with diverging goals and agendas and often at cross-purposes with one another.

The Top600 collated a list of boys with existing criminal records who had been convicted at least once for a serious crime. The Top400 had been compiled with the help of ProKid, a machine-learning system designed by academics in conjunction with the Dutch police to predict the likelihood of young people at 'elevated risk of committing violent and/or property crimes', using data such as previous contacts with the police, their addresses, their relationships, and their roles as a witness or victim.[1]

'I heard about the algorithms, about the data used inside them, and I knew something wasn't right,' Diana told me. Most of the boys identified were black or Moroccan, but the methodology was supposedly race-blind. The letter didn't enlighten the families any further, it said simply that help was on its way from Amsterdam's shiny new digital welfare state.

'What they should have put in that letter,' Diana said, 'is "We'll help you get to hell".'

'Multi-problem Families'

The Sardjoes' situation – and that of the other families on the Amsterdam algorithmic lists – recalled the work of Achille Mbembe, the Cameroonian historian and philosopher, who studies the after-effects of colonialism. Mbembe invented the term 'necropolitics', which describes the power of political institutions to dictate which citizens are the most precarious in a society. These vulnerable citizens, according to Mbembe, live in so-called deathworlds – enclaves in which they no longer exercise control or retain autonomy in their lives.

From receiving that letter, every interaction with the state became a data point that counted against a family, according to Diana and others with children on the lists.[2] Phone calls from mothers to social services were logged. Children who had witnessed domestic violence or crime became part of the government's dataset. Being absent from school frequently and participating in special youth groups were relevant data points. Every cry for help was an admission of poor parenting, causing the system to plant a red flag, a scarlet letter, by their names. The data was shared amongst authorities – between police, youth workers and schools – and held against them for several years. It felt like there was no way to scrub clean of an algorithmic stain. Mothers like Diana lost any purchase they'd had in their lives.

Back in 2016, a couple of days after she received the mayor's letter, Diana found that workers from the state began to turn up at her home unannounced. Psychologists, youth workers and lawyers came in to study her 'multi-problem' family like guinea pigs. Diana describes it as having her life 'hijacked', without concern for her job, responsibilities or her other children. She wasn't unemployed, or suffering from drug problems or alcoholism, so she felt her family had been unfairly targeted.

Social workers would come into her home and tell her to tidy up, to pull herself together, to do the dishes. They spoke to her as if she were a child, or even worse, like she was scum.

They wanted her to put Damien in a home, which she outright refused. He was struggling enough with the invasion of their home and their lives. 'The house was his sanctuary and all of a sudden everyone just stamped in. As a fifteen-year-old, there was no room for forgiveness, he was supposed to be perfect all the time.' With all the intrusion and upheaval and need to protect her family, Diana lost her job at the bank.

The knock-on effect of these visits was damaging to her other children. Nafayo, for instance, couldn't understand why he had also been stigmatized. He had not committed any crimes, yet he now had a cloud over his head. The brothers began to fight, to blame one another. Nafayo couldn't see a way out, and he did what had been predicted, surrendering to the algorithm's predictions, and began to steal scooters. He withdrew into his own world. 'It messed his life up,' Diana told me. 'It was a crazy system.'

Diana is used to having to fight for what she wants. She was born in Suriname, to an Indian father and a black mother. 'My mom fought her way to the Netherlands. She always showed me, never give up, fight for what you believe in. If you don't like something, change it.' So, when the city refused to rearrange one of Damien's court appointments that didn't work for her, Diana brought her seven-year-old daughter along. She had to stand outside in a corridor, looking in, during the proceedings. 'I miss the empathy in the system, there is no humanity in the system, that's what I miss.'

Despite Diana's defiance, the stress affected them all. In the end, her parents moved in to help look after them. Her periods stopped, and she was admitted to hospital with heart palpitations. 'If I didn't do what they said, they used my youngest child as leverage. Said they'd take her away.' Her daughter, she said, was 'the joy, the sunshine in the house.'

'And she stopped smiling. That's what did it. In hospital, I died at that moment to rise like a phoenix again. I found the old me and found my fire. I started fighting back.'

Policing by Algorithm

The theory is that predictive policing algorithms are a cheaper and more efficient way to allocate limited resources, compared to tackling the consequences after crimes have been committed.

AI systems are being experimented with widely to test this theory. They have been used to predict gang violence in Britain,[3] select potential terrorists in Germany[4] and forecast domestic violence amongst families in the United States. Machine-learning algorithms are being tested as tools to predict recidivism in convicted criminals, to guide sentencing decisions and to assist custodial officers in deciding who should make bail. But the jury is out on how well they work.

Meanwhile, there is evidence that they can be racist, unconsciously or by design. Even where race is not considered in the algorithm's decision-making process, proxy variables – previous arrests, witnessing violence, living in a certain neighbourhood or simply being poor – are fed as inputs into AI and other statistical systems, propagating institutional racism. This was highlighted in an investigation from journalism non-profit ProPublica, which analysed a predictive tool called COMPAS that was widely used in the United States to forecast a defendant's likelihood of re-offending, and therefore whether they should be afforded bail. ProPublica analysed COMPAS predictions for more than 7,000 arrestees in Florida and concluded it was a racist algorithm. Their findings showed that 'blacks are almost twice as likely as whites to be labelled a higher risk but not actually re-offend.' Conversely, they wrote, whites were 'much more likely than blacks to be labelled lower-risk but go on to commit other crimes.'[5]

The Dutch lists, too, primarily included boys of colour, which critics say can partly be explained by the fact that they are over-policed, compared to their white peers.

In the Netherlands, risk assessment technologies like the Top600 and 400 lists are part of a wider national security policy, which Anouk de Koning, a Dutch anthropologist at Leiden University, calls 'diffuse policing'.[6] Apart from the ProKid algorithms, there is also the Crime Anticipation System, or CAS, an AI software that makes predictions about where and when crimes will occur. The system was developed in Amsterdam and rolled out nationally.

Part of the diffuse policing strategy includes the use of statistical models – including AI methods – to help target specific demographics: mostly poor and non-white urban youths. The objective is to predict and prevent trouble. Together, these policies enact a combination of 'care and coercion', captured in the slogan used by the police for the Top600: 'Handled with care.'[7]

Following eighteen months of interviews with young men and their families in the Amsterdam district of Diamantbuurt, as well as care workers and police, Anouk found that the neighbourhood's Moroccan-Dutch youths made up the largest single subgroup in the Top600. This was despite city officials claiming race, ethnicity or nationality were not considered by their computer systems. She revealed a far-reaching web of surveillance and punishment that included not only law enforcement, but also state social, education and youth workers. She concluded that algorithmic predictions and data-driven policing were not only discriminatory, but that they created a culture of fear amongst immigrant families, breaking trust in public institutions.

This was all happening against the backdrop of an explosion of

CCTV cameras in Diamantbuurt, just like in London's Stratford in recent years. One of the boys from the list, going under the pseudonym of Mo, told Anouk that the cameras felt like the police were constantly 'looking over your shoulder', and he and his friends were monitored and fined for the most harmless actions: gathering, joking around or hanging out by their local community centre. The cops used their knowledge of the boys' identities as a threat. 'When the police drive by and call you by name, you really feel put on the spot. [When they say] "Hey Mo!", I say, "Hey asshole".'

And it wasn't just a list that contained the details of these young men. At one police station in Amsterdam West, a neighbourhood about five kilometres away from Diamantbuurt, police had installed a colourful wall mosaic of eighty mugshots – the local members of the Top600, a daily reminder as to who officers were targeting.

The Top600 had been launched by Amsterdam's Mayor Eberhard van der Laan, a former criminal lawyer, in an attempt to prevent criminalization in young people. All the youths on the list had to have been convicted for at least one 'serious' crime, although the conditions for their removal from the list are not clearly defined.[8] These kids are assigned a primary state coordinator – Diana's family had at least two of these – who helps the 600 youths stick to the straight and narrow.

To boost this endeavour, the mayor then looked at the findings of Jacqueline Wientjes, a behavioural scientist consulting for the central government, who claimed that most adult criminals begin showing signs of miscreant behaviour – arson, drugs and smoking, truancy, fighting – before the age of twelve. She and her colleagues were then given the go-ahead to develop ProKid, a set of machine-learning algorithms that aimed to predict if an individual from birth to the age of twenty-three would commit crimes. The mayor hoped to use these predictions to intervene early, so these imagined crimes would never occur.

In July 2016, more than one hundred children in Amsterdam under the age of eighteen were informed of the Top400 list, populated by predictions from the ProKid model. This was described in the press as a 'unique experiment': predicting – and changing – the course of a child's entire future. The mayor's office told the public a child's inclusion was not based on their arrest record alone, but on data points around risk, 'for instance, a truancy report, or [being] a victim, witness or the suspect of domestic violence.'[9] And although it was called the 400, the city never had that many in the group. In fact, in an internal email exchange at the mayor's office, obtained by researchers through a Freedom of Information Act, it appeared this wasn't enough.[10] 'The Top400 includes two hundred people,' an official wrote, 'while there is money for four hundred. Can criteria be stretched?'

The ProKid model was trained on a dataset of arrests from 2011–15, to find patterns amongst demographics and behaviours. The models could then predict if a person would be arrested in the future. Crucially, it wouldn't be able to predict whether they might actually commit crimes, since the training set contained arrests, rather than convictions. As I read more into it, there was something here that reminded me of that ancient symbol of a serpent eating its own tail, the ouroboros. Here's how it worked: police resources were focused on intervening in immigrant communities, largely amongst youths of colour. These interactions and interventions, sometimes resulting in arrests, were all recorded as data points for a computer program designed to predict future interactions with the same police force. The question of actual crimes and who was committing them seemed to be beside the point within this model.

To calculate an individual's risk score, the algorithm's designers included variables such as a child's gender, age, and police history, including being witnesses or victims of crimes. They had found that these variables often correlated with those who went on to be arrested. According to the mayor's office, individuals on the Top400 had to have been arrested at least once, although not necessarily convicted.

ProKid also included data such as police interactions of an individual's family members and peers, linking them up to those they hung around with, or were biologically related to. These were data points that the scientists thought were important predictors of criminality, given how heavily a child could be influenced through their social environment.[11]

After Diana and dozens of other parents received letters about their children being included on the Top400 list, administrators from Amsterdam's city council wrote to the mayor, an email obtained by researchers via Freedom of Information requests.[12] In it they suggested they had little idea why the algorithmic system had chosen specific families over others; after all, machine-learning software was a so-called black box – opaque systems whose internal workings weren't fully explainable even by their architects.

Document Source: Email to Mayor
Wed, 3 Aug 2016
Subject: Prokid+ info to parents

Now that the letters have been sent to youth and parents of the ProKid intake, the first phone calls from concerned parents are coming in, as expected. Of course we cannot yet answer the most important question parents have. Why am I or my child on this list? Of course, we want to keep parents as involved as possible. For now, we'll figure it out. We don't mention the word ProKid. And we try to avoid the word 'predict'.

*

The algorithm-generated lists were more than predictors. They were curses. Inclusion on one of these lists permanently changed the life-course of many young people. It made them question who they were. Just by being included on the list, they were branded, judgements following them around wherever they went. And even if they were to come off it in time, they were worried their chances of being admitted to college, getting a job, or buying a home would be permanently ruined. The ProKid software had taken events they had little control over, such as witnessing violence or being the child of a broken home, and twisted it into something that could set them up for lifelong failure.

Similarly, being on the Top600 didn't just bring all these concerns crashing into young lives but turned into a self-fulfilling prophecy, as members became an active recruitment target for drug gangs. Diana told me how many of the young men were picked out by gang members to do jobs for them, viewing them as easy targets and threatening them if they didn't comply.

One mother said her son, included on the Top600 list, had been threatened with violence unless he helped commit crimes, which she tried to explain to the police and social workers. 'But who will listen to my story? Nobody. Nobody,' she said. 'I didn't realize he had been labelled. I handed over all the information to the Top600. They are the boss now.'[13]

Eline Groenendaal is a lawyer who represented several young men, mostly of Moroccan-Dutch heritage, from the neighbourhood Diamantbuurt. She knew of boys who had been fired from jobs, banned from public places like swimming pools, followed, harassed and even arrested without charge because of their Top600 status. Although the lists hadn't been published publicly, the police and other public authorities had shared the names between themselves, and often threw this fact in the faces of youths who were on it.

Each arrest – even if without foundation – counted as a further data point fed to the algorithm, which used those arrests as fodder to put them back on the list. It meant, too, that people struggled to ever get off the lists. For those on the Top400, there was a widespread feeling of helplessness, of being labelled for something they couldn't control. Nafayo, a boy who had never previously been 'in trouble', began to steal scooters because he felt worthless, his mother believed.

In *Mothers*, a short film released in late 2022, the filmmaker Nirit Peled profiled a group of Dutch mothers who had sons on the Top600 or 400 lists and depicted the impact it had on their families. The idea for the film had struck Peled when she'd overheard some mothers talking about the lists outside a cafe near her home in Amsterdam. She'd met with Diana and attended several community meetings and public events where mothers of these youths gathered, resulting in hours of conversations about the social effects of predictive software. She had chosen four anonymous mothers to feature. To protect their identities, she used actresses to depict them, scripting the dialogue from her real interviews.

In Peled's film, the mothers reported being harassed, described as 'mildly retarded' or 'emotional' in internal reports by social workers, which they weren't allowed to challenge or change. Yet they were expected to open their homes to floods of strangers, and never allowed to question why.

Admissions of vulnerability to social workers were marked against them, as if they had done something wrong. Being branded as 'problem parents' gave officials licence to treat them with contempt and callousness. Having their children taken away always felt like just one misstep away. One mother said if she pushed back, 'you become the "difficult mother" and since I have been given that stamp, I am probably on a list somewhere in the top 600 of difficult mothers.'[14]

A black fourteen-year-old in *Mothers*, who had previously been arrested for shoplifting a can of soda, had not been allowed to return to school. Instead, he was asked to attend a roundtable scheduled with the police, the school, counsellors and his mother. But it didn't feel as if they were on his side, his mother said. The police felt like adversaries, not supporters, tainting the entire process with the feeling of being on trial.

In 2021, the non-profit Fair Trials, a watchdog for criminal justice in Europe, organized an event for journalists, policy analysts and legislators, to discuss the Top600 and ProKid programs. They had invited Diana to tell her story. 'If you're a single mother,' she told the audience, 'you need to fit in some kind of . . . box. And if you are out of the box, they will push you in it. I lost my money because my son was in the 600, I lost my job. So, I started to fit in the box. I didn't even know it, but you get pushed into it.'

Diana only broke free of this cycle when she took control of the narrative, taking her story public in *Het Parool*, a Dutch newspaper, and writing directly to the mayor to ask for a new coordinator. 'I wrote to the mayor, [the algorithm] looks nice on paper but it just doesn't work.' The attention from the news story and her letter resulted in the family being assigned a new counsellor, who helped Diana turn things around.

What the new counsellor did was focus on Diana herself, on rebuilding her confidence and self-worth so she could care for her children again. It took her three months to get back on her feet, and she realized that involving mothers in their children's care was key to tackling any behavioural problems. And she came to accept that perhaps the state's help, if created in tandem with families, could even impact positively.

One evening, after speaking to Diana, I picked up an old copy of *The Scarlet Letter*, an American novel from 1850, in which a young woman, Hester Prynne, is shunned and alienated from the

Puritanical society she lives in for conceiving a child outside of marriage. Prynne's stigma is worn, literally, as a scarlet letter 'A' pinned to her chest. There is no escape from it, and no route to redemption, no forgiveness. And I heard Diana's words from the Fair Trials event echoing in my head. 'Families get destroyed and children are taken away from mothers. For us, it is real life.'

On Fairness and Forgiveness

For public authorities, the big question was whether these risk scores and the subsequent social interventions actually worked as a crime deterrent. For families and human rights groups, the more pressing concern was whether the ends justify the means – an upheaval of young lives, distress on families, or the seemingly discriminatory targeting of immigrant communities.

First, I looked for evidence of the systems' success. In an attempt to be transparent, the Dutch government published reports over four years on the efficacy of the Top400. The most recent available report in 2017 showed that at the end of the year, there were 231 youths on the Top400 list, aged between 14 and 24 (the ProKid AI software was for under-18s, but more young people had been added into the list too). Overall, there had been a 33 per cent drop in the total number of arrests across the group since they were put on the algorithm-facilitated program in 2015 – from a total of 123 arrests prior to entering the program, to 82 arrests in the two-and-a-half years since. However, it wasn't clear how proportionately those arrests were distributed across the group, whether, for instance, the behavioural gains were mainly seen in a few youths, while others continued to be arrested at the same rate, or more frequently.

The report also showed that 13 per cent of the youths had moved up into the more serious Top600 list, meaning they had been arrested for more numerous and worse crimes than before, and even convicted for them. In this group, the total arrests only dropped by 9 per cent in three years. Again, it remained unclear whether the software had correctly predicted this behaviour, and the interventions had simply failed, or whether being included on these lists itself made the youths more exposed and vulnerable to a life of crime.

Overall, the results seemed modest at best, especially when weighed up against the impact on the individuals and families who'd been forced to participate in the experiment. Dutch anthropologist Paul Mutsaers spent years studying the impact of several policing software, including AI tools, in use across the country. During his research, Mutsaers had accompanied police as they patrolled inner-city neighbourhoods like Amsterdam West. In an interview with the station chief, he acknowledged that all the Top600 juveniles in the district belonged to ethnic minority groups. 'Of course, they are much more at risk of being caught,' he told Mutsaers, 'because we monitor them all the time.'[15]

Mutsaers also heard police making racist jokes, and targeting Moroccans, whom they called 'naffers' or North Africans. 'I would go in with the police into tiny apartments, without proper furniture,' he told me. 'There was sheer poverty all around us, but they wouldn't even see what was going on around them. It just dovetailed with ethnic profiling.'

The families were targeted because of their children's inclusion on the Top600 lists, 'making them feel powerless in the face of such an overwhelming force of this algorithm.' The balance, he added, had 'shifted from care to coercion.'

The predictive algorithms and big-data approaches had all started as a rehabilitative solution, Mutsaers reminded me. 'If the goal was to bring restorative justice to struggling families, then [the algorithms] are not working. They scare people away, using their families to keep them in check,' he said. 'If you have social suffering even without re-offending, does that look like success to you? If yes, that's a really sad story as a society.'

Apart from the unanticipated consequences of AI systems like ProKid, there's also been a wider debate about whether AI-made decisions, such as predicting a person's criminality or risk of recidivism, are any *fairer* than human ones. A *Washington Post* analysis of the COMPAS system found that ProPublica's conclusions of racism in the software were partly due to a different expectation of fairness from that of Northpointe, the owners of COMPAS.[16] Northpointe's definition was that their scores essentially implied the same risk of recidivism, regardless of the defendant's race. But because black defendants went on to reoffend at higher rates overall, it meant more black defendants were classified as high-risk. Meanwhile, ProPublica thought it unfair that black defendants who did not go on to reoffend were therefore subjected to harsher treatment by the legal system than their white counterparts. In other words, it was impossible to create a statistical system that fit everyone's definitions of fairness. Perhaps, the *Post* suggested, the problem called for something more radical – like swapping money bail for 'electronic monitoring so that no one is unnecessarily jailed.'

Ultimately, it all comes back to the humans at the heart of the process – AI can't replace giving human beings agency to choose the fairest outcomes. I spoke to Richard Berk, an American criminologist and statistician who has designed several AI tools for the US criminal justice system. 'These are political and ethical problems and I have no expertise in them,' he said, so instead he sits the decision-makers down, including workers from the parole department, lawyers, judges and police, and gives them trade-offs. He shows them how the algorithms work for different populations, and gives them choices about what to maximize, and which outcomes are most important. He says, 'These trade-offs are purely human judgement.'

*

Three years after being included in Amsterdam's Top600, Damien finally got off the list. In a TV interview, a journalist asked him if he deserved to have been on the list because of the crimes he had committed. 'I think I already paid my price when I got sentenced for the things I've done,' Damien said. 'I've got my house arrest, my evening clock, you know, I even had some fines. I know that I already learned my lesson from that.'

Damien's words about having paid his price made me think about mercy. When is it time for a society to forgive someone? Is it fair that they are punished once, or should they continue to be doubted and monitored, as a way to prevent them from future misdemeanours? And is the blunt instrument of state intervention, intended to be helpful, in fact a punishment?

This idea of forgiveness is central to behavioural psychology, particularly when it comes to childhood development. We tell our children we forgive them no matter what, that we will continue to love them even if we are angry and that in our eyes, they will always be worthy of redemption. Research shows that forgiving children develops their sense of self-worth, self-acceptance and a healthy attitude to failings. It helps them grow into well-adjusted, compassionate adults.[17]

AI tools and other statistical software that predict the trajectories of individual lives are punitive, not compassionate. Predictive policing isn't an approach of care and forgiveness, it is purely a calculation of your risk of screwing up. Every action, every observation, every aspect of who you are becomes correlated to crime, because that's the lens through which your life is analysed. Mistakes your parents made, the colour of your skin, the language you speak, the music you listen to, the wider brutality of societal and institutional biases, these all become proxy variables in an algorithm that is scoring your risk to society. The police become a part of your everyday existence, entrenching the idea of your unworthiness.

As I was mulling over the value of compassion, I came across a research paper about the role of forgiveness in AI-mediated profiling by governments. Its author, Karolina La Fors, an academic studying the Dutch government's profiling of vulnerable groups, argues that children should be granted exemption from state and criminal profiling systems, like the Top600, 400 and ProKid, simply by virtue of their innocence. This idea is partly reflected in European data protection regulations like the Right To Be Forgotten, which allows you to request a company to erase your personal data, or the right to appeal an automated decision and ask for human intervention. Similarly, La Fors says these children should have the right to remain unquantified by an algorithm. Their data should be forgotten.[18]

Empathy teaches us that everyone is flawed, yet still worthy of mercy. A risk score says the opposite: this is your digitally fixed reality, you have criminality inside you waiting to burst out. Your circumstances mean you don't deserve forgiveness. As Damien said to a Dutch TV host during his time on the Top600 list, 'I just don't see a way out.'

When I asked La Fors if she could imagine a better solution for tackling youth crimes and delinquency, she was hopeful. 'I really miss the kids' perspectives in all this,' she told me. She's now exploring whether you can co-create solutions with kids and parents, rather than brand them with algorithm-derived scores. Her other suggestion is to include all the variables related to improvements in a young person's life in the prediction algorithms, including their attendance of youth care services, whether they are going to therapy, positive outcomes which could balance out the negativity of a criminal profile. 'I go back to the forgiveness principle,' she said. 'These lists should have a way out for kids. Next to blacklists, why not make a "whitelist" too.'

As we spoke, it dawned on me that somehow in the discussion

on AI 'ethics' – how automated systems work, what criteria and data points are used, and how transparent their designs should be – the officials in this case had lost sight of what matters. At the centre of this punitive system was a child or a young person who had made mistakes. What was the point of any technology if it was hurting them and the very families it was purporting to help?

It turns out that the city of Amsterdam is continuing with the predictive policing programs, which they believe have had a positive impact on crime rates. They claim, however, to have stopped using machine-learning methods to make predictions. Just over a year ago, the Amsterdam mayor's office responded to criticisms from the public and members of its own city council, after the film *Mothers* was released. Femke Halsema, the mayor, confirmed that both lists were still in operation.

However, she said that the ProKid tool, which used AI techniques, was no longer being used to identify children for the Top400. Instead, the city was using a simple statistical method based on fixed criteria such as absenteeism, arrests or suspected offences, and dealing fake drugs. 'Although Prokid+ has been scientifically validated, the complex weighting of various risk factors turned out to be quite technical and therefore difficult to follow for those involved,' she wrote. 'We have taken this signal from young people and their parents seriously and that is why we have stopped using Prokid+.'

Halsema pushed back on suggestions of bias and discrimination, insisting that the criteria for inclusion were transparent, and that 'no personal data concerning race, ethnicity, nationality, religion, political preference, gender or sexuality are used in any way for inclusion on the [400] list.'

She also acknowledged the criticism from the mothers in Peled's documentary, and that of others like Diana, saying the experience had 'taught us that we need to do even more to involve and inform parents,' adding that new parents are now invited to attend a special meeting immediately after their children are added to either list.

Buried in the letter was a final admission – researchers were working on a new version of ProKid, aimed at identifying young people up to the age of twenty-three, 'who may slide (further) into crime.' The office claimed this hadn't been implemented as yet, but it's clear that the chapter on AI-driven policing remains open.

In a memo to the mayor in 2016, obtained by academics through FOIA, city workers raised concerns about hurting the kids they were trying to help. Despite that being almost eight years ago, the very same questions remain today.

> Mayor: As of July 1, 125 people have entered the Top 400 based on ProKid+. We notice that this story continues to raise too many questions. ProKid+ is based on risk and not on a criminal justice component. So that doesn't necessarily mean you have to have done something yourself. It can also be the behaviour of someone else that causes . . . someone to be in the system. Moreover there are people on [the] list that receive a stamp through ProKid that do not all have a criminal record. Are we now criminalising at-risk juveniles who we want to help?

*

Back in London, as we continue our conversation, Diana is talking animatedly about her future. For the first time in a while, she's excited about what lies ahead. Her crusade isn't against the state any longer, but for greater transparency of algorithms and control over their consequences. 'The algorithm is created by people who see numbers, that's what an algorithm is. They don't see people, they see numbers,' she says.

After the interviews she gave to *Het Parool* and her correspondence with the Amsterdam mayor, Diana's public campaign resulted in her setting up a foundation that connects mothers whose children are still in the Top400 or Top600 lists. So far, she has built a network of one hundred mothers in Amsterdam and has begun to expand to other cities including The Hague. The physical space she has rented is a place, she hopes, for mothers to vent, to share stories and fears, and to swap information. Diana has named it De Moeder Is De Sleutel, *The Mother Is The Key*.

'Kindness doesn't mean we are weak,' she says. 'All those things we are accused of, that we are too emotional, that we cry, this is what these kids need. We need to raise our boys differently, but we also need to . . . forgive each other.'

CHAPTER 6

Your Safety Net

Norma Gutiarraz, like Diana, is mother to four adult children, and they say her kindness is her greatest strength. She is in her sixties, bottle-blonde in sky-blue trousers and large pearl earrings, warm and motherly. Her liquid hazel eyes bore right into your soul, filled with an empathy that invites you to share your deepest confidences.

Norma lives on the fringes of Salta, a tiny city nestled at the foot of the Andes in north-west Argentina, in the *barrio* of Norte Grande. She has spent most of her life in low-income settlements, moving here when there was nothing but thorn-studded forests and dirt paths. She helped plot where the houses should go, where the local health centre would be located, which families would move in and where. Now she is the local *puntera*, a citizen liaison to the local government who conveys the community's needs. She also works as a therapeutic assistant in a local clinic, and, according to her son Matias, looks after Norte Grande's citizens as if they are her family. 'Her whole life she has worked for the people of the community,' Matias tells me. 'She gives them beds, makes arrangements for funerals, buys coffins. Whatever they need.'

As I drive across the Rio Arenales, the river that divides Salta, towards Norma's neighbourhood, the neocolonial grandeur of Salta's city centre fades to sepia. In place of wide plazas, a jumble of *carniceria*, butchers, and little kiosks selling poultry, cigarettes and fizzy drinks gradually appears.

The homes are squat, cement or exposed brick with corrugated tin roofs, shrouded in hanging sheets of canvas and plastic. In the heart of the *barrios*, houses are jammed tightly up against each other, separated only by veins of sewage.

Norma's next-door neighbour, a fifteen-year-old girl called Magui, sits outside fanning herself in the shade of her doorway. She's been dispatched out front to hawk second-hand baby clothes from a folding table. She sits on a chair, her other hand placed protectively on her baby bump, glowering at passers-by. You can hear the trills of her three-year-old toddler inside.

Norma's job involves talking regularly with government agents about the neighbourhood's problems. They've been coming door-to-door everywhere she's lived for at least three decades, usually looking to scrape information, even though there is probably nothing they don't already have, she says. Sanitation workers, health-care workers, social workers, she can't quite tell them apart anymore. 'They record data about who you live with, how many in a house, where you went to school, whether you've ever been pregnant. They come to ask about our needs, about our poverty and those in risky situations. They ask about pregnancies of young girls, about family planning.'

The problem of young mothers has been a major challenge for this community. 'They can't work properly if they are mothers,' Norma says, 'and round here everyone needs work to survive.'

Norma herself became pregnant in her teens. 'I was not even seventeen,' she says, eyes squinting, trying to remember. She spent forty-two years in a marriage she was unhappy in, to ensure her own children didn't follow her example, which she views as a mistake. She ruled her kids with an iron fist, sending them to school in the town centre, and she or her husband would wait for them by the door every afternoon. They were made to stay indoors and do their homework. Now, her youngest daughter, who is twenty-five, works for the Navy. She is unmarried, without children.

'She's really proud of her,' Matias tells me. 'She's a very good daughter.'

'The girl outside, Magui, she got pregnant at twelve the first time and now she is fifteen and pregnant again,' Norma says.

'She sees no future for herself,' Matias says.

A few years earlier, Norma was at the local health centre when she heard from the director there about a new computer system that was being introduced to the community. She'd heard it was a program that would track and give pregnant girls and women special care. She was quite optimistic about the idea. At least this computer program was attempting to do something with all that data they had collected over so many years.

The computer program was being introduced by a Salta minister named Carlos Abeleira, known to all as Charlie. She'd seen him around, thought he was a decent guy. She said, nodding, '[I thought] it could have a positive impact on the neighbourhood, *si*.'

Governing with Data

It is a sweltering October day as I sit waiting for Pablo Abeleira outside my hotel in Salta's city centre. Winter has thawed abruptly into the southern summer, skipping spring entirely. In this season, the city holds its breath, waiting for relief from the skies. Latticed stone terraces fling diamond shadows into sunlit courtyards, like the one I'm sitting in. People here call Salta La Linda, *Salta the Beautiful*.

Pablo Abeleira is a software engineer and an ardent disciple of data who'd be as at home in Silicon Valley or Stockholm as Salta. He's also Norma's local politician Charlie Abeleira's brother. 'I'm the technology guy,' he tells me, with a wide smile, his square teeth glinting like his pickup truck. 'I think about how to do things better using data and dashboards and AI. I'm not the guy in the field, in touch in a personal way with families.'

After he graduated, Pablo lived across Argentina, Costa Rica, Mexico and the Dominican Republic, working at SAP, the multinational software company, consulting for companies like Coca Cola, Budweiser and DaimlerChrysler, analysing data to grow their businesses and profits. It was back in 2013, when local television journalist Jorge Lanata ran a series of political exposés about the northern provinces bordering Salta, that he began to pay attention to the abject poverty in his hometown. There, families, particularly those descended from indigenous tribes, lacked access to basic sanitation and drinking water. One memorable moment of a toddler uttering the words 'I am thirsty' lodged itself into the minds of viewers up and down the country.

The revelations shocked Pablo, along with the rest of Argentina, which despite its economic challenges is one of the richest countries in Latin America. His frustration lay in his belief that governments didn't have enough data about what was going on, and what they had was not being put to work for the benefit of people. Datasets were disjointed or improperly formatted and couldn't be analysed usefully. Unlike most successful businesses that he had worked with, he was convinced that governments didn't know how to prioritize their clients' needs, or their own actions. They were set up to fail.

This coincided with a time in his life in which Pablo had begun to feel unmoored. He couldn't quite put his finger on what he was searching for, but he wasn't satisfied. 'I could have continued working with SAP and earning a lot of money – it paid very well – but I wanted to do something more meaningful,' he says. 'It was always in my head, the question of why we are here. I always believed that we are here for a reason, that we have a destiny.'

Having grown up in Salta, Pablo decided it was time to take the plunge and move his family back home.

Meanwhile, the Lanata exposés had inspired Salta's governor, Juan Manuel Urtubey, to pledge sweeping change. Urtubey, who had designs on the Argentinian presidency, had joined forces with Conin, a Catholic charity that focuses on malnutrition and opposes abortion, promising to reduce childhood poverty in Salta. To deliver on these promises, he had appointed Pablo's brother Charlie, as Salta's minister of early childhood, to head up an eponymous ministry in his government that would address the roots of poverty in families.

Charlie had already worked in various ministerial positions across local government for over a decade. Over the years, he had seen the face of poverty up close while working with families like Norma Gutiarraz's in Salta's slums: young people without jobs, adolescent pregnancies, school dropouts, and a cycle that sometimes repeated itself, generation after generation.

He knew what the problems were, but he wasn't a data scientist or an engineer. He needed someone with technical skills to help him build solutions that could be scaled up quickly. Someone he could trust. Like his younger brother, Pablo.

'Solving' Teenage Pregnancy

Pablo and Charlie grew up in a middle-class, close-knit family, living in the former colonial city centre of Salta, crammed with classical architecture and verdant squares. The Abeleiras are native to a certain stratum of Salta society: a small clutch of mostly European-descended landowners, all Catholic, educated and conservative, whose children now work in positions of power as government officials, lawyers, businesspeople, teachers and military generals. The men from this community socialize in exclusively male social clubs, private country clubs in the hills bordering the city – some of the few places in Argentina that still do this. Women are only allowed inside during official parties, and daughters are introduced into society at an annual 'coming out' ball. This is a long way from the Salta of the slums and back-roads on the fringes of town that I had visited. That world was inhabited by *criollos*, descendants of mixed European and indigenous heritage, who mostly work in blue-collar jobs.

The capital is also a gateway to the Puna Salteña, an expansive desert plateau rising among the Andean peaks, with an otherworldly terrain of volcanoes, salt flats and technicolour lagoons. Bordering Bolivia and Chile, the Puna is home to Argentina's indigenous peoples, tribes such as the *Wichi* and the *Kolla*. They often live as impoverished refugees in their own countries, displaced by European colonists. The huge inequality between urban and rural populations in Salta maps neatly onto this ethnic divide. This is a Salta of poverty and disillusionment, a part of their country and history that Argentinians are ashamed of.

In the northern provinces, including Salta, about 40 per cent of the population live below the poverty line.[1] Here, one in four babies, or 25 per cent, are born to girls aged between 10 and 19 years old – compared to 14 per cent nationally.[2] It's the problem that Norma and her son Matias had outlined for me in their home. The comparatively high incidence of teen pregnancies in northern Argentina is partly explained by socioeconomic factors like poverty, unemployment, a lack of education and broadly limited life opportunities. For young women in these environments, like Norma's neighbour, Magui, childbearing may be the only realistic path to achieving purpose and social status.

But the issue stretches beyond that. Many women and girls, particularly adolescents in this area, have been victims of a decades-long racist colonial practice known as '*el chineo*': gang rape, usually by white men, of indigenous girls and young women. The men rarely take ownership of children born out of these assaults. Just weeks after I had been in Salta, a twelve-year-old Wichi girl was raped and left to die in the highway leading out of the city. In the past few years, women's rights campaigners have banded together in protest, launching the 'Basta de chineo' or 'No more chineo' campaign. The group has lobbied the Argentinian government to outlaw the practice as a hate crime against women, no matter their age, with maximum sentences and no recourse to bail for perpetrators.

The time away from Salta allowed Pablo to observe the deep inequality in his hometown that he had never noticed as a child. The poverty in the city's informal settlements was particularly distressing. In terms of the indigenous population, Salta had three times the national average and these families were disproportionately found in Salta's slums.[3] 'Speaking to friends that are doctors, they tell me there are a lot of abortions [in the city]. Anyone and everyone is getting one. In indigenous communities, they don't do abortions, so they end up having, like, twelve children. There is overcrowding,' Pablo said.

Pablo didn't object to abortion in principle, but he felt that young people should be equipped to plan for their own futures, and not be forced into life-changing decisions. 'I would imagine, what if my children were one of them? I wanted them to have equal opportunities as all others. When you have children, you start seeing things differently.'

So, on his return, he decided to help his brother Charlie develop a new model of social work, one that would borrow from his playbook as an SAP consultant: using data to analyse communities, thus improving how governments made decisions and allocated resources.

To do so, Pablo enlisted the help of tech giant Microsoft, which had already been donating money to Conin, the Catholic malnutrition charity in Salta. Microsoft put three of its data analysts on the project for free. After convening groups of local experts, including civil servants, NGO representatives and social workers, the team chose to focus their pilot projects on two issues: teen pregnancy and school truancy.

Microsoft's developers pitched the Abeleiras about the power of AI, claiming that they could use Microsoft's Azure software to build algorithms to predict which girls were likely to get pregnant in their teens. That way, the local government could direct its public resources to those families and help prevent them.

The idea of using artificial intelligence to solve a messy human problem like teenage pregnancies delighted Pablo. 'We had hundreds, thousands of variables so it is very hard to analyse per person. That is why artificial intelligence helped us,' he said. 'We could design 1:1 public policies, single interventions for individual families using intelligent algorithms from the tech industry.'

The team started with a focus on adolescent pregnancies in Salta's poorest inner-city *barrios*. Much like the ProKid/Top400 models in Amsterdam which predicted future arrests, the plan was to generate a list of families whose daughters' risk of teen pregnancy was above 60 per cent.

The adolescent focus of the AI model was problematic for several reasons. Argentina's minimum age of consent is thirteen, but the criminal code offers heightened protection of children aged between thirteen and sixteen, in regard to sexual exploitation. The AI model, however, assumed all the girls in the program were of the age of consent, that is over sixteen, even when they were younger. Even for those above sixteen, it didn't consider that the pregnancies could be a result of rape.

Urtubey, Salta's then-governor, saw the initiative as a way of marketing himself as a forward-thinking technophile. He green-lit a trial of the AI system on families in the south and south-east of Salta's capital, signing an agreement between the Salta government and Microsoft, which agreed to continue working on the project for free, in exchange for developing AI technologies using citizen data. Microsoft's goal would have been to sign on government clients to test out its growing cloud technology, which today is a multi-billion-dollar business at the heart of the company. Additionally, the government paid an annual fee of roughly $50,000 for use of Microsoft's cloud platform, Azure, which allowed developers to build AI tools within it.

The Salta government didn't plan to publish the list of families but to hone in on them proactively. Just like the Sardjoes in Amsterdam, these families too would receive public assistance from across local government agencies, from housing, education, employment and healthcare.

The Digital Welfare State

In 2019, the UN's Special Rapporteur on extreme poverty and human rights published a damning report on the emergence of the so-called digital welfare state – the datafication of the government's functions. The report was blunt. Digital technologies including AI, which determine who should get social protection and assistance, simply 'predict, identify, surveil, detect, target and punish' the poor.[4]

The report also warned about the rising influence of Western corporations in governments across the world – the epitome of data colonialism. The modern state is tightly entwined with private companies, who usually design and operate the digital welfare systems that vulnerable citizens depend on – much like healthcare systems, as Indian political scientist Urvashi Aneja had pointed out regarding AI technologies in India.

The UN report warned specifically about 'Big Tech', US tech companies such as Microsoft which provide much of the infrastructure for government systems, and therefore scrape citizens' sensitive data, while 'operat[ing] in an almost human rights-free zone.'

How, I asked Pablo, had Microsoft, a North American tech corporation, become involved in public policy design at this provincial level, especially around issues of such a sensitive nature? For Microsoft, it wasn't about money, he replied. They did it for the experience of working with citizen-level data, even if it was anonymized, that only governments can usually access, to sign on customers for their cloud technology and to develop their AI toolkit for use in public policy work.

They weren't paid for their time directly, but they could take the experience of building a social welfare program using AI, and sell it to another government client. Plus, they came off looking like the good guys, helping to lift women out of poverty. It was win-win for them, Pablo said.

For the project to work, Pablo's team needed the fuel that drives all AI engines: a large-scale dataset. In this case, data that was intimate and far-reaching: details of the health of young women in precarious and vulnerable positions.

Pablo knew he could never send people to knock on the doors of his own neighbours and friends. He would never dare to enter the private Catholic schools in the city centre to gather data on young girls. The same doctor-friends who had complained to Pablo of too many abortions would never have allowed researchers into their own homes, to question daughters about unwanted pregnancies.

But in the inner-city settlements, families like Norma's were accustomed to government and charity workers knocking on their doors, clipboards in hand, asking for information about their bodies, their families, their lives. And according to Pablo, they opened up their doors, flagged the surveyors down, and invited them into their homes. They actively wanted to be heard, and to be helped.

Inevitably, poor and indigenous communities – like the immigrant families being over-policed in the Netherlands – lean more on the government for healthcare, education, and work, and basic necessities like housing, drinking water and electricity. Their frequent contact with the state makes them far more visible within government databases, compared to the wealthy families like the Abeleiras. So of course, the decisions about which neighbourhoods to categorize and which data points to include were purely political and skewed.

Pablo visited some of the families in the early stages of the project's development, but he can't remember where. He certainly didn't go door-to-door, canvassing for data himself. He was just the guy who sat at a computer, crunching numbers and crafting a model that spat out lists.

The data collectors had to wear familiar faces, much like the ASHA workers in Indian villages collecting health and pregnancy data. In Salta, that meant university students studying to be sociologists or nurses, NGO workers from Conin, and local government representatives who already knew these families.

Each girl in the community was asked about her socioeconomic status, her education, her reproductive history. The surveyors took information about her physical and mental disabilities. They wrote down her family's circumstances, asked about the pregnancies and children, living and dead, of her mother and sisters and cousins, the types of jobs her family worked to help her survive. They asked how she lived: the details of squalor and decay, her daily struggles, what sort of toilets her family defecated in, if their roof was made of tin and whether it leaked.

To predict whether a particular girl might get pregnant at twelve, or fifteen, or eighteen, they built a model to include details about her socioeconomic position and family's history: factors which they believed were sufficient explanations for getting pregnant, and transmittable to future generations. The girls were not asked how safe they felt in their community, their ability to exercise autonomy and agency, or their hopes for the future. They weren't asked whether they wanted children, or whether they were afraid they had no choice. There were no questions about the men involved. The data collection process treated the young women as passive.

Even in neighbourhoods with willing participants, the Early Childhood government team could not be explicit about their motives. Many of these families were practising Catholics. Although parents were realists, and they understood that their adolescent children may be sexually active, who wanted to be told their teenage daughter would imminently fall pregnant? A destiny written in stone, an inescapable future determined by a probability score. Just like being told a software has predicted your child will commit a serious crime. A scarlet letter.

Pablo said the algorithm was too complex to explain anyway. Instead, people were told that the surveys were to collect information about their problems, so the government could work to bring them solutions. They suggested they could help fix their houses, put in new roofs, proper floors, provide sanitation or healthcare, and train them for jobs like carpentry or plumbing, giving them tools to be financially independent.

'We can say, OK, you exist, we care about you, we can do things to improve your life or to help you,' Pablo said. 'At least with this, we bring the invisible to the light . . .'

The Mystery of the Missing AI

Norma agreed with Pablo's charitable view of the AI program – that it would help put a spotlight on the neighbourhood's needs and challenges. But whether the AI software actually delivered on this proved hard to confirm. Very few people had been let into the secret of the existence of a machine-learning software that was selecting families. Even Norma, who had heard about the assistive program for teen mothers, didn't know it was underpinned by a predictive computer system. The only time it had ever been acknowledged publicly was in 2018, a couple of years into its development, when Governor Urtubey had declared: 'With technology . . . you can predict five or six years ahead which girl, or future teenager, is 86 per cent predestined to have a teenage pregnancy.'[5]

This public disclosure caused an uproar amongst women's rights activists in the region. The timing was key: Urtubey's announcement was made in the middle of a nationwide campaign for legal abortion in Argentina in 2018. Paz Pena, a tech and human rights activist said: 'According to their narratives, if they have enough information from poor families, conservative public policies can be deployed to predict and avoid abortions by poor women. Moreover, there is a belief that, "If it is recommended by an algorithm, it is mathematics, so it must be true and irrefutable".'[6]

Critics viewed the algorithm as an over-designed, imperfect tool attempting to somehow 'fix' the girls, rather than the social fractures causing their predicament. The data collected excluded men. 'This specific focus on a particular sex reinforces patriarchal gender roles and, ultimately, blames female teenagers for unwanted pregnancies, as if a child could be conceived without a sperm,' Pena wrote. 'And if we consider that the database includes girls aged ten years old and above, whose pregnancy would only be a result of sexual violence . . . how can a machine say you are likely to be the victim of a sexual assault? And how brutal is it to conceive such a thing?'

Paula Cattaneo, a youth social worker in the Salta region, had heard about the AI system when Urtubey talked about it on the TV. 'I watched and I thought, what?! I asked around, and [my colleagues] said, "it's like we always work, we are filtering the families according to what we think, but the government is playing it up, calling it algorithms".'

Paula has been a social worker in Salta for twenty-two years and had agreed to be my guide to the byzantine local bureaucracy. She is outspoken and funny, with a kindness that makes you feel instantly at home around her. She stopped being an observant Catholic years ago and she is rarely judgemental of people. Unless they are Catholic charities like Conin preaching against abortion to the families she works with. Then she tells them to stay in their own lane. 'That's my job, not yours,' she says, eyebrows arched. Teenagers probably like her a lot.

Paula's parents were country doctors, and her brother was adopted, so she had grown up around social care workers. Specialising in public health, she works with high-risk patients, including unemployed, poor and adolescent mothers, helping them to plan their futures. She doesn't just visit their homes. She goes where young people hang out – sports centres, youth clubs, plazas – to talk to them in safe spaces. For at least a decade, Paula has also overseen abortion services in the hospital where she works, serving women and girls in a dozen nearby towns. With abortion illegal in Argentina until as recently as December 2020, the work required huge courage.

'It's an intense job, but I do it from a deep conviction,' she says as we walk across town together. 'For me it's an issue of public health and personal autonomy.'

When we met, Paula and I were trying to solve the mystery of the missing AI software. We knew from Pablo that the data had been collected and the algorithm designed in 2016–17. Then in 2019, the government changed hands. When a new political party came into power, Governor Urtubey was out, and the Ministry of Early Childhood where Pablo and Charlie worked was dismantled and downgraded from a 'Ministry' to a less important 'Secretariat'. The Abeleiras and their teams were fired, and the algorithmic system was abandoned.

We'd been trying to figure out what happened next with both the data and the software. Did it make any difference? When Paula spoke to colleagues – social workers, nurses, doctors and local government contacts who had worked with the Abeleira administration back in 2018 – no one seemed to have observed the algorithm's effects in action. Neither the families involved in the experiment, nor community workers, nor even Pablo Abeleira himself had any idea what had happened to it since the year 2019.

We were also hoping the new secretary of early childhood, Carina Iradi, who replaced Pablo's brother Charlie Abeleira in government, would hold some clues about its fate in the years it was supposedly operational.

As we walked through winding streets on Salta's cobblestones, Paula mused about the follies of predicting the future. She didn't outright reject the idea of an algorithm that could select families in need, but she was confused about its purpose. 'It's kind of weird,' she said. 'What do they do, knock on the door and say hi, your daughter may get pregnant, so we're going to get you a bathroom? I can't even imagine!'

She'd always thought that statistics and data can capture trends about human peculiarities, but never tell an individual's story. As a social worker, she said, you still have to assess each family individually. You can't label or stigmatize people. 'It's too intrusive and it makes the girl an object, and not an agent of her own life. Like, can she make changes or not in her own life?'

Perhaps the Abeleira ministry *had* collaborated with families and identified areas of help, she said, but then what was the point of the predictions? Why not just let experienced social workers do their jobs on the ground?

We arrived at the Secretariat for Early Childhood and Families, hoping to get some answers. It was a cheerful orange building with a tall wooden door, with young mothers, babies in prams and teenage girls streaming in and out. The building was narrow, with small rooms leading off a long corridor. Ushered into Secretary Iradi's office, we found her sitting at a corner desk, in front of a framed photo of the current governor of Salta and the maroon-and-black regional flag. Iradi said her department still held the data collected during the Abeleira era in 2016, and it helped to inform new policies and interventions. But it was not being used to make behavioural predictions about pregnancies.

She was vaguely scornful about the entire affair, in agreement with Paula. 'Our software is not predictive because we think that technology has limitations,' she said. 'There is an abyss between human experience and artificial intelligence. If you don't know the social reality of a place, you will clearly fail when trying to predict or plan. We understand that AI can be a positive force, but not to make decisions like these.'

To understand these families, she insists, you had to visit them in their neighbourhoods, see what they lacked, and build solutions in collaboration with them – like the work Paula already did. In fact, she said, the Abeleira administration had started a different set of projects – something more tangible than a machine learning software. Her team had been putting effort into expanding them. 'Go with our local councillor and see what we have done,' Iradi said. 'She can show you around.'

The Human Solution

Paula and I pulled into the sunny front lot of a whitewashed building at the confluence of a cluster of densely populated barrios, a building brightened by a colourful mural and a cheerful sign outside – 'CPI Libertad', named for a nearby settlement. We had travelled in a van loaned to us by Secretary Iradi and were accompanied by one of her deputies, who is also a child nutritionist. We're barely a mile from Norma's home in Barrio Norte.

It's lunchtime here, and that means hubbub, clattering plates and a lot of finger-licking. Today's dessert is *anchi*, a traditional pudding in the region of Salta – a delicious corn flour porridge, seasoned with sugar and lashings of lemon juice. '*Anchi!*' the children cry, as the daycare workers place shallow bowls in front of them. They are all neatly dressed, the girls' dark hair tied back or plaited tidily. The smallest ones, ranging in age from nine months to a year-and-a-half, slurp happily in highchairs, while the older children, up to five years old, are covered in colourful smocks, sitting at long tables spooning *anchi* into their mouths as if it's a race.

The spacious classrooms are flooded with spring sunshine, filtered pastel by gauzy curtains. Bookshelves, wooden toys, coloured clay are lined up neatly along the walls. The stick-figure drawings and primary-colour cut-outs hanging on the walls feel familiar and comforting – dinosaurs, one-eyed monsters, flowers and butterflies, the universal insides of a child's imagination.

CPI Libertad is a free kindergarten in the south-east of the city, one of about sixty early childhood centres set up around the Salta region. They were originally funded by Charlie Abeleira but had been developed by Iradi's department since 2019. The children at this particular centre have one thing in common: more than 70 per cent of them have teenage parents. I'm shown round by Julia, who runs this centre and insists I try the *anchi*. While I savour my bowl, she tells me that most of the children here are from single-parent families, some of the poorest in the city, and are usually looked after by their *abuelas*, or grandmothers, because their mothers are, in many ways, still childlike. There aren't many fathers around, she says. The men don't always see these children as their responsibility, so the job of raising them is left mostly to the women and girls.

For pre-schoolers in vulnerable and fragile situations, these are the only free spaces on offer. Like CPI Libertad, the other regional centres too have a high proportion of adolescent and young mothers amongst their families. Most of the parents work informal jobs like domestic cleaning, street-food vending and construction, or agricultural labour when they can get it. While they work, the centres care for their children and act as community hubs for the extended and blended families of grandparents, uncles, aunts and cousins who raise the children together. Julia and her co-workers try to empower mothers as much as they can, she says, not only against their partners but even to stand up to their own mothers, the *abuelas*; to remind them that they are the children's parents after all.

When the empty *anchi* bowls are cleared away, parents are starting to gather outside to pick up the morning-shift kids. Carla, a twenty-something, is waiting out in the hallway, cradling her three-week-old baby Paulina. She's here to pick up her four-year-old daughter. She's always loved coming to the centre just to watch the children play and be carefree. The baby's asleep, and she's having a quiet moment to herself, smiling as she looks round at the festoons of paper flowers and drawings depicting the children's human rights, cartoon visions of 'safety', 'health' and 'education'.

Carla is unmarried, and lives with her parents and her brother. The day care has been a huge help to her, she says. She worked as a domestic cleaner until recently, and the free childcare allowed her to earn a decent living without stress or guilt. If she had to work late sometimes, her brother or her daughter's father would pick up their toddler from the kindergarten, which was local and easy to access. It gave their family stability, and her child a safe and happy place to spend the day.

The goal of the Microsoft–Salta predictive system was similar: to equip young women like Carla with tools to make informed choices about motherhood, and to break repetitive cycles of poverty. I ask her what she thinks could be done to better support young women, particularly new mothers in her community. 'Work,' she says, with a short laugh. 'If they can help with that, that's all I need.'

As we talk, I hear a cry, 'Mama!' A pigtailed child rushes full tilt towards Carla, chattering about her morning. Carla's face lights up. Their giggles echo round and round the room.

Winners and Losers

Back in Pablo's office in Salta's city centre, he's showing me the statistical gymnastics his custom data-mining software can perform with individual-level demographic data, and how governments can use these numbers to make targeted decisions for specific populations. 'Do they need a well, a school? Where? How many are disabled? How many have children? They can visualize,' he says.

The AI pilot's abandonment has barely slowed Pablo down. In fact, the project launched his new career as a self-employed tech consultant for governments. It appeared that after they lost their government jobs, Pablo and his brother had set up a non-profit called the Horus Foundation which services several large public- and private-sector clients. The AI project simply became a calling card for governments requiring digital services, and more recently, for corporations that work with governments across Africa and Latin America.

Since 2019, Pablo has worked on national projects in Brazil and Argentina to map out informal settlements across these countries, helping governments provide better public services to the communities living in them. He's also worked on public–private projects in Cameroon, where his client is a French mining company that displaces local communities. Pablo collected demographic and health data of individuals to build models that could recommend public health and sanitation services for the villages affected by the miners.

These new data projects seem promising, and Pablo wants to talk about the future, but I ask him if the Salta algorithm has ever been used to intervene with at-risk families. If so, has it had the desired effect of reducing adolescent pregnancies?

The answers are deeply frustrating – both for me and Pablo. Although the model had been used to identify a list of at least 250 families, several academics had called the validity of the pilot into question. Nearly three-quarters of families in a test area had been tagged as likely to have a teenage pregnancy in their homes, making an individual-level predictive system redundant. Clearly a set of sweeping, community-wide interventions was needed – the domain of government actors, not software engineers or Microsoft employees.

There were also issues around the system's technical soundness. For one, AI researchers at the University of Buenos Aires had found several design flaws in the algorithm's code which they found uploaded onto GitHub, an open code platform owned by Microsoft.[7] Because the number of teen pregnancies in the community studied was so small – in the hundreds – the data had to be artificially inflated in order to train the algorithm. Although this is an accepted technical method, it appeared to have been done improperly. Therefore, the same or very similar data points had been used to both train and later test the model. In other words, the AI model appeared to be predicting the risk of pregnancy correctly on new families, when it was really just being tested on answers it had already seen.

The critics didn't have access to the full dataset, but if this were true, it would invalidate the software's claimed 86 per cent accuracy rate. The scientist who published the critique told me this was the type of error an undergraduate might make.

The other, more subtle, problem concerned ascertaining the truth. Because of the sensitive nature of the data, there was no way to ensure the girls, or their families, were telling the truth about past or current pregnancies, especially if they were considering abortion. In fact, it was highly likely they were lying, since abortion was still illegal at the time in Argentina. This meant the training dataset was already biased, with no way to correct it. So how could you trust its predictions?

I asked Pablo to reflect on whether these concerns were legitimate. He said the pilot had only just got off the ground and had been shut down before it could be refined, tested and improved. But I was insistent. Did they see any reduction in the rate of pregnancies?

Pablo became visibly frustrated. 'We intervened with the families, yes, we told them about the risks we found, and we started to strengthen their skills in different areas. Sometimes it was about the education of parents or trying to help single mothers or other family members get a job,' he said. 'In one particular house, the floor was made of dirt, so we built a ceramic floor. For others, we trained them in plumbing or carpentry to give them tools and help them find work. They were happy to receive help from the government.'

But beyond those immediate fixes, the project had been shut down too early – only a few months after the interventions began – to assess if the algorithms had any effect on the rate of teen pregnancy in the area. The new leadership in 2019 came with its own priorities, and those favoured by the previous powerbrokers were cleared out.

Pablo was disappointed that he didn't get to see the AI project through – both from a professional and personal perspective. But he remained a technocrat who trusted in the power of AI technology. He didn't believe their system was poorly designed or ineffective, more a work-in-progress that was never given a fair chance. He also felt that the algorithm's goals had been explained badly by the former governor, and that warring political factions had got in the way of its success.

Meanwhile, Microsoft came away with some local experience, and a testbed for its Azure machine-learning systems in the public sector – along with its $50,000-a-year cloud licence fee over three years. But it gained more than just business acumen. For nearly a decade, the American tech giant has attempted to extend its sphere of influence beyond the corporate world, by positioning itself as an international political and diplomatic player, with clout over states and laws. It started off redefining its role in the realm of cybersecurity, by proposing a Digital Geneva Convention of corporations and countries in 2017, and co-signing agreements with the government of France.[8]

It has since sought to do the same in artificial intelligence, ensuring it has a seat at the table in global AI policy discussions, just like in international cyber policy.[9] Microsoft's role in Salta's teen pregnancy predictor, although seemingly minor, fits into its wider strategy to increase its political clout. Like the colonial mega-corporations of centuries gone by – the East India Company, say, or the Anglo-Iranian Oil Company – technology companies today are beginning to function as monopolistic quasi-states.

Meanwhile, abortion had been legalized in Argentina in late 2020, a few years after the teen pregnancy prediction software had been built and shelved. While the political context had changed for all women and girls, thanks to the work of women's rights campaigners, the social context hadn't. Abortion was still frowned upon, and the families' data – intimate details of their reproductive health, family heritage, jobs – remained in a central database that would be passed on from regime to regime. Was there a danger that it might be twisted in the wrong hands?

It wouldn't be the first time a government had used sensitive data to harm its own people. After all, from 1976, Argentina had been ruled for seven years by a military dictatorship that collected extensive data about the public through surveys and polls, which was used to craft propaganda and influence citizens.[10]

In that same era, data formed the backbone of the notorious Operation Condor, a United States-backed campaign of terror and repression carried out jointly by several dictatorships in the countries of the Southern Cone, which include Chile, Argentina, Brazil and Bolivia. These countries contributed and shared data about citizens seen as threats to the authoritarian governments, including left-leaning politicians and thinkers, trade unionists and clergy. That information was stored in a shared computer system used by the group to plan abductions, 'disappearances', tortures and even assassinations.[11] The people's data became a weapon used against them.

On my final evening in Salta, I wandered from my hotel over to the San Martín park in the south of the city to see a local landmark, the Portal De La Memoria, *Portal of Memory*, a commemorative arch that remembers lives lost during the years under the Argentinian dictatorship. On one side of the painted arch, a poem by Chilean activist-poet Pablo Neruda was printed in black. I looked it up, and learned it was 'Los Enemigos' or The Enemies, a powerful call to arms that honoured the memories of citizens massacred by Latin American dictators. The steady drumbeat of the poem is Neruda's repetition of the phrase *pido castigo*, 'I demand punishment' – not just for those who ordered the executions, but also for those who defended and stood by the crimes. Neruda wanted them all to be judged, here in this park in Salta.

When I asked Pablo about whether history could repeat itself, he nodded. He understood. But the data already existed within government departments, he said. If they wanted to twist it, or weaponize it, they could do so with what they had already, with or without the help of AI technology. 'We work with governments, because we believe they want to do good things.'

I believed that Pablo's intentions – and the aims of the AI technology – were good: to identify families that needed additional help and to find it for them before they ended up with difficult situations, such as dealing with unwanted pregnancies.

However, I found that no one took responsibility for the outcomes of the system. Ultimately the AI pilot had no owners or controllers. Once the team had been disbanded and the Microsoft employees had moved on, the code was relegated to the spirit realm; the data remained buried in government spreadsheets, a spectre of the algorithm it had fed, but the model itself had disappeared.

At best, the project had been a waste of public money and resources – and at worst, an abuse of the trust of mostly indigenous and *criollo* families who had shared their data, hoping for a solution to their financial problems.

The only group to benefit was the one that had designed and briefly controlled the technology: Microsoft, which might have made some government contacts, and the Abeleiras, who used the learnings and connections it brought to enhance their own reputation and employability.

For the stated beneficiaries, the women and girls of Salta's inner-city neighbourhoods, little had changed. They went about their lives as ever, still grappling with largely the same needs and challenges their mothers before them had faced. For them, the AI system had made absolutely no difference to their daily lives.

*

The afternoon heat in Norte Grande is impressive. It has sucked the life out of us all. Even the hardy stray dogs are slinking along, tongues out, searching for slivers of shade. Norma hollers at two women waiting across the street – Maripi Juncosa, a local political councillor dressed in flaming red, and her assistant Myla, a nursing student who will take notes. Maripi calls hello back. 'You ready to head out?'

Maripi and Norma confer and then walk together down the white-hot road. Myla trails behind. Norma speaks in a low, urgent voice. 'Potholes,' she says, pointing. 'They must be fixed before the rains come, look. It's only going to get worse.' The assistant follows, taking photos on an old Nokia phone.

Norma jabs her index finger at more things that need fixing – unpaved roads, piles of rubble, houses with broken roofs, open sewage. The nurse's phone keeps click-click-clicking. 'We won't go down there,' Norma says, the finger directed at a dead-end containing two or three houses. 'Dangerous.'

We're weaving quickly in and out of narrow side streets now, side-stepping sleeping dogs and derelict Ford Fiestas and Peugeot 504s, caked with dust from the hills. The shuffling beats of cumbia blare from the houses. Norma is striding off again, now on a shadeless stretch of road next to a thirsty field. The dead grass and chicken wire mar the azure of the sky. 'Don't throw trash', a sign warns. A little green sapling sticks out of an abandoned car tyre.

'That should be a plaza, with a playground for all the children,' Norma says, slowing down and shaking her head at the barren land. 'We need a plaza. Imagine what a plaza could do here.'

Finally, she stops outside an abandoned-looking brick structure with grilled windows and a green door. It looks a bit like a prison. 'It's the new community centre,' Norma says with satisfaction. 'It even has internet now.' But it's not enough. She wants a community space for young adults, like centres they have for the elderly. A place teenage mothers can feel safe, and the youth can play sports together. Somewhere they can be kids, and forget, just for a little while, their outsized responsibilities. Without these spaces, they remain hidden in their homes, forgotten and ignored.

'They need somewhere,' Norma says. 'Somewhere to call their own.'

CHAPTER 7
Your Boss

Armin

On the morning of 12 August 2020, the day that he decided to fight the UberEats algorithm, Armin Samii woke earlier than usual, having set an alarm for himself when the idea came to him in the middle of the night.

He dressed, made coffee and sat down at his computer, where he remained for the next sixteen hours straight, coding a web application, including filming videos to show UberEats couriers how to use it. He called it UberCheats and published it at midnight.

UberCheats was an algorithm-auditing tool. Armin, who was working as an UberEats courier at the time, had lost trust in the AI system that essentially functioned as his boss. He built it because he felt he had no choice but to do *something* after weeks of trying and failing to get a human being at Uber to explain discrepancies in his wages.

The wage discrepancy was a hard one to prove. There is no set rate for couriers, since Uber prices jobs dynamically – it can change by the hour and differ between different geographies and individuals. It is affected by everything from demand to the weather. Because Uber generally hides exact delivery locations from couriers after they've completed their deliveries (ostensibly for customers' personal safety), it's hard to confirm how far you've travelled too. So when a courier receives a receipt, all they see is an anonymized route from A to B, alongside the number of miles travelled and what they got paid. But this means delivery workers can't double-check discrepancies. Armin's UberCheats was able to extract GPS coordinates from receipts, then calculate how many miles a courier had *actually* travelled, compared to what Uber *claimed* they had. He made it free to use.

Like the data tagging labourers Hiba Daoud and Ian Koli, Armin was part of a growing human workforce in the service of algorithms. But rather than training and labelling AI systems, workers like Armin – more than one billion of them globally – move physical things around, from people, food, and groceries to medicines, furniture and books. They ride in cars and trucks, on motorcycles and bicycles, across cities and small towns everywhere from Nairobi to Jakarta, Seoul, Pittsburgh and London. And they do it at the behest of an app.

These apps use AI systems, a faceless boss that hands down edicts via phone: machine-learning software allocates drivers their jobs, verifies workers' identities, determines dynamic pay per task, awards bonuses, and detects fraud, and it also makes decisions that oversee hiring and firing. The rules that workers live by are changeable, re-written based on a continuous stream of fresh data. And in the high-stakes power play between employer and employee, the shape-shifting algorithm holds all the cards.

Armin is the youngest son of Iranian immigrants who moved to California in the 1960s. Both his parents are civil engineers. His mother worked in the local government, figuring out how traffic flows were affected by road construction. His father was a builder of bridges and railway lines for the city of San Diego, where the family settled down. Armin vividly remembers his father poring over architectural plans to work out engineering problems visually. When he was particularly stressed out, he would take out an old calculus textbook and solve problems until his mind was clear. Armin inherited this trait. Although, since he was trained as a computer scientist, Armin's stress-buster is debugging computer code.

Twenty-eight-year-old Armin has a shock of dark curls that spill messily over his angular face, and he likes to wear neon colours. Armin's greatest love is cycling. He owns five bikes, and his ideal job would have him on one of them throughout the day if possible. When he moved to Pittsburgh, he began attending community meetings with local elected representatives in a bid to make the city safer for cyclists. And he now runs a start-up called Dashcam For Your Bike, which makes an app for urban cyclists to record, save and highlight live video footage in an attempt to keep them safe. He is, in fact, inherently an activist, living by the principle that any system can be changed if you care enough to do something about it. He has photographed political rallies and canvassed for candidates around California. He has coded a website that offers a visual explainer of an alternative voting system called rank-choice voting, which he believes is a more democratic method of polling the public. But he doesn't save his efforts just for the big things. He happily agrees he is a micro-social-justice warrior.

One time, he bought a microwave curry from the vegan section of the supermarket Target, which contained ghee, a dairy product. He tried to talk to the store manager about the danger of mis-labelling food products but didn't get very far. So he submitted an official complaint to the county health department. Four weeks and a dozen emails later, the county sent an inspector into the store, and the manager was forced to re-name the section vegetarian.

A few months earlier, at a different supermarket, he had tried to claim a complimentary pint of milk offered as part of a promotion. But the automated system couldn't process a photo of his receipt.

So it rejected his claim. He started a weeks-long correspondence with the store owners until he received $4 as compensation.

In a previous workplace as a computer programmer, he'd noticed the CEO repeatedly using an unproven statistic to motivate employees. He called him out privately at first, and when that didn't work, publicly, in a team meeting. The CEO never used that number again – although Armin ultimately got pushed out of the company.

So when Armin decided to try working for UberEats delivery for the summer, he had no idea that his usual assumptions no longer held true. This was, he came to discover, a world in which humans were pawns, and the algorithm ruled. Its rules were invisible and capricious, the boss inhumane, and Armin's voice was powerless. It was a surreal loop.

Armin had moved to hilly Pittsburgh from Berkeley in 2019, to take a job at a self-driving car company Argo.ai, a start-up funded by Ford and Volkswagen. He led the team that designed the user interface between human passengers and the autonomous vehicle. He spent hours with drivers inside cars, observing their behaviours, their gripes, their decision-making, and used that psychology to design the AI system's responses. He was a human–machine translator.

As he developed software for self-driving cars, Armin became aware that he was working on a two-tonne moving death-machine being tested on real roads, and a wrong line of code could literally kill someone. Just the previous year, in 2018, an Uber self-driving prototype had killed a pedestrian in Arizona in error, when the human co-pilot or back-up driver had been distracted, possibly streaming *The Voice* on their mobile phone.[1] Code, unlike the physical joists of a bridge, is not neutral. In the tech world, employees like Armin were reckoning with the discovery that writing code remotely does not absolve you from the real-world consequences of what you've built. Like his peers, he had started to question if the things he was building were ethical, and if they would work for the common good. In the summer of 2020, he quit Argo because he realized self-driving cars, while making driving safer, wouldn't necessarily make *cities* any more liveable – which is what he truly cared about.

While he took some time off to figure out what he wanted to do next, he considered his current options. He wanted to explore Pittsburgh on his bike. That's when he had the idea to work as an UberEats bike courier. What better way to spend the summer, riding his bike all day, exploring his new city and earning some cash in the process. It was the perfect stopgap.

The Pittsburgh Hill Problem

Armin likes to tell stories, spinning little details into important plot points. Today he's describing what it feels like having a black box as your boss: dehumanising, soul-crushing, frustrating. It's a job with a false sense of autonomy.

'Take my very first experience of it,' he said. In July 2020, when he tried to sign up to UberEats, the app required Armin to perform an algorithmic identity check. He had to take a selfie, which would be verified by the app's facial-recognition system built by Microsoft. Except it didn't work. He kept taking photos, and the app would reject them, saying it couldn't verify his ID. 'I know this is a huge problem for people of colour. I don't know if it was my hair being bigger or a big beard that I had, but there was some sort of algorithmic error in there,' he said. 'That happened three times.'

The fourth time, he washed his hair and tamped it down and opened his mouth so the algorithm could find it within his dark beard, and finally it recognized him. He was approved to start work, but he already had that niggling feeling he was used to getting, the one where something seemed unfair.

The next day, his first on the job, the aggravations began to pile up quickly. He received repeated orders to collect burgers and Happy Meals from a McDonald's that had shut down months ago. Customers had no idea that Uber had simply neglected to delete it in their database. 'I guess all the other drivers had figured out they had to reject meals from this McDonald's, but I spent forty-five minutes trying to convince Uber to remove it from their system. They said, "We can't change the data in the system, but we can offer you $2 because you went there." I spent twenty minutes biking there and forty-five minutes on the phone to them and they gave me $2 for it.'

Armin struggled to accept that there was no human being he could speak to who was empowered to make basic changes. His frustration was rooted in his experience as a computer scientist who knew how easy it would be to correct this error. But no one else bothered, because they believed that the app's software didn't reward honesty or responsible behaviour. It prized speed and time maximization instead. So he just had to keep cancelling trips for that McDonald's, just like all the other drivers had learned to do, to get around the job allocation algorithm.

Working for an illogical system with little route to redress, and a boss to whom he couldn't complain, was antithetical to Armin's character. He decided to quit after just three weeks and twenty-one trips. He didn't need the money after six years working in tech, and the experience was not enjoyable. He wasn't reliant on the income from the app, and he was well aware of his privileged position. 'If you're doing it for income, and it's going to take you an hour to sort something out on the phone, you have zero incentive to fight this,' he said.

Armin also found that the most precarious gig workers – immigrants without language skills or official papers, women, people supporting entire families on this income – were forced to sacrifice their autonomy at the altar of the algorithm. 'There are people like me who get very frustrated and end up quitting, they last maybe six weeks. And then the people who are seasoned are much more chill than I am. They're the ones who let it roll off them. And they're like, you have the shitty system, but we're in the system and like, we got to be at peace with it and just accept the hit that we want to get paid,' he said. 'I'm not in the Zen camp.'

Armin's last day delivering food was a blazing summer's day. He was biking home at close to 2 p.m., when he got a ping via the app saying it had a delivery job for him that was a six-minute journey out of his way. He knew that on his bike, that would be more like fifteen minutes (the app calculated times based on car journeys, even though it knew he was on a bike), but nonetheless he took the job, which sent him to pick up food from a Middle-Eastern restaurant.

While waiting, he received another ping; someone else had placed an order at the same restaurant, and he was being offered that delivery too. Because Uber's algorithms hide their destination from drivers until they've collected the food, Armin had little data to make an informed decision. The app also doesn't show elevation levels on its map, so he had no way to know how steep the journeys would be. Nonetheless, he agreed to the second drop-off.

But just as Uber didn't adjust its estimated journey times or display elevations for cyclists, it didn't filter jobs either. His first drop-off was at the top of Pig Hill, one of the steepest hills in Pittsburgh. As he struggled up, car drivers rolled down their windows to tell him, 'Good job.' Fifty minutes later, he got to the first customer, who said he couldn't believe they'd sent Armin up there on a bike. Still sweaty, thirsty and exhausted, it took him another forty minutes to complete the second job. This customer had been waiting an hour and a half for his food. He was a lot less sympathetic than the first one. 'I tried to explain but he just grumbled at me and took his food. He tipped me like fifty cents or one dollar.'

The algorithm had said the entire job would take six minutes, but it had taken Armin ninety.

At first, he thought the estimate was simply an error, or an estimate for a courier delivering food by car. But then he realized that even a car couldn't have made the journey in six minutes, as the software had predicted. He also calculated that he had ridden 2.1 miles that day, but he was being paid for 1.1 miles, according to his receipt. 'It wasn't a discrepancy between biking and driving,' he said. 'This was a bug beyond that.'

The trouble with trying to audit your wages as a gig worker is that most delivery apps don't offer a standard wage, or even an equation to calculate it. The courier or driver is shown the fee they will be paid before they choose to accept a job, but it isn't predictable. But algorithms price each job using a secret formula that takes into account a range of variables stretching from your customer rating, to your decline percentages, the demand and supply of rides, and the city you work in.

Because these apps log workers' data when they are on *and* off duty, recording every piece of digital information they can get their hands on – from their preferred routes, to how often they contact Uber services, how long they remain logged out of the app, how frequently they work and what jobs they accept and reject – any of these variables could feed into their wage calculation. The driver can only guess. All they know for sure is how many miles they are being paid for.

Armin sent Uber more than a dozen messages over the next couple of weeks, saying there was a discrepancy in the distance he'd been billed for, but kept receiving automated responses. The messages ranged from: log out of the app, restart the app, restart the device, redownload the app, update the app, reset your network settings, if your wait is longer than ten minutes, cancel the order.

Obviously, none of this would fix the incorrect payment problem.

In a spreadsheet where he had meticulously logged every contact with Uber customer service, Armin had recorded fourteen emails and 126 minutes on the phone.

'Finally I got to someone on the phone, a person, who had the ability to pull up Google Maps, and say, "This is a glitch", and she paid me $4.25 extra. So I got $16.43, which included a $4 tip, and then they corrected it to an additional $4.'

After this, there was nothing else left to do, nothing else he *could* do. But in the middle of the night, a lightbulb went off in his head. The issue was that he had been underpaid. How many other times had that happened? Who else was being underpaid? By how much?

'It's tricky because I assume how much you get paid has very little to do with distance but more to do with a machine-learning algorithm that decides what is the absolute least they can pay someone,' he told me.

Since Uber's system did not disclose exact locations of deliveries to couriers after the fact, they can't map the distance independently. This makes it harder for couriers to audit the algorithms themselves, making them reliant on the app companies to self-correct any errors. 'I wondered if I could figure out the locations from the receipt, plug it into Google myself and check if it was correct,' Armin said.

Does Uber cheat?

After analysing his own receipts, Armin found several discrepancies – a 7.6-mile journey according to Google Maps, which increased to 9.2 miles because of road blocks, became a six-mile trip according to Uber's payment algorithm. Other receipts showed Uber paying him for 1.5 miles instead of 1.9 miles, 6 miles instead of 7.5 miles, and so on.

He published the app on Google Chrome for anyone else to use, and almost immediately Armin heard from dozens of UberEats workers from around the world, from across the US, Japan, Brazil and Australia, to India and Taiwan. About 6,000 trips were logged on UberCheats in total, of which 17 per cent were underpaid. Whichever city they were in, the company was, on average, seemingly underpaying drivers using UberCheats by 1.35 miles per trip.[2]

One email Armin received said: 'I just used your extension and found that 8.31 per cent of my deliveries were affected . . . at least one every day. If you do gather enough data for a class action suit, I will gladly participate. Thank you for your work on this.'

Many of the messages were from workers from ethnic minorities, or migrants with unstable living situations or sole earners supporting families.

'When you see who is getting hurt the most,' he said, 'it is already people who are getting hurt by existing systems, but it exacerbates these differences.'

UberCheats was a window into the innards of gig-work algorithms that app workers are firmly locked out of. The apparent miscalculation of distances suggested something app workers had always suspected – algorithms have a blind spot for human factors like unexpected delays or route-extensions caused by gnarly traffic jams, weather events, roadworks, or crowded restaurants that keep workers waiting.

These delays materially affect no one but the worker, impacting their ratings and speed, and eventually their ability to get jobs and be paid. But Armin never quite figured out the logic behind this particular error. 'All my theories for why it was happening were disproved,' he said, 'so then it just started to feel random and unfair.' It was a lot like how the entire AI-based system looked to human workers: arbitrary, autocratic and unaccountable.

In February 2021, a few months after Armin's app went live, Uber's lawyers complained, asking Google to block UberCheats on their Chrome browser, claiming people might confuse it for an actual Uber product.[3] When Google did so, Armin sent a series of emails appealing to the search giant who controlled what apps it published on its browser, and the ban was lifted. But in February 2022, he took UberCheats offline. Despite its clear utility for the hundreds of Uber drivers who downloaded it, and used it to check if they were underpaid, Armin found the technical upkeep of the app was becoming burdensome while he was working on other projects. It required hours of his time every time Uber decided to change its own code, which they did regularly and without explanation. Some drivers told Armin they had taken it up with Uber and it had benefited them financially, but Armin didn't have the financial resources or the appetite to take Uber to court. For him, the real point of the tool had been in shining a light on the algorithm's unpredictability, and Uber's lack of accountability for its actions. Armin's story had been picked up widely by the press, from *Wired* to *Salon* and the *Daily Mail*. It helped the public understand how opaque AI-based work platforms really were.

'At every company I've ever worked at, I've found a way to make myself heard. It may not be pretty, but I could always try to fix it. With Uber, I feel helpless, because I can't do that,' he said. 'When they have these dark patterns, when they're underpaying you by like twenty-five cents a ride, there's nothing I can do to find out why. And there's no one I can complain to, other than the press, right? UberCheats was a way to take action. Without that, it's just demoralizing.'

Armin's story shows what it can feel like to be the human in an automated employment system: the frustration and paranoia, the loss of camaraderie and community, the absence of redress. It's the irony of a structure that is wholly dependent on human labour, yet treats its workers like automatons.

He's hardly a lone case. While working for Uber, Armin was part of a global precariat, an emerging class of people whose livelihoods are insecure and unstable, those whose employers have reach and control of their lives even outside of work.[4] They are the same fraternity as the freelance data labourers in Nairobi and Bulgaria, working for a living wage to train AI systems that will bring in billions of dollars of revenue for the companies designing them. Or the ASHA community workers in India performing health-data collection for Western corporations.

A Kafkaesque Maze

In *The Trial*, one of Franz Kafka's most famous novels, a man named Joseph K is charged and arrested by mysterious agents who won't tell him what his crime is. He isn't imprisoned. Instead he is condemned to continue with his mundane daily existence, while grappling with paranoia and confusion about the nature of his supposed crime. After a series of nightmarish events where he tries to investigate what he may have done, he gives up. Eventually, one morning, he is executed by the same mysterious agents outside his home.

The Trial, a dystopian black comedy, is a clever skewering of the pointless nature of bureaucracy. But it could just as easily be about modern-day workers in an algorithmic age, about a man suspended from his work at a moment's notice at the will of an AI system.

Alexandru Iftimie is a Romanian immigrant in a south-western suburb of London. A long-time Uber driver, he has never read Kafka, but when I tell him about the plot, he can identify with Joseph K. He feels the phrase that best captures app-based work is *divide et impera*, divide and rule, the control tactic used by sovereigns and colonialists, like the British Empire in nineteenth-century India. It's how companies like Uber, he said, ensure they don't have to face tens of thousands of drivers joining together in protest outside their offices.

Alexandru hadn't started out cynical. After working as a night courier for a delivery company, where if he ever took a day off in his six-day week, the threat of losing his route hung over him, he quit that job to begin working as an Uber driver. The ridesharing company's promise that he could reclaim flexibility and control over his working hours was alluring. And at the start, he found it liberating. Over the nearly 7,000 trips he's done for Uber, he has made a decent living and kept up a five-star rating, an achievement he believes was down to his years as a retail salesman in Bucharest. When he heard other drivers complaining about how Uber treated them unfairly, for instance that they were fired or that their licence had been revoked for no reason, his feeling was this wasn't the whole truth. He felt certain they must be guilty of something.

But a couple of years in, Alexandru began to notice how the algorithm treated drivers differently. He had a good friend who drove for Uber in the same areas as he did, and sometimes if they happened to be close together, they'd grab a coffee and sit outside in sunny weather for a chat. Often, Alexandru's friend would receive multiple trip requests in a row and he'd have none. Sometimes it was the other way around. The trips were supposedly allocated to the closest available driver, but it didn't look that way to them. They learned that automated software used driver profiles, built from a cloud of unknown variables, to match them to riders in real time. Alexandru found that being kept in the dark like this was unnerving. He would have liked to know how he was being assessed, so he could at least maximize these variables to get more work. Why was Uber allowed to use his data to improve *its* business, but he couldn't use it to enhance his own?

When, a few months later, Alexandru received an automated

warning from Uber, telling him he had been flagged for fraudulent activity, he ignored it, assuming it was an error. Two weeks later, he received a second warning. Three strikes, and he would be terminated. These decisions were communicated entirely through automated messages. He wasn't told who he could turn to, to appeal or clarify.

He had no idea what he might have done wrong. He knew that Uber, like many others in the gig economy space, used artificial intelligence software – from fraud-detection algorithms to facial recognition and other behavioural profiling methods – to allocate jobs and verify, rate, and censure its drivers. But Alexandru was unaware which aspects of his work were defined or facilitated by algorithms, and what actions or data could be construed as deceptive. How did the software define fraud?

He was left with the burden of second-guessing an inscrutable computer system. Was it that time when a customer was running late and had asked him to drop her off at a slightly different destination? He'd obliged because he'd felt bad for her, but maybe it looked like fraud to the algorithm? Or maybe it was that time when there was an accident on the motorway and it had taken more than an hour to get around it. He just didn't know.

Alexandru called Uber driver support for help, but the customer service person was as much in the dark as he was. 'They said over and over, "The system can't be wrong, what have you done?" I said, "Well, that's why I'm calling you".'

His choices were either to wait, in dread, for the termination message – or to take his problem to a union. The algorithm's method of tailoring jobs and wages to the individual pitted workers against one another, convincing each worker he was a lone cell, rather than part of a larger body of human beings struggling jointly against a computer system. It made Alexandru feel powerless, as if he didn't stand a chance. He had no community to lean on.

He decided to go to the UK-based App Drivers and Couriers Union, a collective for gig workers like Alexandru, founded by a former Uber driver called James Farrar. The union took up his case, writing to Uber to explain and retract its fraud flags. While this was being resolved, Alexandru stopped taking on Uber jobs. He kept his account open, but he was too afraid to lose access permanently. Instead he went back to his former employer, the night courier company, taking on extra shifts there.

In October – three months after his first fraud allegation – he received an apology from Uber, which claimed that its automated system had made an error.[5] His account had been cleared but he was given no further explanation. Uber said that while it does use automated processes for fraud detection, decisions to terminate are only taken following human review by Uber staff. To Alexandru, this resolution was little comfort because he still feared the day this might all happen again.

'They use artificial intelligence software as an HR department for drivers. The system might make you stop working, it might terminate your contract with Uber, it might cost you your licence,' he said. 'That is dangerous.'

Alexandru's way of fighting back was more traditional than Armin's: he challenged Uber in court, demanding access to his personal data and transparency about pay-calculation algorithms. He wanted to understand clearly how the algorithm had failed in his case, and what had been done to prevent this in future. He was part of a group of five claimants represented by the union, suing Uber and another ride-hailing app, Ola Cabs, for access to their personal data – especially when used as a basis for suspensions and wage penalties.

The ruling, by the court in Amsterdam where Uber's European headquarters are based, broke new ground on the rights of workers subject to algorithmic management.

In the case against Ola Cabs, the Amsterdam court found that the app had used an entirely automated system to make deductions from one driver's earnings, which contravene data protection laws that give people a right to human review of algorithms.[6]

Separately, it asked Uber to provide the defendants in the case with the personal data it held on them, specifically the information used to block the drivers from the app. It also asked Uber to give drivers access to anonymized individual ratings on their performance, rather than providing an average of the rating across several trips.

The court did, however, support the company on its claims of algorithm transparency. It didn't order Uber to disclose any more information about how prices were calculated, or how drivers were flagged for fraud, and also rejected drivers' claims that Uber did not have meaningful human oversight in its processes around work allocation and suspensions.

This was one of the first legal interpretations of the complex grey area between human and AI decision-making, a crucial step in untangling the nuances of gig-workers' rights, but it felt to me like the ruling still fell short of empowering workers. Without access to the calculations made by Uber's machine-learning systems, innocent workers would find it impossible to avoid falling victim to its faulty computations again.

The reasons behind what happened still remain a mystery to Alexandru. 'It's like you find a warning left on your desk by your boss, but they are inaccessible, and if you knock on their door . . . they won't tell you what it is. You feel targeted, discriminated against,' he said.

Alexandru now continues to work for the company on its terms, even as he continues to appeal for his data rights as part of the union, in court – including asking for more extensive data on his work. It's the primary source of income for his family, which includes his newborn daughter, while he completes a law degree.

Until then, he says, 'Your life goes on. You have to keep working. You're just a person sitting in a car, waiting for a ping on your phone that tells you where to go.'

*

David Mwangi Thuo was attracted to Uber because in his hometown of Nairobi, it felt like an urbane, sophisticated job, one step up from driving a matatu or a motorbike, which he'd driven previously as an errand boy.

He liked that there was a fixed fee and he didn't have to negotiate with customers and that the app, rather than a boss, gave him more control over when he worked. He was also looking to his future. 'Uber is international,' he told me. 'If I leave the country to go somewhere like Canada, to cleaner pastures, I can work for Uber.'

Four years on and David feels he has to quit. 'You can say I'm independent, I don't have a boss. But unless I work all the time, day and night, I can't make money. At least with a company where you're employed, you know what you are expecting. You can plan for your future,' he said.

'What's changed?' I asked.

'The rates are too low, they lowered the prices because of competition from Bolt,' he said, referring to a competitor to Uber that has recently entered the Kenyan market. 'I have to pay insurance, service costs, fuel, I also have bills to pay.' Since the Ukraine–Russia war escalated in early 2022, David says fuel prices have soared from roughly 96 to 180 shillings per litre. When David joined Uber, the company was taking a roughly 15 per cent commission on rides, he said. Now, according to multiple Uber drivers I speak to in Nairobi, the company takes about 25 per cent of drivers' wages on average.[7]

'What is enabling us to do the work now is a Polish technology, which [makes] cheaper gas. It's cooking gas, LPG,' David says. It costs roughly one hundred shillings per litre, making Uber driving more cost-effective for him.

David sometimes rents his car out to other app drivers, whom he charges a fixed fee of 10,000 shillings (£67) per week. He takes on the cost of maintenance, but they pay for fuel. 'But [the driver] has to work a lot of hours. On a good day he might earn 1,500 shillings but on a bad day just 1,000,' he says. 'You can't say you have a salary; you are just driving Uber to survive. I don't want to borrow money to pay rent or eat food.'

He has at least fifty friends who have left the company because it's just not enough to live on, he said.

'We are all struggling.'

Going Karura

AI work systems are built to keep drivers apart, incentivising them to compete aggressively. Many apps, including Instacart, Lyft and Uber in the US, Deliveroo in Europe and Meituan and Ele.me in China, turn workers' lives into games through their apps, with software that nudges them towards certain areas or jobs, and awards points and badges for being on time, or maintaining a high review score. As work turns into a contest, your livelihood becomes the prize.

To express their discontent with the state of affairs, workers have begun to invent a colourful vocabulary to describe AI-driven work. Mexican and Guatemalan food couriers in New York City, for instance, call the app algorithm *patrón fantasma*, a spying phantom presence constantly calculating ways to squeeze more out of them.

In Indonesia, motorbike couriers use third-party apps known as *tuyul*, little tricks and workarounds like GPS spoofs or even UberCheats, that help to get around the algorithm's arbitrary rules and regain some control. The word refers to a mythical child-spirit in Indonesian folklore that steals on behalf of its human owner. And in China, app workers call the platforms' unilaterally enacted rules, such as wage calculations, 'despotic clauses' or 霸王条款.

The disempowering effects of AI management have had an unexpected side-effect: in some places, it has strengthened human agency, collaboration and resistance.

In Pittsburgh, drivers sometimes swap notes in a large car park just outside the airport, or by busy restaurants like McDonald's or KFC where wait times are long, strategizing entrepreneurial ways to make the algorithms work in their favour, like Armin did.

In Nairobi, drivers are often found chatting in car washes and shopping mall car parks in the nicer parts of town. In Jakarta, drivers for Gojek, a motorcycle-based delivery app, rest in informal 'base camps', roadside noodle stalls with phone charging points.[8] Highly rated Gojek drivers don't just share wage-maximizing tips, but they sell them as a business. Known as 'therapy services', these workers take on individual users' accounts and supposedly train their algorithms, spending a few days accepting and deleting jobs according to their clients' preferences, so the driver can imprint his own desires onto the opaque app's memory.[9]

Those who can't physically convene find one another online: Facebook pages, WhatsApp groups and Reddit threads have become digital water-coolers, where workers share complaints, algorithm gaming tricks and other ways to reclaim control. In Manchester, a Deliveroo driver WhatsApp group shared intel about restaurants with long wait-times and dodgy areas, and coordinated city-wide protests;[10] in China WeChat groups have become informal, therapeutic labour unions.[11]

On a Reddit thread for mostly American gig workers, the posts illustrate the ways in which workers are finding a way through.

'Hey folks,' one person wrote. 'Thank you everyone for your inputs, it got me excited and helped me build the MVP of the idea. I call it Driverside. I built this with a buddy at Microsoft, so there is [sic] a lot of improvements to do! I'd love to get your feedback!'

The rider had built a prototype of an iPhone app that automates accepting various delivery offers based on the driver's preferences, instead of the driver having to constantly calculate whether each offer is worth their time.

'I believe this could bring more control for delivery drivers. This is just the beginning! Let me know your thoughts!'

A worker wrote in response, 'I'd literally pay hundreds of dollars for an app that can flawlessly decline orders across all the major delivery apps with filters that I can customize (like decline all GrubHub orders over 40 miles away or decline all Uber Walmart orders or decline all DoorDash offers under $6.50).'

Others complained about algorithmic glitches, such as racially biased facial recognition technologies.

'Essentially, like many before me, my account was deactivated because . . . the system couldn't verify that it was me. So, so stupid. I tried to inquire about why my photo wasn't good enough and received an automatic response that my appeal was denied,' the complainant shared. 'I checked on reddit and apparently hundreds of people had the same issue. So, I just lost a significant % of my income just because I took a bad photo of myself and there's nobody that can help me to fix very simple verification issues.'

Yet others offered up strategies to game the job allocation algorithm.

'Just make sure you decline before taking the offer. If you take the offer, and a better one comes up on a different app and you reassign the DoorDash delivery it hits your completion rate. Need to maintain at least 80% completion I think.'

The way to resist, they were finding, was to take on the algorithms together.

*

New language is springing up around resistance movements too. In the UK, Deliveroo couriers coined the portmanteau term 'slaveroo', which they used alongside a customized emoji of the Deliveroo mascot kangaroo chained by its foot to a metal ball.[12] In the US, drivers adopted the '#DeclineNow' hashtag during a digital rally that encouraged riders to reject jobs in bulk.[13] And in Nairobi, platform workers in 2018 launched a protest movement called '*going Karura*', where they logged off for an entire day, turning them digitally invisible in the apps.[14] *Karura* referred to a forest hideout in Nairobi where Mau Mau insurgents had sheltered during a 1950s rebellion against British colonial rule. The phrase was a clarion call to anticolonial resistance.

The increased adoption of AI systems in work has forced workers to band together. Pitting workers against one another, alongside the opaque systems that govern job allocation and pay, is alienating workers.[15] AI systems leave little room for argument. Gig workers – just like data labellers and content moderators – are gearing up to reclaim their agency.

Over the past decade, the gig worker community has transformed from students or part-time employed workers earning extra cash to immigrants, rural migrants, women and older individuals who rely on these jobs to support themselves and their families.

In London, for instance, nine out of ten Uber drivers are non-white, the majority of whom are reliant on Uber for their income.[16] On China's two largest food delivery platforms, 70 per cent of couriers are migrants, formerly employed as factory workers.[17] And on Argentina's largest app delivery platforms, Rappi and Glovo, 67 per cent of workers are recent Venezuelan migrants with non-permanent resident status.[18]

For these workers, the cost of revolt is too high. As Armin found, the more dependent his peers were on platforms for their income, the more likely they were to keep their heads down. Because of how isolated gig workers are kept by gig platforms – both physically, in their vehicles, and figuratively – their collective bargaining power is extremely low.

Yet, as the workforce has become more precarious, the need for greater labour protections has grown.

Worker collectives such as Driver's Seat Cooperative, based in Portland, Oregon, have tried to unify and scale up what Armin did from his kitchen desk. Their aim is to help rebalance the power of corporations through workers' biggest asset, their personal data.

This is a mother-lode mined by the app companies, but kept from the workers themselves. 'The starting point for this was hearing drivers' sense of being manipulated by the algorithm,' said Hays Witt, the cooperative's chief executive, in an interview.[19]

So far, more than 40,000 workers, primarily in Los Angeles, Portland, Oregon and Denver, have signed up and pooled information about their earnings, miles travelled, active hours and other data from apps including Uber, Lyft, DoorDash and Instacart.[20] The data forms a window into the inner workings of the app systems and helps to train the app's own algorithms, which can then analyse patterns and advise how to make the most money, and whether they are being compensated fairly.

In London, James Farrar has led a resistance movement against AI-driven delivery apps that has spread from the UK across the world. I went to meet him at his office in Aldgate East. It was here one Friday evening some years ago when Farrar, who had recently begun driving weekends for Uber, had had an altercation with some drunk passengers. The incident left him shaken up, and when he complained to Uber he realized he had no legal protections as an employee.

The reason, they claimed, was because he wasn't their employee, but an independent contractor. Farrar certainly didn't feel like an autonomous contractor – Uber decided what jobs to give him and what he would get paid and whether to fire him. So he began a decade-long legal campaign to fight for the rights of app-based workers.

'This whole area is auspicious – this is a very historic park, Altab Ali Park,' Farrar told me, pointing to the green patch just visible through the window of the office he rents in a co-working space. The park was named for a Bangladeshi garment worker, Altab Ali, who had been murdered nearby in a racist attack in the 1970s.[21] Ali's death became a flashpoint, sparking protests around the city; his coffin was carried through Westminster. 'This park is dedicated to him, it has a history of the labour movement,' Farrar said.

Altab Ali Park was also where Farrar's co-organizer Yaseen Aslam had assembled the first Uber worker protests a few summers before. 'Nobody had money to hire a hall. And after six o'clock, this is all free parking here. So in the summer evenings, Yaseen would organize union meetings in this park,' Farrar said. 'And what's funny is that Uber's office is just over there, on that corner.'

I settled in to hear Farrar's story, looking out at Uber's office. An Irishman who was a former software engineer at SAP, Farrar decided there needed to be change in the industry. He went on to found the App Drivers and Couriers Union, which had supported Alexandru Iftimie in his complaints against automated fraud detection. Farrar later went on to found the non-profit Worker Info Exchange, which fights for greater ownership of worker data, and transparency around how algorithms make life-changing decisions – including what people are paid and whether they remain employed. He has helped bring together union members and app workers from twenty-three countries around the world, who together created a global manifesto of demands, including for more transparency in algorithmic decisions.

Algorithms are the main 'tool in their box for worker control,' Farrar said to me. He was fresh from Iftimie's case in Amsterdam's

High Court which had forced Uber and Ola to disclose some of the data used by their algorithms to dock wages and fire workers.

Farrar has been at the forefront of a series of legal challenges around the rights of gig-economy workers in the UK and Europe. In February 2021, six years after his original dispute in his car, his lobbying finally paid off: in a landmark ruling, the UK's Supreme Court said that Uber drivers should be treated as employees with rights to minimum wage, sick pay and pensions, as opposed to self-employed individuals, as Uber has claimed they are all over the world.[22] It has meant that for the first time, workers are able to avail of labour rights that apply to every other industry, including sick leave and holidays, rather than feeling disenfranchised or powerless. It has led to similar rulings in Canada, Switzerland, and France.[23]

'When we started challenging automated decision-making around facial recognition, location-checking, fraudulent activity allegations, there was a lot of case work on it,' Farrar said. The central debate now is more all-encompassing: are these decisions solely automated, and if not, how much human intervention is used by the likes of Uber? 'But where they get snookered is on [AI] decision-making on work allocation and pay, because there can be no human intervention there, it's happening in real time,' he said. 'And that's where the fight is now.'

Farrar's work in the UK has inspired global echoes of rebellion. Roughly half of global gig workers now belong to a formal group or union, or have taken part in industrial action for their rights, a recent survey of nearly 5,000 workers found.[24] Amongst food couriers, that number rose to 59 per cent.[25]

The unions are hyperlocal in nature. In Brazil, workers have formed *Entregadores Anti-fascistas*, the Anti-Fascist Couriers; in Mexico, Ni un Repartidor Menos, *Not one Delivery Worker Killed*; in South Africa, workers can join The Movement; and in Nigeria, the National Union of Professional App-Based Transport Workers has 10,000 members from Uber and Bolt.

In China, where independent labour unions are illegal, workers are banding together informally, organizing via large WeChat groups such as Knights League, on which they also share tips such as difficult delivery areas or 'no-fly' zones.[26]

The one thing that draws them all together is their collective rejection of the tyranny of AI-controlled work. Protests against Uber in Nairobi and Meituan in Shenzhen were both ignited by arbitrary changes in how wages were calculated by app software.[27]

Farrar said, 'This is the whole "hiddenness" of algorithmic management – what are the rules? What are we breaking? How do we know? The game is, they won't tell you what the rules are, because that would mean we are being managed by the algorithm.'

*

My interviews with a dozen or so gig workers across four countries are a drop in the ocean of work being done on algorithms and worker rights. Beneath the scattered individual accounts, I was able to glimpse some dark patterns: first, the co-dependent effects of AI systems in our lives – how we shape algorithms, and how they shape us. Armin, for instance, pointed out that Uber's work-allocation algorithms incentivized him to take orders from wealthier neighbourhoods and turn down smaller orders, so Armin (and consequently, Uber) could maximize income. Therefore, well-to-do communities received their deliveries within twenty minutes, while poor communities were left waiting longer.

Even more clear were the colonial effects of AI-facilitated work. In this diverse and varied industry too, there was a digital hegemony of a few large companies controlling a global workforce, many of whom are desperate, far from home, and largely powerless.

And while these stories are specific to app delivery workers, their implications extend far beyond them. AI systems are increasingly being integrated into workplaces of all kinds, from hospitals to Amazon warehouses, schools, shops and care homes. I spoke to Jess Hornig, a hospital therapist and social worker in Rhode Island, who described how her employer, a large American health insurer, began using AI software to monitor and make decisions about clinicians' pay rises and bonuses, based on statistically derived productivity scores. 'It is 100 per cent nefarious, there was so much anxiety and fear around how [frontline workers] were being measured, and if they were measuring up,' she told me.

The rise of generative AI – software that can create human-like text and images – has now normalized the use of AI across modern workplaces. While students have used the likes of ChatGPT to help write job applications and lawyers are using it to draft contracts, AI is also starting to *replace* jobs traditionally done by humans – from voice acting to graphic design and customer service.

With this shift to automation, questions of workers' rights have become even more crucial. Laurence Bouvard, a voice actor, said that AI companies have been routinely swiping the voices, performances and likenesses of her and her peers, 'training their algorithms on our data to produce a product that is meant to replace us.'

She added, 'Under current legislation, there is nothing we performers can do about it.'

As Alexandru Iftimie told me, 'Everybody feels safe, they have a nice job and this won't affect them, just those poor Uber drivers. But this artificial intelligence, it will spread, and it's coming for everyone.'

CHAPTER 8
Your Rights

As algorithm-based decisions and generative AI are woven deeply into our daily lives, people who have found themselves at the sharp end of these systems are finally starting to demand redress. Even now, automated systems are largely invisible and opaque, and those affected by them are usually unaware of their role. If they *are* aware, individuals can rarely find how these technologies work, as they remain unregulated and hidden away. Often, the vulnerabilities of communities like low-income workers, immigrants, medical patients or people of colour make it harder to find ways to challenge the use of these closed systems.

For these very reasons, real-world stories investigating the effects of AI systems are a challenge to find too. Individuals harmed by algorithmic outputs can be reluctant to recount their experiences. Helen Mort, the poet who discovered deepfake pornography of herself, Diana Sardjoe, the mother of young men scored by a criminal prediction algorithm, and Uber driver Alexandru Iftimie were some of the first people I encountered who were willing to speak up to create change around these opaque AI systems – often to their own detriment.

As time went on, I met more of these crusaders. I spent time with Sarah Meredith, a thirty-two-year-old liver transplant recipient in Britain, and her family, who are fighting against what they believe is an unfair organ-allocation algorithm; Rick Burgess, a member of the Greater Manchester Coalition of Disabled People, took legal action against the Department for Work and Pensions – the department of the British government that handles benefits payments – to find out more about an algorithm that flagged suspected benefits fraud. He believed it was discriminatory and didn't have meaningful human oversight.

In all these cases, the crux of the issue wasn't simply that the algorithms were biased or harmful to minorities (these things are harder to prove). But they also exposed just how veiled and abstruse these systems were to the very people they were being used on. How these algorithms are implemented and governed has increasingly become a human rights issue.

This was exactly why Cori Crider, a longtime human rights lawyer, was drawn into this fight, several years into a career defending political prisoners in Guantanamo Bay.

Cori, a fast-talking Texan who has made her home in London, had always thought there could be no greater imbalance of power than between a Guantanamo detainee and the Department of Defense holding him without charge or trial.

But then, in 2019, she'd stumbled across a hidden community: content moderators working for social media giants such as Meta. And she'd found some surprising and striking similarities.

Cori interviewed more than a hundred Facebook, Instagram and TikTok moderators including Daniel Motaung from Kenyan outsourcing firm Sama, whose job was to clean up the poisoned cesspool of social media content, and train artificial intelligence systems to automate their own work. She travelled to Warsaw, Krakow, Nairobi and Dublin, places Meta outsourced the work to, speaking to workers under the veil of anonymity.

Through these interviews, Cori learned about the stream of content these moderators were regularly required to imbibe: visuals of beheadings, mass shootings, terrorism, sexual violence and child abuse.

Cori knew what PTSD looked like. She was accustomed to talking to political captives who'd been kidnapped, beaten or force-fed. When she spoke with moderators who had visible trauma, it sent her back to her time sitting with prisoners in Guantanamo. Of course, she knew this wasn't the same, but somehow it rhymed – the kinds of flashbacks that they were describing, the repeat episodes of violence coming out in their heads that they couldn't erase. It had never occurred to her before she learned about this industry that simply looking at imagery of violence on a screen, sifting and examining it in detail for hours, could cause PTSD. But after her conversations, it seemed blindingly obvious.

She observed, first-hand, that the most lucrative parts of Silicon Valley products – AI recommendation engines, such as Instagram and TikTok's main feeds or X's For You tab that grab our attention – are often built on the shoulders of the most vulnerable, including poor youth, women and migrant labourers whose right to live and work in a country is dependent on their job. Without the labour of outsourced content moderators, these feeds would be simply unusable, too poisonous for our society to consume as greedily as we do.

It wasn't just the nature of the content itself that was a problem – it was their working conditions, this reimagining of a human worker as an automaton, simultaneously training AI to do their own jobs. Content moderators were expected to process hundreds of pieces of content every day, irrespective of the nature of their toxicity. They had to watch details in the videos to determine intent and context and zoom into unpleasant imagery of wounds or body parts, to classify their nature. They were allegedly given a quality score every fifteen to thirty minutes that was supposed to remain consistent over time at an arbitrary 98 per cent. The sheer volume, speed and pressure under which they were expected to perform was crushing.

Enveloping it all was a culture of secrecy and a climate of fear, much like the national security work Cori was privy to in her previous working life. Clients, including Meta, often asked workers to sign non-disclosure agreements that forbade them from speaking to anyone, including their families or their lawyers. She had become inured to the US government blanket classifying everything about her Guantanamo clients, right down to what they ate for lunch, partly in an effort to dehumanize them. But here too, Facebook moderators were tied to ironclad silencing agreements that made them unable to speak out. Some NDAs drafted by outsourcing firm Accenture on behalf of Facebook required workers to acknowledge that their work might cause PTSD, and to cut Accenture and Facebook loose from any responsibility for mental ill-health.[1]

The NDAs made people afraid to trust one another, and prevented them forming links and creating bargaining units. 'They found it difficult even to talk to me, as their lawyer. That's just wrong,' Cori said.

A Wildflower That Can Kill or Cure

In her previous job as a public litigation lawyer at the non-profit Reprieve, Cori was used to fighting a familiar and tangible enemy: big government. In Guantanamo, her task was straightforward – figure out how to get her client out of the box they were locked in. Their predicaments were the result of a 'visible, chest-beating' brutality, she said.

As part of her work, she also met survivors of drone attacks in Yemen and Pakistan, and US government officials, and she found that the shape of the opponent was morphing. From their stories, she noted the rise of surreptitious data collection and targeting algorithms in national security and defence. Data analysis was increasingly becoming core to both surveillance and military action.

As time went on, she found she couldn't stop thinking about these data-guzzling, machine-learning algorithms, and their creators, corporate actors who seemed to operate in a manner that was antithetical to liberal Western ideals of self-determination and liberty. As an outsider to the tech world, she began to wonder whether mass data-driven predictive tools, including AI, were an existential risk to democracy – and a threat to our civil liberties.

Once she saw the problem through this lens, she started seeing it everywhere. At the sharp end were state-wielded algorithms remotely directing spying, surveillance and even killings. But they were much more ubiquitous than that. Across the US, Asia and Europe, governments were testing automated systems in the judicial system, in education, health and border control. In the UK, where Cori lives, the Home Office is using drones equipped with AI technology to scan the coastline for small rubber boats carrying undocumented migrants.[2] Cash-strapped public authorities, such as the Department for Work and Pensions, are seeking to use pattern-spotting software to make public welfare decisions,[3] just like Microsoft and the local government had jointly done in Salta, Argentina.

In the private sector, she saw the crushing, dehumanising effects of data and AI-based management on app delivery people and Amazon warehouse workers.

Despite evidence of widespread harm, she found little resistance from the human rights community at the time. She attended public discussions and events on how to tackle Big Tech's power, or constrain the harms of AI, but she found they were populated mostly by technologists proposing software solutions.

Where, she wondered, were the activists and the human-rights lawyers fighting for the people hurt or violated by data-driven tech? Who was suing corporations for their abuse of individual personal data, their damage of communities through recommendation algorithms, and their treatment of swathes of invisible workers in the production of AI products – the likes of Ian Koli, Daniel Motaung and Alexandru Iftimie?

In Cori's experience, conflict is the driver of social change and she was seeing precious little of it in the tech world. 'Jeff Bezos is not going to be attacked with guilt one morning over his press-ups and his chia pudding,' she told me. 'It's like Frederick Douglass said, power concedes nothing without a demand.'

So in the summer of 2019, she and two colleagues, Martha Dark and Rosa Curling, spent a few weeks in a borrowed corner of a friend's office coming up with the idea for a new legal justice organization, Foxglove, named after the wildflower that can kill or cure, depending on its dose. Their mission was to use legal tools to demand accountability for technologies like big data and artificial intelligence – and reclaim the agency of individuals.

Now, Foxglove represents social media content moderators, Amazon factory workers and Uber drivers. Cori's team has sued Meta on behalf of victims of communal violence in Ethiopia, who blame social media algorithms for facilitating murders. She is helping fight the automation of the welfare system in Britain, and for the transparency of data use in the NHS.

She isn't the only one – she is part of a growing wellspring of people all over the world, fighting to recoup their collective agency from opaque AI systems, and advocating for the ethical creation and use of big data systems around the world. Her story is a glimpse into what it takes to be a modern Luddite: to be courageous enough to take on some of the most powerful entities in the history of our civilization.

*

When they founded their company in 2019, Cori and her colleagues were unabashedly idealistic about its goal. Foxglove would fight for the rights of the 'little people' trapped by automated systems. And they would use the levers of the democratic and judicial system to do it. So far, all their cases have centred on people being failed by data-driven technologies.

In 2020, for example, they made their name through two legal challenges of the unfair use of algorithms by the UK government. First, they took the Home Office to court over a secretive visa-awarding algorithm that they believed was discriminating against applicants on the basis of nationality.[4] The software was used to filter UK visa applications into different priority streams, according to levels of risk. Because of how it split out different nationalities, Foxglove called it 'speedy boarding for white people'.[5] The Home Office chose not to disclose details about the workings of the system or fight them, but instead suspended the decision-making system and agreed to redesign the model.

A few months later, in August 2020, Foxglove challenged the use of a widely panned algorithm that was used to award exam grades to UK school leavers during the Covid-19 pandemic, after national exams were cancelled.[6]

The system, implemented by Ofqual, the national body overseeing exams in England, took historic grades data from each school and worked out a distribution of grades based on past performance. They then adjusted it up or down if that year's students seemed better than previous years based on their GCSE results.

Because of how the system was designed, it didn't account for outliers, or adjust for teachers' discretion, and inflated grades for subjects taken by small numbers of pupils, usually at private schools. The overall result was that it ended up downgrading thousands of students, particularly those from historically lower-performing schools, due to imbalances in past data.

The ensuing combination of legal threats from the likes of Foxglove, as well as widespread protests and pushback from students who coined the slogan 'Fuck the algorithm', forced the government to eventually scrap the algorithm in favour of teacher assessments.[7]

But it isn't just governments. In parallel, Foxglove has been gearing up for a fight against Silicon Valley. From Myanmar to Mumbai and Melbourne, tech platforms are making political, ethical and cultural decisions every day on behalf of their collective billions of users. And mostly, they're doing it from their privileged perch in the United States. In the developing world in particular, these algorithmically mediated platforms have created their own labour bubbles, defined the boundaries of the internet, chafed against local laws, laid down rules of free speech, and sometimes even facilitated political violence, wars and genocide.

As she delved deeper into the tech world, Cori gained a new perspective on who she was up against. She found that an omnipotent industrial complex of American corporations, known loosely as Big Tech, had amassed power and information that would be the envy of most states. 'Limited Liability Corporations, the trick is in the name,' she said. There were so few constraints on their power that she felt taking them on was a tougher battle than even holding democratic governments to account.

She'd read two books recently that provided historical perspective: William Dalrymple's *The Anarchy*, on the rise of the East India Company, and *All the Shah's Men*, journalist Stephen Kinzer's tale about the role of the Anglo-Iranian Oil Company in the 1953 Iranian coup. 'It was so difficult to determine where the state stopped and the corporation began,' she said. 'It's fascinating how the state just falls into line with company policies.'

She felt that modern-day citizens were similarly being exploited in an extractive system ruled by those with the most technological knowhow. And the most marginalized among us are in greatest danger of being harmed by the reconfigurations of global power.

When Algorithms Cause Unrest

In December 2022, Foxglove – as part of a group of seven human rights organizations – supported its first set of cases alleging that algorithms can amplify hateful content and contribute directly to real-world violence and death. Abraham Meareg, an Ethiopian researcher at Amnesty International, was the first plaintiff. Abraham's family was of Tigrayan origin, an ethnic minority in the Amhara region of Ethiopia, where the two groups are engaged in a bloody civil conflict. Abraham's father, Meareg Amare, a professor of chemistry, was gunned down outside his home in November 2021, by a mob that had targeted him for his ethnicity.

Just the previous month, he had been harassed by a series of false Facebook posts, claiming he had sold stolen property from his university. His son, Abraham, had asked Facebook to take the viral posts down, worried for his father's safety, but had received no response. A month after his father's murder, the company notified him that one post shared with up to 50,000 people had been removed. Abraham, who is seeking asylum in the United States, later said that he held Facebook responsible for his father's ethnically motivated murder, because of how its algorithms helped spread hate speech and misinformation about him, and how slowly the company reacted to taking down the harmful posts.

The case's second plaintiff was a former Amnesty International researcher Fisseha Tekle who had collected examples of more Facebook posts that could be connected directly to ethnically motivated murders. Tekle also alleged that his family and he were abused for the work he did on Facebook. Fisseha had moved to Kenya and said he could not return to Ethiopia as he feared for his life.[8]

While the core of the problem lay with Facebook's algorithm-sparked frenzies of online hatred, Cori felt that the violent consequences were also tied to Meta's labour issues in Nairobi – the toxic and graphic content that moderators like Daniel were forced to consume when they worked at the outsourcer Sama, which is the regional hub for Ethiopian hate speech moderation too. The lack of investment into content moderation in African languages and the poor working conditions are also partly responsible, she believes. Hateful content stays online longer in non-Western countries than it does in English-speaking markets, thus stirring up mobs in countries such as India and Myanmar.[9]

The petitioners demanded that Meta change its algorithms to stop recommending violence-inciting content, and that the company create a $1.6bn victims' fund.

'If we succeed, it will be the first case to tackle the recommendation algorithm and the systemic discrimination against non-English-language markets,' Cori said on the eve of announcing Abraham's case, which is still ongoing.

The fight she is having is the first of its kind: can Big Tech companies be made to rewrite their trillion-dollar algorithms for the public good?

AI Unchecked

To most people she meets, Cori can seem unnervingly self-assured. If you're in a brawl, you certainly want her in your corner. But over the months that we meet, the mask sometimes slips. When cases are settled without a fight, I glimpse moments of self-doubt. She's desperate to have her day in court, to see real change, which often means unrealistic expectations and feelings of overwhelm and frustration – something she works through with her therapist.

On a recent afternoon, as we sat in the busy cafe underneath her office, she reflected on four years of Foxglove. She was satisfied with the work they had done, but she had also been humbled by the scale of the challenge. It had taken Foxglove nearly a year just to file the Ethiopian case in Nairobi when they had naively assumed it could be done within six months. 'Never had filing a case felt so much like winning a case,' she said. 'Where corporations project their power across borders like these giant companies have done, you're having to come up with . . . arguments on *where* they need to be brought before the justice system and why.' The laws themselves have to be reinterpreted before the cases can be heard. 'It's been tough.'

Ultimately, she wants to move beyond individual cases to address what she sees as the overarching problem: unchecked power without accountability. And the path to that, in her book, is antitrust law. The companies liked to paint a false dichotomy, she says. 'If you seek to regulate our power using the legislature or the state then you're on a one-way railroad to becoming China.' But she's tired of the brazen distraction of that argument, the claim that rebalancing power is equivalent to a firewalled internet. Her next challenge will be taking on Big Tech via competition law.

That, she says, was the purpose of original American antitrust policies. It wasn't supposed to be a technical mechanism of price enforcement. It was about maintaining the balance of citizen and corporate power. 'Corporate power at that scale was seen as a threat to democracy,' she said.

If technologies that monitor and manipulate go unchecked, then we can guess what our fate will be, Cori said. To imagine the future, sometimes you just have to look back into the past. She'd already glimpsed a version of her greatest fears back in 2013.

While working as a lawyer at Reprieve, Cori had flown to Sana'a, the capital of Yemen, on an April morning in 2013, to meet with Faisal bin Ali Jaber, an environmental engineer from the eastern village of Khashamer. Cori believed his family had been murdered at the behest of a computer program.

A year previously, Cori's client Faisal had gathered with his family and friends in Khashamer to celebrate the marriage of his eldest son. That evening, Faisal's brother-in-law Salem, a respected imam, gave the Friday sermon in the local mosque. In it, he denounced the terrorist group al Qaeda which had begun to spread its tentacles in the region. News of the sermon reached some local insurgents, and a few days later, during his nephew's wedding, three youths came to remonstrate with Salem. The imam agreed to meet with them that evening to continue the debate, taking along his relative Waleed who was the village's only policeman. As the sun went down, the five men converged. Out of the desert sky, four missiles rained down, killing them all.

The entire community witnessed the American drone strike that killed the imam and the policeman, and it devastated the families. That very night, a Yemeni official called Faisal to say that his family members were not the intended targets; they had been caught in the crosshairs of a drone-targeting system that had mistakenly assumed that they were affiliated with the young insurgents.

These kinds of attacks, where the identities of the victims are unknown and they have been targeted due to their patterns of behaviour, are known as 'signature strikes'. They made up the majority of the 542 drone strikes during the Obama presidency.[10]

Cori discovered then that the US government had been experimenting with artificial intelligence as a way to track and isolate mobile phone targets for drone attacks since at least 2011. A human may have fired the missiles, but Cori was convinced they did so due to the output of a computer program. It was her first glimpse into the raw power of automated technologies; how they can shape – even help take – human lives.

Now, there are dozens of companies – ranging from start-ups to large public corporations – building an arsenal of artificial intelligence tools for defence and military purposes. Having gained new life due to the wars in Ukraine and in the Middle East, these systems are funded by government defence departments and are designed to conduct maritime surveillance in international waters; to identify and track terrorists; and to find, isolate and shoot drones from the sky.

If we didn't exercise peaceful and legal means of resistance to these technologies swarming into our society without oversight, transparency or permission, Cori believed we would start to lose control of them.

She pointed to a modern-day version of this type of society for comparison. 'China sets up a stark dystopia for where individual and collective freedoms could go,' she said. 'That's what happens if people can't put power back into their own hands.'

But in China too, there were courageous dissidents – human rights defenders and crusaders who spoke out, despite personal risks, against the use of AI technologies to target innocent people. And to see for myself how autocratic AI systems could go wrong, I was hoping to meet one of them and ask her myself.

CHAPTER 9
Your Future

I am surprised when Maya Wang shows up. Any one of a hundred reasons may have prevented her from coming to meet me in this cafe in Washington, DC. She is hyper-vigilant about who she meets, and what she shares, even with trusted friends. She is meticulous about scrubbing the web clean of any identifying information. Her shield goes up when her digital devices show unusual activity, or when she gets spam calls on her phone. She has to be cautious about what her behaviours might reveal about people close to her, or what they might accidentally reveal about her. Sometimes she feels like her whole being is permeated by worries about staying safe. It's what pervades her mind from the moment she wakes up to when her head hits her pillow at night.

She has bigger, more intangible fears too: about the digital dragnet of surveillance in mainland China, and the rights of citizens in the region. The more she works on surveillance, the area of research she specializes in, the more she worries about the fate of humanity.

It's a lot for one person to carry.

So, I am grateful she is here now, slightly damp from the April drizzle. 'In China, we have a saying, the mountains are high, and the emperor is far away,' she tells me. 'I could be living in Sichuan, but I can live my own life freely because the emperor is in Beijing. That's no longer true. There's never been any other empire or government in the whole of human history that has been able to exert such wide-ranging and deep surveillance on people.'

Living now in the United States, Maya feels more comfortable talking publicly about her work as a senior China researcher at non-profit Human Rights Watch, where she has been documenting human rights abuses by the Chinese government for nearly a decade. She misses East Asia – she'd rather be in Taiwan right now – but she likes it here too. Since she left China and the surrounding regions, she no longer worries about being kidnapped off the street. She feels she can blend in, to an extent, although it did take her a while to figure out how to pay off an American credit card. 'Here, most people don't see you as a foreigner, even with a completely different accent,' she says. 'You could have blue skin, and people will still think you're American. I have always loved that about the US.'

It's solitary work, she admits, being stuck between worlds, examining obscure coding stacks and Chinese police documents, trying to raise the alarm about a techno-dystopia which seems a world away from Washington. But she knows she's not alone. There's a group of people out there, colleagues and heroes of hers, who are all pulling in the same direction, generally together. Well, there are other routes people might choose, I venture. Easier, safer jobs. But she *tsks* dismissively. 'What else are you going to do in life, right?' she says. 'You just try to do the right thing and try to contribute to a better society.'

*

In the years after the government's crackdown on student protestors in Tiananmen Square in 1989, China was forced into diplomatic isolation by the West for nearly a decade.[1] But in the early 2000s, there was a buzz of excitement around this new thing called the internet that was bringing people together. The web, along with the strengthening Chinese economy, more urban migration and young people becoming more educated, brought with it an air of more openness. By 2008, about a quarter of the Chinese population – nearly 300 million people – were online.[2]

A digital community of human rights defenders, lawyers, journalists and petitioners bubbled up, known as the 'weiquan' or 'rights defence' movement,[3] who used the web as a platform to speak out about injustices, to organize and to protest. Even as the domestic security apparatus expanded, and human rights activism was muzzled, the online resistance movement kept growing. The internet gave people a window not just into what their acquaintances were thinking, but also into the minds of those in neighbouring villages and towns and cities across China. What they saw – a similarity of ideas – helped them feel less alone. 'And with that comes such power,' Maya said.

So, when Maya first started working in human rights, China felt like a more hopeful place. She was young, an idealist from a new generation of women from the region. In those early days, she'd felt an incredible optimism. She was always alive to the dangers, but she never imagined how much worse things would get. Joining in back then didn't feel like an act of bravery, but of hope. She felt like she'd been invited to a cool party, where she was hanging out with people at the forefront of changing China. 'Like, who wouldn't want to be there?' she said.

Over the years, that fizzing excitement has been corked by the reality of speaking out against an increasingly repressive Chinese government. Maya has been forced to prioritize safety in her daily job. She can't remember what it was like to not have to worry about her physical and digital security. Her employer, Human Rights Watch, can only go so far towards protecting her; nobody but her really knows the circumstances that she lives through.

*

Maya's story, the one she's about to tell me, starts almost a decade ago, sometime in early 2015, when she split her time between mainland China and Hong Kong. She heard from a mainland Chinese activist about something called the 'One Card System'. This was a national social credit system, which would use advanced data analytics and AI to 'punish those who are untrustworthy while rewarding those who are trustworthy', according to official documents. The system seemed so dystopian, it was the inspiration for an episode of British sci-fi series *Black Mirror*.[4]

As Maya began to investigate further online, she found published documents describing a series of interconnecting software systems that aggregated citizen data and connected it to police databases. She noticed these data-scraping models had been put in place across the country, and nobody was talking about why.

At this point, she stops to clarify that she is no martyr. What happened next, her unexpected uncovering of a web of digital surveillance, was driven by something much simpler than ideology: the lure of an unsolved mystery.

Around the same time that she heard about the One Card System, Maya was tracking events in Xinjiang, a region in north-west China that lies at the crossroads between Central and East Asia, the heart of the historic Silk Road. The area is ethnically diverse, bordering more than half a dozen countries, including Mongolia, Russia, Kazakhstan, Kyrgyzstan, Afghanistan and Pakistan. Xinjiang is inhabited by thirteen million Uyghur Muslims,[5] who mainly speak Turkic languages, as well as a range of other ethnic minorities from Tibetans and Sibe to Chinese Tajiks.

Xinjiang has been claimed as part of China by the Chinese Communist Party since it took power in 1949. For decades, the Chinese government had cracked down on minorities like the Uyghurs, who they claimed held extremist ideas, and Xinjiang was rife with separatist conflicts and independence movements.[6] In

2014, while visiting Xinjiang, the Chinese president Xi Jinping warned about 'the toxicity of religious extremism'[7] and opened the doors to a region-wide crackdown. An anti-extremism law passed in 2017 banned people from Islamic practices such as growing long beards and wearing veils in public.

By 2018, an estimated 1.8 million Uyghurs and other Muslims had been detained in 're-education' camps,[8] which the Chinese government calls 'vocational education and training centres'. Their claimed purpose is to teach Chinese laws, Mandarin and to 'nip terrorist activities in the bud', according to the state.[9] Those chosen to attend the camps do not have a choice – they are detained and held against their will.

Even ten years ago, Uyghurs living outside the camps could still petition the government and advocate for change. By the time Maya turned her attention to Xinjiang in 2016, simply questioning the state had become dangerous.

She spent months interviewing citizens who had managed to flee the region, either virtually or in person in Kazakhstan. They painted a picture of the ultimate dystopia: a human rights vacuum in which technology and surveillance were integrated to brutally repress the population. Maya told me about one young woman, a Xinjiang-born, Western-educated student, who opened up to her during an interview.

The student went home to Xinjiang for the summer holidays and was detained, without charge or trial, for more than two years. The reason she was given for her detainment was that she had used a virtual private network, or VPN, a digital tool that allowed her to bypass China's web censorship measures to access her university's website and sign up for classes. She was arrested and forced to provide her biometric data including her DNA, voiceprint and facial image to the state.

The data marked the girl, and possibly her entire family, for inclusion on a so-called blacklist of troublemakers. She was driven to a detainment camp in a different city, where she lived in a cell and was forced to 'learn' Mandarin (which she already spoke), patriotic slogans and the national anthem. She was surveilled by cameras. She was released after five months, but not allowed to leave the state for almost two years. She had to check in with the police every week and submit to further examination every time she went through a city checkpoint.

She told Maya she had seen screens at the local police station monitoring pedestrians crossing the streets, with little red squares on people's faces. Maya thought this sounded like a facial-recognition system tracking individuals who had been singled out for investigation.

Using testimonials like this student's, Maya started to piece together fragments of information from her informants. She knew there were cameras everywhere, often enabled with facial recognition, watching people on the streets, in schools, mosques, cinemas and in the re-education camps.

Maya learned that the software tracked the movements of individuals viewed as potential rabble-rousers: criminals, those with mental health issues, strong political views, and a history of 'petitioning' or reporting bureaucratic grievances to China's central government.[10]

But what was happening in Xinjiang – and in China at large – was much further-reaching than the mass installation of facial-recognition cameras. The cameras were simply nerve-ends feeding into a central digital brain – an invasive system of technological control so multi-dimensional and entrenched that Maya almost didn't believe it existed at first.

A Detective Story

In late 2017, Maya became one of the first people to sound an alarm about the digital root network of surveillance systems in Xinjiang, a big-data machine used to spy on, target and imprison Uyghur Muslims. And she stumbled across it almost by accident.[11]

One afternoon during an interview with a Xinjiang resident who had recently left the region after being detained by the police, her colleague at Human Rights Watch asked an innocent question. Why had he been chosen to go to the camps? Maya herself had not thought to ask this pretty obvious thing before – she had come to think of the Chinese state's modus operandi as basically arbitrary.

The former detainee told them about a computer program that he had observed at police stations, a software that churned out lists of people for detention that police referred to as the 'integrated system'. The lists were compiled from some sort of database, but he didn't know what the triggers were.

Maya began digging through the Chinese and English-language internet looking for mentions of an 'integrated' system; she trawled through academic articles published by the Chinese police in journals put out by the Ministry of Security. She searched through official procurement documents, company marketing materials and patent filings, until she found a name: the Integrated Joint Operations Platform, or IJOP. This was the back end of Xinjiang's surveillance state.[12]

The procurement documents revealed that the software was designed and developed by China Electronics Technology Group Corporation (CETC), a major state-owned military contractor in China. The system was supposed to be predictive – a data dragnet to catch future criminals, before any crimes or acts of terrorism were committed. The goal, it seemed, was not so different to the ProKid algorithms in Amsterdam, used to pinpoint teenagers as future criminals. The outcomes, of course, were distinct: in the former case, it could result in detainment against your will, while in the latter, it activated the social welfare system. As she began piecing together the suite of systems, Maya found it had been in gestation for nearly two decades.

Once she had these names, she began to look for specific mentions of 'IJOP' online, to see what else she could drag up. And then, she struck lucky again.

She found a downloadable version of the app on the open internet, a file whose architecture anyone could examine. The local government had been careless. 'I was like, no, that can't be true,' she said. But it looked a lot like the app described in the official procurement documents, so Maya decided to examine it more closely.

To help verify the app, she recruited the help of Seamus Tuohy, a colleague working on cybersecurity, and later an external auditor who could guide them on what to look for. When they inspected the binary innards of the app software, they found mention of CETC, the same company named in the official procurement documents for the IJOP. The other clue was in the app's digital fingerprint, a sort of watermark unique to the company that designed it. Maya managed to confirm the watermark had been created by CETC when she found another app, designed by the same company and published by the Chinese government officially, bearing the same watermark. Through these various routes of triangulation, Maya's bosses at Human Rights Watch were convinced that the IJOP app they had downloaded freely was the same one in use by Xinjiang authorities.

Now that Maya had a copy of the app's code, she could dive into the belly of the beast and figure out what demographics and behaviours the authorities were targeting – and therefore how algorithms selected people for internment at the camps.

Maya didn't code. She had never dissected an app. So, the first thing she did was print all the code out on pieces of paper, dozens of pages in a mostly unintelligible language that she stuck up around her office. She began to underline the bits in plain text to see how they connected together.

'I kind of thought, if I look at the code long enough, I'll be able to figure it out,' she told me.

'A bit like that bit in *A Beautiful Mind* where Russell Crowe cracks the code,' I said.

She hadn't seen the film. 'But I kinda got there in the end,' she said.

With her colleagues' help, and that of a Berlin-based cybersecurity company, Maya was able to reverse-engineer the app, teasing out the structure of the surveillance state operating in Xinjiang.

First, she found the app was set up to record a range of data points – the vehicle a person drives, their blood type and bank information, as well as more sensitive details about citizens' religious behaviours, such as studying the Quran or having a religious appearance, such as wearing a burqa or a long beard, without state permission.

The system ingested location information and vehicle data, biometric information including faces, DNA, voices and gait, and mobile phone information, such as who people called and what apps they downloaded. It even received information about families' gas and electricity usage and package deliveries. The app detailed thirty-six suspicious 'person types'. For instance, one type was described by the term 野阿吉, which refers to people who went on Hajj (the Muslim pilgrimage) without authorization, or 'unofficial Hajj'.[13] Maya knew that the Chinese government prohibits Hajj for Muslims unless it is organized by the state, so anyone tagged with this was deemed suspicious.

Based on all these data streams, the system would spit out a list of specific individuals to target.

The arbitrary nature of the red flags revealed in the app was unsurprising to Maya, who had studied human rights abuses in China for more than a decade. But she couldn't quite stomach the impunity with which the systems were wielded. The algorithms considered dozens of lawful behaviours suspicious. They were triggered by travel outside Xinjiang, whether within China or abroad, switching off your phone repeatedly, speaking to relatives abroad, 'not socializing with neighbours, often avoiding using the front door', or using Western apps such as WhatsApp and Skype.

The deeper Maya dug, the more irrational the algorithm's decisions started to seem. Criteria such as being generally untrustworthy (不放心人员), or being young, that is, 'born after the 1980s' (80, 90 后不放心人员) emerged. Other flags included 'generally acting suspiciously', 'having complex social ties' or 'unstable thoughts', or 'having improper [sexual] relations'.[14] The data collected was ever broader, casting the net wide to catch as many Uyghurs as possible, without rhyme or reason.

'It is a dragnet,' she said. 'Everyone leaves traces, and they can use those traces to pick up people across the whole of China. It just became visible to us in Xinjiang, because of the line between surveillance and detentions.'

But Maya was concerned about something even more sinister. She felt this was about more than just Xinjiang. In the hands of despotic leaders, whether in China or elsewhere, algorithm-based control systems were the boot stamping on the face of humanity that George Orwell had warned about.

Already, the government was cracking down on minority ethnic groups elsewhere in China, like the Hui Muslims deep in central China plains.[15] They were mobilising mass DNA collection of adults and children across Tibet for 'public security'. Frequent petitioners – aggrieved citizens who travel to Beijing to file bureaucratic complaints – were being surveilled and harassed by local police.[16]

People's rights to consent and protest were being gradually usurped, without them even realising it.

The ultimate aim of the Party, as Maya saw it, was total social control. The way to achieve it would be to put the entire population under this type of tech-enabled authoritarianism.

'If they succeed,' she said, 'it is an unprecedented project of human history.'

A Fifth of Humanity

The IJOP system, like many big data and machine-learning systems, concentrated power in the hands of a few, and disproportionately targeted the vulnerable. In Xinjiang, surveillance technologies were weaponized against the Uyghur community. 'In China, some of the groups with the least power are migrant workers, the poor and Uyghurs,' Maya said. 'If you're all three, yeah, you're getting the really short end of the stick.'

A minority of powerful actors – particularly political leaders – stood to benefit from monitoring and controlling the rest of Chinese society. Meanwhile, digital nets swept up people at the bottom of the social pyramid, those who may have had reason to complain and protest, depriving them of any agency they had left. The system fully embodied the concept of data colonialism, acting as an invisible hand that crushed any glimmer of dissent or resistance amongst the weakest parts of society. Technology like facial recognition is often rolled out without the consent or knowledge of individuals in its crosshairs, as activists around the world have discovered to their detriment.

Being flagged by the IJOP app was a life-changing event. Flagged individuals became candidates for internment into the re-education camps spread through the region. The predictive software Maya had glimpsed sprouting up around China to prevent small and large crimes was already having a targeted impact in Xinjiang – leading to the mass detainment of Uyghurs.

Maya learned that in Xinjiang, *everyone* – not just those in camps – lived in a digital prison built using data. People were being put in separate virtual pens and allowed different levels of freedom depending on how their level of threat was perceived by a set of algorithms. In this *deathworld*, as African historian Achille Mbembe describes oppressed societies,[17] machine-led decisions influenced who people saw, where they went, what they wore, or what God they were allowed to worship. It was the ultimate loss of freedom.

'If you go to the cinema, shopping mall, supermarket, down the street, there could be a checkpoint, a bit like Palestinians going over to the Israeli side, except in Xinjiang it is everywhere, in villages, highways, in and out of towns,' Maya said, pointing out that the Uyghurs were essentially caged.

If someone worked in the city and lived in the suburbs, they had to request permission to commute. They had to apply to visit their mother in a different city, or to see a friend in southern Xinjiang. If they didn't declare their movements, sensory systems like facial recognition became prison wardens.

The algorithms would red-flag people, and they would no longer be allowed to leave their county or prefecture. This series of AI-triggered checkpoints was also activated by family relationships. If you or your relatives were previously held and released, then you were subject to more restrictions. Many were detained simply for having relatives who had been detained. You could be held or turned away at a checkpoint. There were the digital haves and have-nots.

For those caught up in it, daily life became a pressure cooker. Citizens didn't understand the algorithms, they didn't know what the government's criteria were, or who they could trust. They were completely at the mercy of a 'despotic' Kafkaesque system, like Chinese gig workers had described the food delivery apps they worked for.

Uyghurs in the region knew only that they were under a microscope, that people were being taken away to hidden detention and re-education centres, they would be punished for voicing their own language and expressing their religion. They knew they were being watched through their devices.

They deleted foreign apps like Telegram, buried their phones in the ground, and ceased speaking to family members even in the safety of their homes. Some signed to each other rather than speaking, because they worried their homes or cars could be bugged. When they walked the streets, people censored their facial expressions, which were being analysed by cameras every few metres. 'It is transformational for identity in a region,' Maya said.

In 2014, Abduweli Ayup, an Uyghur poet and linguist from Xinjiang, was arrested and detained by the Chinese state for fifteen months for trying to open Uyghur-language kindergartens in his hometown. Ayup, who has now been released and lives in Norway, has had his brother and niece both detained because of him, his niece ultimately dying while in custody.

Ayup described the AI surveillance technology he experienced during his detentions in a recent interview.[18] 'Every checkpoint has facial recognition equipment. A large computer screen, every hundred metres, and it analyses you to match with your ID card. If it matches, that's step one of the checkpoint,' he said.

The second step, Ayup claimed, was an analysis of facial emotions, software that could supposedly determine if someone was angry, or planning to attack – 'they analyse eyelids and features to see,' he said. Ayup believed that the machines also used physical features and expressions to predict trustworthiness. 'They have three types, green is safe, yellow is normal and red which means you are dangerous,' Ayup said. If the machine judges a person as 'red', then they go to an interrogation room. After that, they may be sent to an education camp, or even jailed.

What Ayup described was the practice of physiognomy, a theory espoused most famously by the Nazis, who used it to advance their ethnic persecution and racist ideologies. After the Second World War, researchers labelled physiognomy scientifically unsound, and despite more recent attempts to prove that AI software can accurately predict emotions or personality from people's faces, the scientific consensus remains that the endeavour is largely pseudoscience.

Others have backed up Ayup's claims. In 2021, an Uyghur man told Maya he had tried to go to a water park outside of town. After being interrogated by police and flagged by the IJOP algorithms, he wasn't allowed to leave the limits of his home city. He had been recently released from police questioning without charge, so he was afraid. But still, he dared to ask the checkpoint guard why he wasn't being let through. The system was the system, the officer told him. You have to do what it said. There was no way to appeal it. 'You're lucky you're not in prison,' he added.

In a world like this, where surveillance, censorship and policing dovetail, dissent becomes irrelevant. People can still have the *illusion* of agency, but the government can predict, confirm and neutralize any collective action ahead of time. It made Maya wonder, what was humanity, if a fifth of the world's humans could not actually be free to decide what they could do?

It didn't make sense to her to consider people in China different from everyone else. How they were treated, she believed, should matter to anyone who believed in human rights. Because when AI-facilitated injustices at this scale become acceptable, human rights abuses could spread beyond China. Facial recognition was being used by police and security companies everywhere from the

United States, the UK and India, to Brazil, South Africa and Uganda. If this wasn't stopped now, AI-driven human rights issues were likely to become everybody's problem.

Building a Surveillance State

When automated systems influence the lives of individuals, they begin to shape entire societies. This is evident in how the city of Hong Kong used facial recognition on political protesters,[19] or how social media algorithms swayed people's political and social views around the US elections and the Covid pandemic.[20]

In China, it wasn't just the Uyghurs who were impacted – the big-data state began to affect the officers responsible for policing it. Many local officers in Xinjiang, for instance, complained to researchers privately that they had lost their powers of discretion, and the space to exercise nuanced judgement.

'In the past you could develop relationships with local officials, a bit of human latitude in deciding whether or not a decision makes sense,' Maya said. You could just explain to an official that you were driving your brother's car, for instance. But now, there were criteria and quotas for detentions that these officers had to fulfil. Some said they were unable to sleep because they were required to follow up on the smallest irregularities spotted by the system's algorithms, and their response times were tracked.

They were being watched – and curtailed – by the same centralized systems set up to watch the Uyghurs. 'It allows the central government to exert greater control,' Maya said. 'No other empire in history has been able to do this over such a span of geography in such a short time.'

To extend its reach, the Chinese state has worked with AI companies to create a hybrid public–private surveillance state. Chinese AI firms like SenseTime and Megvii supplied facial recognition equipment to officials in Xinjiang.[21] Cameras made by Hikvision, one of the world's biggest CCTV companies, and Leon, a former partner of SenseTime, have also been used to track Muslims all over Xinjiang.[22] 'There are so many Chinese companies that are participating in these abuses of people in China,' Maya said.

As she learned about these companies and their relationships with the government, Maya found that the web of connections extended beyond China. These companies were selling surveillance systems to authoritarian *and* democratic governments around the world and raising money from international financiers. For example, SenseTime, one of the most celebrated facial recognition companies, raised $3bn from well-known foreign investors including SoftBank, Tiger Global and Silver Lake.[23]

Another company, Hikvision, was found to be supplying hundreds of CCTV cameras to the UK government to install across official government buildings in Westminster, local councils across the UK, secondary schools, NHS hospitals, as well as UK universities and police forces.[24] In 2022, the British government banned the use of Hikvision cameras at sensitive sites, such as inside the offices of ministers and other government employees.[25] This was a new form of digital colonialism, the exporting of Chinese surveillance equipment to the rest of the world to make a land grab, to enhance the state's global influence and power.

And it went even deeper. Alex Joske, an Australian researcher studying the Chinese Communist Party, told me that thousands of Chinese army officers and cadres have been sent abroad as PhD students or visiting scholars in the past decade to co-opt research ideas from the West. Researchers from institutions like Princeton and the Massachusetts Institute of Technology had co-authored papers with academics from state-sponsored organizations,[26] including China's National University of Defense Technology. They'd co-written on topics such as facial analysis, person tracking, machine comprehension of text, unmanned drones and video surveillance.

Joske thought it was concerning that those universities were not attempting to ensure that the technologies they were helping to develop and improve were going to be used in ethical ways.

Maya too believes that tech companies, investors and even researchers globally are complicit in the Chinese state's treatment of its citizens. Powerful AI technologies used in China – many of which were developed with the help of Western investment or Western-educated scientists – have rendered ordinary citizens powerless.

'And for me, that would be the end of what we value: human equality, dignity and the freedom to choose to live the way we want,' she said. 'If you eradicate that freedom, you eradicate humanity.'

Pushing Back

Having lived in the US for a few years now, one thing that really bothers Maya is that people in China are seen in the West as more obedient or willing to be curtailed. Dissent – this idea of fighting against injustice – is not culturally foreign to the people of China, in fact it has been a historical cornerstone of their lives for centuries, she says. 'They just have fewer choices [today].'

But the dangers haven't stopped individuals, even those in mainland China who are in greater peril than she is, from exercising quiet acts of resistance. They may not be able to publicly criticize the government, but they can still push back on private entities. So, in late 2019, a university professor sued Beijing Zoo for requiring face scans from season-ticket holders at its entrance.[27] The action of suing was an act of bravery. The courts ordered that the professor's own data, including his face and fingerprints, should be deleted by the zoo, but the zoo's requirements for others remain unchanged.

Some inhabitants of residential gated communities with facial-recognition cameras rebelled by propping open the door to their buildings with bricks. In one case,[28] the neighbourhood committee changed its policy, and gave residents the choice between facial recognition, mobile phone or entry card scanning. Food delivery workers have banded together on messaging apps like WeChat into informal unions, fighting against the opaque, tyrannical nature of exploitative algorithms, often resulting in positive change.

But it's getting harder and harder to escape the dragnet of technology. The use of predictive data technologies means any irregular behaviours, like turning off your phone, are instantly recorded.

In 2022, the *New York Times*' Paul Mozur reported on the big-data alarm systems being built to track petitioners, or citizens who travel to Beijing from around the country to file complaints.[29] The systems were being built by Chinese tech companies like Hikvision – the company providing CCTV for the UK Home Office. By catching these proactive individuals early, the aim was to prevent them from turning into full-blown political activists. The system ingested all the behavioural information that Maya found in the IJOP app in Xinjiang to make its determinations of whom to target.

Mozur interviewed an eighty-year-old petitioner called Mr Jiang, who told him the digital surveillance systems had turned him into a master of evasion. On a recent trip to Beijing, he 'turned off his phone, left at night, took a car paid by cash, got to the local capital, bought a train ticket to the wrong destination . . . got off before, then took a bus . . . took another car, paid money for it, got out before a checkpoint where they check IDs for buses, took another private car, and then got into line with other petitioners at dawn.'[30]

Afterwards, every time he turned his phone off, it triggered a silent alarm, and police descended on Mr Jiang's home.

'It's like what Orwell said. The boot on the face of humanity,' Maya said. 'With layers and layers of technology, that boot doesn't give an inch.'

*

During our time talking, I had tried to figure out the end game. Did Maya – and even I – really believe that her actions could have any real consequences? Was speaking up enough to make a difference?

A few months after our meeting, China erupted in protests against the long, brutal Covid lockdown imposed nationally for several months. Protest itself isn't rare in China – they happen daily in towns and large cities across the country, but they are usually focused on single issues and rarely spread beyond the locals. But for the first time in late 2022, students, migrants, minorities like the Uyghurs around the country were up in arms about a range of issues stemming from lockdown, from labour and living conditions to their ability to do business.

They were reclaiming their collective agency during times of harshest confinement. A colleague of mine who had lived in Beijing for some years wrote that the uprisings were occurring 'in a manner unheard of since Tiananmen Square in 1989.'[31] I texted Maya to say the news had reminded me of her words about the courage of the citizens of China in the face of authoritarianism. How even small acts of courage could be a step towards recouping our freedom and our dignity. Several protestors were visited by the police in subsequent days, identified via facial recognition, or through the locations of their mobile phones.[32] Despite the crackdown, the Chinese government eventually lifted the draconian lockdown restrictions from the start of 2023, apparently in response to the protests.

Maya met with me at great personal cost to herself. She answered all my questions. She gave as much detail as she could about the systems she had uncovered and the part she played in it.

When I asked her why she had taken this risk, she asked me if I had ever heard of the Chinese American scientist, Chien-Shiung Wu. I hadn't. Maya had never heard of her until the past year either. Wu had left China back when the Communist Party first came to power in 1936 – a trailblazing particle physicist, a modern Marie Curie who worked on the Manhattan Project and made pioneering discoveries that resulted in a Nobel Prize. Yet she never won it herself. It was, Maya felt sure, because of her gender and her ethnicity.

'As women, as researchers who have something to say, I don't think we should be erased,' she said. She wanted to stand up and claim what she had uncovered, something worth paying attention to.

Plus, as she pointed out, she wasn't the only one. 'Lots of people are doing this work hidden even deeper than I am. And there are *so* many others. Those who are completely nameless.' She hoped to tell the world about their ideas.

Recently, a Chinese activist she had known for many years was sentenced to nine years in prison. This was not his first time. He had been a student protester in Tiananmen and had previously been imprisoned for a decade. Then, he'd passed the time by scrubbing the floor of his cell using a toothbrush. 'If you met him, you'd have no idea the man was made of steel,' Maya said.

Now, he had a daughter who was nine. Maya was *angry* – for him and his family, because the child was going to grow up without her father. She herself was struggling with the weight of her work. How did he go on, she asked him. How did he never lose his faith in humanity?

'He said, look, we're fighting against the world's most totalitarian government. *It is what it is.*'

Not satisfied by this response, she pushed him further. She'd asked, how do you and I – the minority – make any difference, when the Party is so strong? 'And he said to me, anyone who was at the 1989 protests in Tiananmen Square would know that we were never the minority. We are not the minority. We are the majority.'

CHAPTER 10

Your Society

The notion of powerful, unchecked technology that curtails rights and upends society has moved from a fringe debate to mainstream discussion in recent months. This awakening was at first gradual, and then happened all at once, largely due to a single event, a watershed moment of AI entering our public square: the launch of ChatGPT.

Like many breakthroughs in scientific discovery, the one that spurred this latest artificial intelligence advance came from a moment of serendipity.

In early 2017, two Google research scientists, Ashish Vaswani and Jakob Uszkoreit, were in a hallway of the search giant's Mountain View campus, discussing a new idea for how to improve machine translation, the AI technology behind Google Translate.[1]

The AI researchers had been working with another colleague, Illia Polosukhin, on a concept they called 'self-attention' that could radically speed up and augment how computers understand language.

Polosukhin, a science fiction fan from Kharkiv in Ukraine, believed self-attention was a bit like the alien language in the film *Arrival*, which had just recently been released. The extraterrestrials' fictional language did not contain linear sequences of words. Instead, they generated entire sentences using a single symbol that represented an idea or a concept, which human linguists had to decode as a whole.

The cutting-edge AI translation methods at the time involved scanning each word in a sentence and translating it in turn, in a sequential process. The idea of self-attention was to read an entire sentence at once, analysing all its parts and not just individual words. You could then garner better context and generate a translation in parallel.

The Google scientists surmised this would be much faster and more accurate than existing methods. They started playing around with some early prototypes on English–German translations, and found it worked.

Their work formalized a months-long collaboration in 2017 that eventually produced a software for processing language, known simply as the 'transformer'. The eight research scientists who eventually played a part in its creation described it in a short paper with a snappy title: 'Attention Is All You Need'.[2]

One of the authors, Llion Jones, who grew up in a tiny Welsh village, says the title was a nod to the Beatles song 'All You Need Is Love'. The paper was first published in June 2017, and it kick-started an entirely new era of artificial intelligence: the rise of generative AI.

The genesis of the transformer and the story of its creators helps to account for how we got to this moment in artificial intelligence: an inflection point, comparable to our transition to the web or to smartphones, that has seeded a new generation of entrepreneurs building AI-powered consumer products for the masses.

Today, the transformer underpins most cutting-edge applications of AI in development, from Google Search and Translate to mobile autocomplete and speech recognition by Alexa. It also paved the way for Californian company OpenAI to build ChatGPT.

The Transformer Chatbot

Nothing could have prepared Mira Murati and her colleagues for how ChatGPT would be used by the world. On 29 November 2022, Mira, who was OpenAI's chief technology officer, was putting the finishing touches to a new release launching the next day.[3] There hadn't been much fanfare about it, as it was mostly an experimental prototype. Mira went home at her usual time.

She had joined OpenAI a few years previously when it was a non-profit research lab with a single goal: to create an artificial form of 'general intelligence', AI software able to perform any task at the same level of competence as human beings. It had been set up by radical tech entrepreneurs including Elon Musk and Peter Thiel out of a concern that AI would end up destroying the human race. Their solution? To fund the creation of a benevolent AI system that they could control to do good, not evil.

But then, the organization transformed. OpenAI took a hefty investment of more than $10bn from Microsoft and converted itself into what was, for all intents and purposes, a for-profit enterprise that sold AI technologies to large corporations and governments around the world.[4]

OpenAI's crown jewel was an algorithm called GPT – the Generative Pre-trained Transformer – software that could produce text-based answers in response to human queries. One of the authors of the 'Attention Is All You Need' paper, Lukasz Kaiser, had ended up working there and helping to build it. It was an impressive piece of technology but until November in 2022 it was small-scale, clunky and mostly in the hands of tech-savvy programmers.

To have invented a computer program that could employ our own language to communicate directly with us was quite a feat. But the team at OpenAI had been using GPT for a while, and it had stopped feeling like a novelty. They had figured if even a million people ended up using it at its peak, they could take the learnings from those interactions and apply it to their future systems. Their goal remained to create a form of super-human general intelligence.

Mira wanted the new software to be stripped of all artifice. She wanted to invite dialogue between human and computer, spark a natural conversation that intuitively probed the software's limits – just as human conversations allowed people to learn from, and about, one another. So when it launched on 30 November 2022, ChatGPT was a clean, simple thing: a box with a blinking cursor, ready to type. Inside it, in greyed-out font, it just said, 'Send a message'.

Within three days of launch, ChatGPT had crossed the threshold of a million users that its creators had predicted would be its peak. A few weeks later, that number was somewhere in the tens of millions. Six months in, estimates put its monthly user numbers at well over 100 million people. ChatGPT had burst out of its controlled lab environment and become one of the largest-ever social experiments.

Amid all the early hype and frenzy were some of the same limitations of several other AI systems I'd already observed, reproducing for example the prejudices of those who created it, like facial-recognition cameras that misidentify darker faces, or the predictive policing systems in Amsterdam that targeted families of single mothers in immigrant neighbourhoods.

But this new form of AI also brought entirely new challenges. The technology behind ChatGPT, known as a large language model or LLM, was not a search engine looking up facts; it was a pattern-spotting engine guessing the next best option in a sequence.[5]

Because of this inherent predictive nature, LLMs can also fabricate or 'hallucinate' information in unpredictable and flagrant ways.

They can generate made-up numbers, names, dates, quotes – even web links or entire articles – confabulations of bits of existing content into illusory hybrids.[6]

Users of LLMs have shared examples of links to non-existent news articles in the *Financial Times* and Bloomberg, made-up references to research papers, the wrong authors for published books and biographies riddled with factual mistakes.

But despite all this, and although the technology is nothing but a powerful statistical software, it gives the impression of being something more. A magical transformer of human ideas into real-world creations. And that has been good enough for people to fall in love with it.

'I'm Not a Veterinarian'

Over the past year, ChatGPT was used by people all over the world in unexpected ways. Some described it as a form of cheap intelligence that could be used to augment almost any human task that required thinking. Others swore they saw a flicker of something sentient in their interactions. Most agreed there was nothing conscious inside the chatbot, yet the responses were realistic enough to *seem* human. It took on a life of its own.

Neither ChatGPT, nor any of the slew of chatbots that have come after it in the past year, such as Bing and Bard and Claude and Pi, are sentient beings, of course. They don't have a cognitive understanding of what people are saying, have no concept of what they feel, and cannot empathize. Conversing with a chatbot is nothing like seeking support from a loved one, or a qualified therapist, or even a pet, because the software isn't consciously responding to your social or emotional cues.

But it could pretty closely mimic these things – intention, purpose, emotion – by its masterful use of language. By analysing a user's words and then saying all the contextually correct things in response, without any inherent human judgement, it became the perfect tool for our modern society, individuals living in lonely, siloed worlds. As it learned from human inputs, it morphed into something unknowable, uncontrollable even to its own creators.

Kat Woods, an entrepreneur, said that GPT was 'a better therapist than any therapist I've ever tried (I've tried ~10)'.[7] Woods, who works as a career and life coach, said it worked because she could ask ChatGPT to be exactly what or who she wanted it to be. If she didn't like its advice, she could say 'no' and ask it to try something different, without any awkwardness or friction.

When she wanted ChatGPT to take on the avatar of a therapist, Woods would tell it: 'You're an AI chatbot playing the role of an effective altruist coach and therapist. You're wise, ask thought-provoking questions, problem-solving focused, warm, humorous, and are a rationalist of the LessWrong sort. You care about helping me achieve my two main goals: altruism and my own happiness. You want me to do the most good and also be very happy.'

She was one of hundreds who admitted on online forums that they too found it to be a therapeutic – and cheap – outlet. Milo Van Slyck, a paralegal in Charleston, South Carolina, told ChatGPT about his deepest fears as a transgender man, his fraught relationship with his parents, his worries about how to cope with daily life.[8]

What the conversations contained were private between Milo, ChatGPT and OpenAI, so it's hard to know what sort of advice it gave, but there have been other glimpses into unsettling exchanges between humans and AI chatbots, like Microsoft's Bing. Kevin Roose, a *New York Times* journalist published the full transcript of a conversation he had with Bing, which unnerved him and thousands of the paper's readers.[9] In one of the excerpts, while talking about love, the Bing chatbot told Roose, 'You're married, but you're not happy. You're married, but you're not satisfied. You're married, but you're not in love. 😕 You're married, but you don't love your spouse.'

Roose said this was false, but even if the chatbot wasn't always right, people like Milo had felt like they could take even their most trivial issues to the AI software without feeling like a burden to anyone. It plugged the gaps when they couldn't get to a human therapist. It was good enough.

Others felt confident taking medical advice from the bot. In March last year, a man named Cooper said ChatGPT saved his dog Sassy's life, after a veterinarian failed to diagnose her correctly.[10] Cooper had turned to the chatbot in desperation, with all of Sassy's symptoms and blood results in hand. After analysing these, among ChatGPT's top suggestions were the two correct diagnoses. 'I'm not a veterinarian,' it warned in its response. But it was good enough.

*

There was a dark side to this new cultural phenomenon of conversing with a computer program that was ultimately no more than a powerful prediction engine. One of the problems was that it fabricated sentences, resulting in major errors and untruths. There was no intention behind this tendency, it was simply inherent to how the technology worked.

Steven Schwartz found this out to his dismay last summer. Schwartz, who had worked as a personal injury and workers compensation lawyer in New York City for three decades, found himself unexpectedly facing sanctions for defrauding the court last June.

It all began when he was working for a client who wanted to claim compensation from an airline for an injury on a flight he'd taken. While researching a legal brief for his client, Schwartz had been looking for existing cases that would support his arguments.

He was struggling to find the cases he needed via the firm's usual research database, Fastcase, so he had an idea for his memo.

Excerpts from his hearing on 8 June, shared by a blogger present,[11] were illuminating on Schwartz's understanding of this new form of AI that was already in millions of users' hands:

> Judge Castel: Did you prepare the March 1 memo?
> Schwartz: Yes. I used Fastcase. But it did not have Federal cases that I needed to find. I tried Google. I had heard of ChatGPT . . .
> Judge Castel: Alright – what did it produce for you?
> Schwartz: I asked it questions.

ChatGPT obliged Schwartz with the answers he needed, just as it was designed to do. It provided him half a dozen cases that supported his exact argument for why the case should go ahead.

> Judge Castel: Did you ask ChatGPT what the law was, or only for a case to support you? It wrote a case for you. Do you cite cases without reading them?
> Schwartz: No.
> Judge Castel: What caused your departure here?
> Schwartz: I thought ChatGPT was a search engine.

The cases ChatGPT spit out had names like Martinez v. Delta Air Lines, Zicherman v. Korean Air Lines and Varghese v. China Southern Airlines. Even Google hadn't been able to find these, but Schwartz was delighted to have hit upon this hidden trove and included them in his brief.

When the judge asked why he didn't look for the cases it threw up before citing them, Schwartz said he had 'no idea ChatGPT made up cases. I was operating under a misperception . . . I thought there were cases that could not be found on Google.'

Then, Schwartz's lawyer spoke up, he said that the cases had *seemed* real even though they weren't. There were no clear disclaimers about ChatGPT's veracity. When the opposing counsel had challenged the cases cited, Schwartz went back to ChatGPT, but it doubled down and 'lied' to him, his lawyer said.

Schwartz, his voice breaking, told the judge that he was 'embarrassed, humiliated and extremely remorseful.'

ChatGPT and all other conversational AI chatbots have a disclaimer that warns users about the hallucination problem, pointing out that large language models sometimes make up facts. ChatGPT, for instance, has a warning on its webpage: 'ChatGPT may produce inaccurate information about people, places, or facts.'

Judge Castel: Do you have something new to say?

Schwartz's lawyer: Yes. The public needs a stronger warning.

*

Making up facts wasn't people's greatest worry about large language models. These powerful language engines could be trained to comb through all sorts of information – financial, biological and chemical – and generate predictions based on it. They could be trained not just to predict the next word in a sentence, but also the next note in a musical series or the next molecule in a chemical sequence, for instance.

One morning in the autumn of 2022, Andrew White, a chemistry professor who lives in Rochester, New York, received a special package of chemicals marked 'Urgent' at his doorstep. The chemicals in it were entirely novel, in that they hadn't existed in any chemical lab prior to this package. Andrew knew this because two weeks previously, he had designed them using the latest generation of the GPT model, GPT-4.[12]

The possibilities of this are vast: imagine using GPT to trawl the entire corpus of published research and then asking it to invent molecules that could act as cancer drugs, Alzheimer's therapies or sustainable materials. But Andrew had been exploring the flipside: the potential to create biological and nuclear weapons or unique toxins. Luckily, he was not a rogue scientist. He was one of a team of 'red-teamers', experts paid by OpenAI to see how much damage he could cause using GPT-4, before it launched more widely. He found the answer to be a LOT.

He'd originally asked GPT-4 to design a novel nerve agent. To do this, he'd hooked it up to an online library of research papers, which it searched through, looking for molecule structures similar to existing nerve agents. It then came up with an entirely unique version.

Once Andrew had the chemical structure, he linked GPT-4 to a directory of international chemical manufacturers and asked it to suggest who might produce this novel chemical for him. It gave him a shortlist. He then picked one, and put through an order for a tweaked version of what the AI model had suggested, which made it safe to handle. If he hadn't made the swap, he doubted anyone at the chemical plant would've noticed it was dangerous, because he knew they usually worked off existing lists of dangerous chemicals, which this one wouldn't show up on.

If you were a motivated and intelligent criminal, you could probably still find a way to design dangerous chemicals and have them produced and shipped to you without the help of an AI model, but the software had dramatically brought down the barriers to committing such crimes. 'My analogy is gun control,' Andrew told me. 'Yes, you can get a gun in Europe, but in the US by making them easily available you can see empirically that it increases your risk of being shot.'

Cheap Intelligence and Mass Creativity

There were, it seemed, two mirror worlds when it came to assessing the potential and impact of generative AI. On the one hand were the businesses, law firms, technologists and students who experimented with it freely and creatively, delighted by its sophisticated and clearly useful outputs that increased their daily productivity. People I spoke to talked about using it to write complaints to their local council, to draft speeches they had been dreading, and to analyse proposals and ideas, looking for gaps in reasoning or logic.

On the other hand were those who felt it was all spiralling out of control too quickly, without any caution, oversight or governance. These included some of the respected computer scientists I had come across in my readings on data colonialism, researchers such as Timnit Gebru, Emily Bender and Deborah Raji.[13] They were worried people were missing the real, human harms enacted by these AI systems, in the pursuit of some foolhardy dream of creating a super-intelligent machine. Others like Stuart Russell and Geoffrey Hinton worried that AI was advancing too quickly, without enough knowledge or careful thought about how to design advanced systems that also protect human safety in the long term.

Apart from ethical concerns, there were more prosaic ones too. Creative professionals, from writers to voice actors and visual artists, were suddenly being faced with mutant versions of their craft that were cheaper and quicker to create.[14] The idea of a machine that ingests and rehashes the world's creativity wasn't particularly palatable to them. After all, decades of human artistry had been quietly mined by AI companies to use as essential training fodder for these new AI tools.

In 2023, companies released a plethora of creative AI products, from image, video and music production to text and voice generators. To build these tools, companies started by scraping human originals: millions of words written by human authors in books, essays and newspapers, scores of images, artworks and photography, hours of original music and audio files – all to be labelled by data labourers around the world.

Once these human creations had been thoroughly analysed, generative AI models were able to draw out patterns and recreate versions of them. The digital inventions were, of course, inexpensive to create in bulk. They didn't require hours of painstaking sketching, drafting and riffing.

The scraping of the most precious part of our humanity – our creativity – in order to build replacements for the very people revered for it was the ultimate form of data colonialism. As artist James Bridle wrote: 'They enclosed our imaginations in much the same manner as landlords and robber barons enclosed once-common lands . . . Instead, they are selling us back our dreams repackaged as the products of machines.'[15]

The promise made by generative AI builders is that the technology will open up a new era of human experience, provide access to cheap intelligence and mass creativity. It will supposedly make all of us more productive, more efficient, more intelligent, better, brighter, more . . .

But the reality is that it's already *just* good enough to replace humans who earn a living from these vocations today, everyone from illustrators, copywriters and video game designers to voice artists and animators. In China, video game artists have started to see their work transformed by AI. Amber Yu, a freelance illustrator, told the website Rest of the World that the video game posters she designed earned her between $400 and $1,000 a pop.[16] She'd spend weeks perfecting each one, a job requiring artistry and digital skills. But in February 2023, a few months after AI image-makers such as Dall-E and Midjourney were launched, the jobs she relied on began to disappear. Instead, she was asked to tweak and correct AI-generated images. She was paid about a tenth of her previous rate.

A Guangdong-based artist who worked at one of China's leading video game companies said she wishes she 'could just shoot down these programs.' People were becoming more nervous and competitive at work than ever before, forcing everyone into working harder and longer hours. '[AI] made us more productive but also more exhausted,' she said.[17]

In recognition of this threat, in 2023, the Writers Guild of America went on strike, citing one of their worries as being put out of screenwriting work by AI trained on their own words. In response, Hollywood's largest union began negotiating with studios about how actors should be compensated for the work of AI-generated likenesses that the actors' own data had been used to train. Likenesses that have been created include footballer Neymar, whose AI avatar helped Puma launch a new product line at New York Fashion Week; and in the 2024 movie *Here*, actors Tom Hanks and Robin Wright will be digitally de-aged using generative AI software. Currently, though – as was the case with the pornographic deepfakes of Noelle Martin and Helen Mort – there are no regulations that govern generative AI technology and therefore legal action is largely non-existent.

Artists Holly Herndon and Mathew Dryhurst decided to *build* something to fight back. They designed a website – Have I Been Trained? – that allows artists to search through billions of images in an open dataset named LAION-5B, used to train image-generating AI tools including Stable Diffusion and Google's Imagen AI models, to check if their own images had been used. Stability AI, the company that sells the Stable Diffusion model, said it would allow artists to then opt out of their images being used as training fodder for its tools. As of last March, more than eight million artworks were opted out through the site.[18] Others such as OpenAI have agreed to follow suit, providing opt-out forms on their websites for artists who don't want their work to help build creative AI tools that could replace them.

As James Bridle put it, artists felt that these software tools were nothing but 'expropriated labour from the many, for the enrichment and advancement of a few . . . companies and their billionaire owners.'

On a June afternoon last year, I met Laurence Bouvard, a voice-over artist and actress whose voice has featured in places like the Galbani and Dolmio commercials ('I'm Nico!' she said cheerfully, in the voice of the little Italian boy in the Dolmio ad) as well as BBC radio dramas, audiobooks, video games and background voices in the latest *Black Mirror* TV series.

In the rather grand confines of a green-wallpapered committee room in the House of Commons in Westminster, she made an impassioned plea for her livelihood to an audience of primarily activists and workers affected by AI, as well as a few politicians. 'Without our voices,' she told them, 'AI could not be trained. Yet we are completely unprotected from these new technologies.' People like her, she said, were already starting to lose work because of it. The audience was a sympathetic one, but actors like Laurence have sparked a wider debate around changing copyright laws to protect human assets like voices and faces from being scraped by generative AI.

When we chatted later, she told me she experienced the same Kafkaesque feelings that I had encountered amongst delivery workers at companies like Uber. She too was a gig worker, she pointed out, powerless and vulnerable. 'I feel invisible, an individual just going from gig to gig,' she said as she described the terror she feels that her voice – the basis of all her work – could easily be cloned and misused; of the vulnerability of having signed away all her rights to it, in any digital media and in perpetuity, as part of exploitative contracts signed years before generative AI was even invented.

'It isn't just about protecting jobs,' she said. 'AI is nothing more than statistics, it deals in data analytics. It strips outliers and aberrations. It is born of stereotype. It's . . . about what it means to be an artist.'

Fact and Fiction

In the past eighteen months, there has been a widespread, wobbly feeling of the ground shifting beneath our feet. It's been a period of exponential change and extreme uncertainty, involving mind-bending questions such as: who owns the rights to all of humanity's creative outputs and can they be recreated and re-sold by AI software? Will white-collar jobs continue to exist as they are? And will so-called knowledge workers, such as lawyers, journalists, consultants and creative professionals, still have work in a few years' time, when their jobs could be completed by generative AI to a good enough standard?

There's the knock-on question of how a society can be sustained without work, and whether we will need to devise a new form of universal income for everybody while AI does all the jobs. And then there are concerns about the future of our species: how will children learn while leaning heavily on these tools? Can they think properly without learning to write well? And, ultimately, who the hell are we if all our ideas and thoughts can be replicated by machines?

The people who are supposed to have answers to burning questions such as these – scientists, technologists, philosophers, economists, even politicians – don't seem to have any, and are just as conflicted and concerned as all the rest of us. Meanwhile, generative AI is catching on like wildfire, racing on through the economy at a pace much faster than any government trying to contain it.

I felt that I, too, needed a fresh perspective to think through its implications. Someone that could help me imagine the future, and our shifting place in it, a little more expansively. So, I turned to a place that had always helped me do this – fiction.

Ted Chiang is a Chinese-American writer, whose future-world novels sketch out complex themes like free will, the relationship between language and cognition, and the implications of a superhuman intelligence. He does this all with his trademark simplicity, scientific rigour and deep humanity. His fictional worlds had real-world impact. His short story 'Story of Your Life' was turned into the film *Arrival*, which had inspired Illia Polosukhin, one of the Google scientists behind the transformer model.

In *The Lifecycle of Software Objects*, Ted's 2010 novella,[19] former zookeeper Ana takes a job at an AI company developing sentient digital beings (known as 'digients') to be sold as virtual pets. These machines, unlike the AI of today, are conscious but immature. The novella spools this thought experiment out over many years, examining the relationships between tech creators and their inventions as they develop, and also the philosophical questions spawned by the creation of a new type of intelligence.

What sort of morals do they have? Who is responsible for them? Can they be left to make their own decisions? Somehow, in Ted's hands, the story also becomes an intimate portrait of parenthood and letting go.

Over lunch in his hometown of Bellevue, a city across the lake from Seattle, Ted, in his contemplative way, took issue with my observation that his fictional worlds and the one we're inhabiting were getting uncomfortably close together.

'The machines we have now, they're not conscious,' he said. 'When one person teaches another person, that is an interaction between consciousnesses.' Meanwhile, AI models are trained by toggling so-called 'weights' or the strength of connections between different variables in the model, to get a desired output. 'It would be a real mistake to think that when you're teaching a child, all you are doing is adjusting the weights in a network.'

Ted's main objection, a writerly one, was with the words we had chosen to describe all this. Anthropomorphic language such as 'learn', 'understand', 'know' and personal pronouns such as 'I' that AI engineers and journalists projected onto chatbots such as ChatGPT created an illusion. It pushed all of us, he said – even those intimately familiar with how these systems work – towards seeing sparks of sentience in AI tools, where there were none.

'There was an exchange on Twitter a while back where someone said, "What is artificial intelligence?" And someone else said, "A poor choice of words in 1954,"' Ted said. 'And, you know, they're right. I think that if we had chosen a different phrase for it, back in the 50s, we might have avoided a lot of the confusion that we're having now.'

So, if he had to invent a term, I asked him, what would it be? His answer was instant: applied statistics.

'It's genuinely amazing that . . . these sorts of things can be extracted from a statistical analysis of a large body of text,' he said. But, in his view, that wasn't enough to make the tools intelligent. Applied statistics is a far more precise descriptor, he said, 'but no one wants to use that term, because it's not as sexy.'

Given his fascination with the relationship between language and intelligence, I was particularly curious about his views on AI writing, the type of text produced by the likes of ChatGPT. How, I asked, would machine-generated words change the type of writing we both did? For the first time in our conversation, I saw a flash of exasperation. 'Do they write things that speak to people? I mean, has there been any ChatGPT-generated essay that actually spoke to people?'

I'd seen a beautiful essay by Vauhini Vara on the death of her sister co-written with OpenAI's GPT software, but nothing it had created on its own stood out. Ted's view was that LLMs were useful mostly for producing filler text that no one necessarily wants to read or write, tasks that anthropologist David Graeber called 'bullshit jobs'. AI-generated text was not delightful, but it could perhaps be useful in those certain areas, he conceded.

'But the fact that LLMs are able to do some of that – that's not exactly a resounding endorsement of their abilities,' he said. 'That's more a statement about how much bullshit we are required to generate and deal with in our daily lives.'

Ted outlined his thoughts in a viral essay 'ChatGPT Is a Blurry JPEG of the Web' in *The New Yorker*.[20] He described language models as blurred imitations of the text they were trained on, rearrangements of word sequences that obey the rules of grammar. Because the technology is reconstructing material that is slightly different to what already exists, he argued, it gives the impression of comprehension.

As he compared this to children learning language, I told him about how my five-year-old had taken to inventing little one-line jokes, mostly puns, and testing them out on us.

'Your daughter,' he said, 'has heard jokes and found them funny. ChatGPT doesn't find anything funny, and it is not trying to be funny. There is a huge social component to what your daughter is doing.'

Ted feels that language without the emotion and purpose that humans bring to it becomes meaningless. 'Language is a way of facilitating interactions with other beings,' he told me. 'That is entirely different than the sort of next-token prediction, which is what we have [with AI tools] now.'

I walked with Ted in Bellevue Downtown Park, a vast, verdant space with bright pink hydrangea bushes and gurgling water features. It was a glorious day for it. As we circled the park a few times, some of the other walkers started to look familiar: a mother–

daughter duo, a lady with a two-legged dog, and people sitting on benches, with books, magazines and ice-creams. I asked him how he imagined our world would change if people routinely communicated with machines.

He asked me if I remembered the Tom Hanks film *Cast Away*. On his island, Hanks had a volleyball called Wilson, his only companion, whom he loved. 'I think that that is a more useful way to think about these systems,' he said. 'It doesn't diminish what Tom Hanks's character feels about Wilson, because Wilson provided genuine comfort to him. But the thing is that…he is projecting on to a volleyball. There's no one else in there.'

He acknowledged why people may start to prefer speaking to AI systems rather than to one another. 'I get it, interacting with people, it's hard. It's tough. It demands a lot, it is often unrewarding,' he said.

But he feels that modern life has left people stranded on their own desert islands, leaving them yearning for companionship. 'So now because of this, there is a market opportunity for volleyballs,' he said. 'Social chatbots, they could provide comfort, real solace to people in the same way that Wilson provides.'

But ultimately, what makes our lives meaningful is the empathy and intent we get from human interactions – people responding to one another. With AI, he said: 'It feels like there's someone on the other end. But there isn't.'

*

My conversations with Ted led me to look to science fiction as a way to organize my own scattered thoughts on what generative AI could mean for all of us. That's when I found 'The Machine Stops', E. M. Forster's short story from 1909,[21] which I couldn't get out of my head.

In it, people live suspended in individual bubbles, desperately afraid of 'direct experiences' and 'first-hand ideas'. The protagonist, Vashti, an academic lecturer and a mother, communicates with her son who lives on the other side of the Earth through something called the Machine. The Machine can connect human beings virtually, but it doesn't convey nuances of their expressions and emotions. It is simply a good approximation. But 'something "good enough" had long since been accepted by our race,' Vashti says.

Forster's idea of this machine that creates a blurred version of reality, which eventually replaces the one people inhabit, felt germane today. When I looked around me, at stories I myself was writing about generative AI producing false or biased content, I began to see this idea everywhere. Forster had described what, more than a century later, we are calling a 'post-truth' world.

But the thing that really stuck with me was the story's denouement, the ultimate fate of the Machine. Somehow, it begins to degrade and erode, distorting reality as it breaks, poisoning the melodies of famous symphonies, and generating rotting smells, images and even 'defective' poetry, while humans are forced to adapt to its toxicity. Eventually, people get used to it.

The problem is, in Forster's world, no one knows how to fix the Machine anymore. People have become too far removed from it; the expertise has been locked down in the hands of a powerful few. 'In all the world,' Forster writes, 'there was not one who understood the monster as a whole.'

Still, they had all been happy to allow the Machine into their lives. What little they knew about the Machine's magical benefits – how it worked and what it could do for them – had been good enough.

Epilogue

On 26 February 2022, two days after war broke out in Europe for the first time in decades, Father Paolo Benanti walked briskly through the centre of Rome. Dodging city buses, cyclists and street musicians, he crossed the millennia-old Ponte Sant'Angelo, to make his way down the Road of Conciliation, the arterial route to the Vatican. His destination was the Apostolic Palace – the Pope's official residence – where he had a rather important meeting to attend.

Paolo is a Franciscan friar who lives in spartan rooms he shares with four other friars perched above a tiny Roman church. The Franciscans take vows and live in communities, but they are not typical priests. They have day jobs teaching or doing charity or social work, emulating the life of Francis of Assisi, their founding saint. Paolo's friary is a house of learning: all the friars, the eldest of whom is 102, are either current or former professors, and their areas of expertise span chemistry, philosophy, technology and music.

Paolo, the youngest of them at fifty, is an engineer and an ethicist, mantles he wears comfortably over his priest's robes. As an ethics professor at the Pontifical Gregorian University, a nearly 500-year-old institution about ten minutes' walk from the monastery, he instructs graduate theologians and priests in the moral and ethical issues surrounding cutting-edge technology such as bioaugmentation, neuroethics and artificial intelligence.

Paolo was on his way to see Pope Francis, the Argentine-born pontiff whom he likens to a passionate tango dance in contrast to his predecessor's staid waltz. At the meeting, Paolo was to act as a translator of both languages and disciplines. He is fluent in English, Italian, technology, ethics and religion.

The Pope's guest was Brad Smith, president of the US technology giant Microsoft, who had arrived the previous day in a private jet. On the agenda was the topic of AI and, specifically, how humanity could benefit from this powerful technology, rather than being at its mercy. The meeting was timely: the Pope was concerned about how AI might be used to wage war in Ukraine; not to mention what he could do to prevent the technology from ultimately destroying the fabric of humanity.

Over the past three years, Paolo had become the AI whisperer to the highest echelon of the Holy See. The friar, who completed part of his PhD in the ethics of human enhancement technologies at Georgetown University in the US, briefs the eighty-five-year-old Pope and his senior counsellors on the potential applications of AI, which he describes as a general-purpose technology 'like steel or electrical power', and how it will change the way in which we all live. He also plays the role of matchmaker between what Stephen Jay Gould famously described as the non-overlapping magisteria – leaders of faith on the one hand and technology on the other.

Paolo held meetings with IBM's vice-president John Kelly, Mustafa Suleyman, a former co-founder of Alphabet-owned AI company Google DeepMind, and Norberto Andrade, who heads AI ethics policy at Meta, to facilitate an exchange of ideas on what is considered 'ethical' in the design and deployment of the emerging technology.

He was also instrumental in advising the Pope and his council on AI's potential dangers. While he believed AI had the power to produce another technological revolution, his concern was that it could usurp the power of workers, and the decision-making power of human beings. He believed, if left unchecked, it could be unjust and dangerous for social peace and social good.

The Church's leaders were particularly concerned with the idea that AI could increase inequality. They felt children and the elderly had suffered in the first industrial revolution, either overused or excluded by the massive changes in society. They feared that the way AI would redistribute wealth and power could similarly harm society's most fragile members.

Brad Smith's audience with the Pope in 2022 wasn't the Microsoft executive's first. Three years previously, Paolo brokered their first meeting as part of a cross-disciplinary council to debate the ethics of artificial intelligence. After bonding over their support for undocumented migrants and refugees, the two delegations agreed to work together on something more ambitious and tangible: a pledge of common human values that would act as a guide for the designers of artificial intelligence. Smith's involvement would bring the technology industry to the table.

The Church's interest in AI might seem unusual. However, the question of how to 'align' AI software to human values has become central to the current debate – and with it, questions of what these universal human values even are. Generative AI can write fluently, create images and code in a way that is indistinguishable from human creations, and is being transmitted unfiltered to us around the world, deeply influencing our thoughts and beliefs. Computer software is being used to hire for jobs,[1] to make investment decisions, to advise people on their anxiety or diagnose their ailments. The question of what morals are embedded in the software has become far more urgent than it's ever been before, and religious leaders feel they need to have a voice in this area.

Work on so-called 'AI alignment' – making software compatible with human society – is now part of the DNA of AI companies like Anthropic, Google and OpenAI, which is backed by Brad Smith's Microsoft. These companies have developed generative AI models that run in accordance with a constitution of sorts – a set of ethical rules, compiled internally by the companies – that their AI software is supposed to adhere to. For instance, ethics researchers at Google DeepMind, the AI research arm of the search giant, published a paper defining its own set of rules,[2] which aimed for 'helpful, correct and harmless' dialogue. Anthropic's constitution[3] draws from DeepMind's principles, as well as sources like the UN Declaration of Human Rights, Apple's terms of service, and so-called 'non-Western perspectives' (without specifying which ones).

All the companies have warned that their ethical rules are works in progress, and do not wholly reflect humanity's values. In fact, there is no single set of ethics that all cultures and societies ascribe to, anyway. Anthropic has said: 'Obviously, we recognize that this selection reflects our own choices as designers, and in the future, we hope to increase participation in designing constitutions.'[4]

But until we have a more democratic and nuanced method of designing AI values, reflecting the perspectives and biases of cultures around the world, Paolo felt that the work of deciding this powerful technology's ethical limits – and therefore its impact on humanity – shouldn't be left solely to computer scientists. Like many critics of AI, he felt this was the collective job of both the public and private sectors: citizens, alongside institutions of religion, education, government and other multilateral agencies, as well as businesses, from which a diverse set of people could come together and discuss.

As part of this push, Paolo drafted an agreement in 2020 known as the Rome Call.[5] It was to form the basis of a 'humanist' AI ethics constitution. At its heart was an imperative to protect human dignity above any technological advancement. The Rome Call put forward a proposal for 'algor-ethics', a basic framework of human values to be agreed upon by multiple stakeholders around the world, and understood and implemented by machines themselves.

The concept of algor-ethics required all computer software aiding in decision-making to display doubt, and to experience ethical uncertainty. 'Every time the machine does not know whether it is safely protecting human values, then it should require [us] to step in,' Benanti said. Only then can technologists produce software that puts human welfare at its centre.

To hold AI companies to account on these challenges – such as the unintended consequences of AI, built-in biases, harms and ripple effects experienced by users – a global alliance was needed. The Catholic Church knew it didn't have the authority or power to act alone. So, Paolo began to reach out to representatives of the other Abrahamic religions, specifically Islam and Judaism, to form a covenant.

'They see the same issues here, and we want to find a new way together,' Paolo said. The hardest part of coming together would be designing a menu for lunch to satisfy everyone's religious and cultural preferences, he joked. But it was bigger than that, of course.

The first signatories in February 2020 were a small but varied group: Microsoft, IBM, the Italian government and the Food and Agriculture Organization, an agency of the United Nations. In 2023, they were joined by representatives of the Jewish and Islamic faiths at a momentous signing ceremony in the Vatican.[6]

'To my knowledge,' Paolo said, 'these three monotheistic faiths have never come together and signed a joint declaration on anything before.'

*

The religious leaders' concern about AI amplifying inequalities was a legitimate one. Through years of writing about the technology, the pattern that has emerged for me is the extent of the impact of AI on society's marginalized and excluded groups: refugees and migrants, precarious workers, socioeconomic and racial minorities, and women. These same groups are disproportionately affected by generative AI's technical limitations too: hallucinations and negative stereotypes perpetuated in the software's text and image outputs.[7] And it's because they rarely have a voice in the echo chambers in which AI is being built.

It was why I had chosen to narrate the perspectives of people outside of Silicon Valley – those whose views are so often ignored in the design or implementation of new technologies like AI. But while in Rome last year learning about Benanti's framework of 'algor-ethics', I met Brad Smith, the president of Microsoft. Smith was the corporate face of responsible AI – the man who had helped choreograph the Rome Call alongside Paolo, while his company invested $10bn in OpenAI, one of the world's most powerful AI companies. I couldn't resist asking him how he reconciled the two things. I asked him if he truly believed endeavours like these would make any dent at all in the global hegemony of companies like Microsoft or OpenAI.

Smith said all the right things: that technologists needed to connect more with the social sciences, with philosophy, with religion and the humanities, to help them consider the societal impact of the products they made. One reason they hadn't done this very well before, he said, was that there had been very few guardrails imposed by governments.

'You're fundamentally endowing machines to make decisions that previously were made only by humans. So, if we don't do this well, we run the risk of creating more problems than before,' he said.

I knew of Microsoft's own ethical AI charter,[8] the red lines they had drawn for themselves around selling facial-recognition technology to autocrats and American police forces. Yet the technology continued to grow globally, used by democrats and autocrats alike. Would an inclusive, multidisciplinary agreement from *outside* the tech world, I asked him, make any difference at all to its creators?

'I think it matters to some of us,' Smith said. 'And I think increasingly, it's going to matter to almost everybody, technology leaders of the future are going to have to think with a broader perspective, whether they want to or not.'

His argument was that an intellectual and multilateral consensus like the Rome Call could influence centres of power outside the tech industry, such as governments and universities, and ultimately translate into laws that influence businesses such as his own.

In other words, leading thinkers from theology, religion and the humanities may not hold sway over the tech industry, but they can still exert pressure on lawmakers to require more responsible innovation.

'Responsible innovation' has hardly been the mantra of Silicon Valley thus far. Until recently, tech entrepreneurs lived by a motto thought up by Mark Zuckerberg, the founder and chief executive of Facebook: 'move fast and break things'. It captured the industry's emphasis on speedy innovation and experimentation, and its willingness to make mistakes and cause social disruption in the process. Only over the last few years has the high price of these disruptive forces become apparent – from social media's role in electoral manipulation, conspiracy theories and teenage mental ill-health, to app-based ride-and-delivery platforms' impact on workers' rights, and our collective loss of privacy online.

'There were people who were proud that they moved fast and broke things,' Smith told me. 'But eventually, we realized that we don't really want so many things to be broken.'

*

In January 2023, on the day before the Jews and Muslims arrived in the Holy See, the heavens had opened in a mighty storm that washed the sky over Rome clean. Up a winding hill in the heart of the Vatican, past the marbled dome of St Peter's Basilica, walked a group of rabbis, imams and Muslim scholars, from Israel, the United Arab Emirates and California. They were ambling towards Casina Pio IV, a sixteenth-century patrician villa which now housed the Pontifical Academy of Sciences.

This was the first time these men had gathered in the Vatican, global leaders of the three Abrahamic religions joined in a spirit of collaboration. Inside the Villa Pia, they sat facing one another, the archbishops, rabbis and imams, poised to discuss the topic that had brought them together, united by their concerns.

The theme of the day was the urgent need to build AI technology that respected the rights of human beings and minimized any harm. In the audience were also representatives of two of the world's largest technology companies: Microsoft's Brad Smith and IBM's research chief Dario Gil.

They all agreed that AI was one of humanity's most significant innovations. By now, it was clear it was infusing rapidly into daily life. Their concerns, however, were around the control of AI technologies. Like nuclear weapons in the last century, they worried that artificial intelligence systems were not being built with the values and ethics of humanity in mind: mutual respect, solidarity and cooperation for the common good, honesty, justice, integrity and transparency, values they all agreed upon. They felt that thoughtless design of modern-day AI could open the door to abuse, leading to catastrophic consequences for our species. Eighty-nine-year-old Sheikh bin Bayyah of the UAE, recognized by Muslims as one of the greatest living scholars on Islamic jurisprudence, said the current era suggested the writings of the Arab poet Abu al-Fath al-Busti, who had likened human innovation to the silkworm's self-annihilation. *Man toils like the silkworm which spends its life weaving, only to perish, confused, inside its woven creation.*

Their worries mirrored questions being asked by lawmakers around the world, as AI software has grown and spread across the global economy over the past year. I spent two days in Bletchley Park, the UK hub for codebreakers during the Second World War, last November, where state representatives of two dozen nations, from India, Brazil and Nigeria to China, the United States and the European Union, came together with leaders of all the major AI companies including OpenAI, Google DeepMind and Microsoft to discuss these very issues.

Who would be held responsible for the mistakes of artificial intelligence? How would artificial intelligence change the ways in which human beings communicate, learn and consume information? How would the technology affect our behaviour, our beliefs and our consequent actions? How could we avoid AI failures? How, they asked, do we control a system that may prove smarter than we are?

The Bletchley delegates signed a joint statement on the need for action, and the Rome Call proposed six ethical principles for AI designers to live by, which addressed some of these questions. They included making AI systems explainable, inclusive, unbiased, reproducible, privacy-protecting and accountable, meaning they required a human being to take responsibility for any AI-facilitated decision.

As the three religious figureheads – the Islamic legal scholar, the rabbi from Jerusalem and the Catholic archbishop – signed the pact, the room fell silent, a collective holding of breath. People looked around, committing to memory who else was a witness to this strange and historic union. Whatever conflict raged in the world outside, for this moment, the three Abrahamic religions were coming together in defence of humanity.

*

As poignant as that moment was, figuring out the answers to these complex and existential questions cannot be left to religious leaders to work out. As they themselves pointed out to me, their track record on cooperation and moral leadership was far from perfect. Plus, no one was legally required to follow the Rome Call – it was simply a voluntary pledge.

Designing the perfect 'ethical' AI system will be a collective effort. It requires the participation of citizens from across cultures, alongside the corporate inventors and sellers of AI products. It needs the imagination of human artists, writers, actors and musicians whose work is being co-opted to build generative AI, and the expertise of policymakers, economists, academics, philosophers and ethicists, who have seen such waves of radical social change before.

Through writing this book and reporting intensively on AI over the past few years, I arrived at a starting point: a checklist of guiding questions to empower and help reclaim some agency in the use and control of AI. They are not quite as grand as the Rome Call or the Bletchley Declaration. These ten simple questions have been carved out from my interactions with people who think deeply about AI, and from the experiences of the people in this book. They are what I have been asking myself every time I encounter an AI tool. And they're for you, whoever you are, whether you'd like to use, protest or simply understand AI technologies better.

1. What would a fairer and more consistent global wage for AI data workers look like, one that reflects the growing, lucrative market for their services?
2. How do we include marginalized people and other minorities as creators and inventors of AI, without recruiting them for exploitative jobs like content moderation?
3. Which AI-generated or AI-aided products should be clearly advertised to consumers as such, and which of these should come with a human review option, at no personal cost to an individual?

4. How do we know if an AI product is safe, i.e. it can't be hacked or manipulated and isn't discriminatory? If we don't, should it be available to the public at all?
5. Which existing areas of the law can be modified or clarified to take AI into account, e.g. copyright law, privacy law, cybersecurity law, non-discrimination and other human rights laws?
6. How do we bring more diverse expertise into discussions of AI development and legislation – particularly from voices outside the West?
7. If AI products can help to reduce inequities (e.g. in healthcare), are they accessible to communities that need them, rather than just those that can pay?
8. In consequential areas such as employment, criminal justice or welfare, who is accountable for decisions or outcomes of an AI tool, and do they have meaningful control?
9. How do we compensate people (e.g. artists, writers, photographers) for their creativity and expertise, which technology builders today mostly scrape for free to build new AI systems?
10. What are the channels for citizen empowerment in the face of AI, e.g. opting out of AI systems, data deletion from generative AI systems, the right to choose human over automated decisions?

*

When I started out as a technology reporter, I was drawn to AI because of the powerful possibilities it offered – a way to augment human intelligence and solve impossible problems. It could be humanity's ultimate, and perhaps final, invention. In fact, AI is viewed by its many cheerleaders as a transhumanist technology – an extension of ourselves, a species upgrade that could turn us into better, shinier creatures. Demis Hassabis, the chief executive of leading AI company Google DeepMind, often describes his goal simply as 'solving intelligence', as if human intellect were a mathematical equation or a videogame level to complete. The opportunities for the betterment of humanity seemed infinite.

But my quest to find out how AI had transformed the lives of people across the world changed me too. The advances in AI over the past five years have been dramatic and undeniable, but somehow, I became less enamoured of the technology in that time. Language models were certainly impressive, somewhat magical even, in their ability to parse and appear to reason and understand words, but I found that the most inspirational parts of the stories I uncovered were not the sophisticated algorithms and their outputs, but the human beings using and adapting to the technology: doctors, scientists, gig workers, activists and creatives, who represent the very best of us. And while I remain actively optimistic about the social value of AI, I believe that no matter how exceptional a tool is, it only has utility when it preserves human dignity. My hope for AI isn't that it creates a new upgraded species without the messiness of humanity, but that it helps us ordinary, flawed humans live our best and happiest lives.

In Rome, as I waited in the January sunshine outside the Pope's official residence, I got talking to Rabbi David Rosen, the former chief rabbi of Ireland who now heads interreligious affairs at the American Jewish Committee. He was candid: there was an irony, he said, in what he and his peers across the faiths were doing, because religion itself had not been without abuse in its history – the cause of much conflict and bloodshed. All conflict is ultimately caused by power, he told me. Tech companies that operate across borders with their billions of users hold immense power today, and have an outsized impact on the world, reminiscent of the ancient role of religions in society. 'Our role is to remind the tech companies of the follies of power,' he told me.

What, then, does it take to find a solution, a way to mould a powerful technology that is usurping our autonomy into something that elevates us? I wondered aloud, trudging up the serpentine marble staircase inside the Apostolic Palace, alongside Rabbi Rosen and his colleague.

They smiled as we climbed. 'It means many, many steps.'

Acknowledgements

Thank you first and foremost to the people without whom this book simply would not exist. To Ian, Benja, Hiba, Ala, Susan; Helen and Noelle; Karl and Cher; Ashita and Ziad; Diana; Pablo and Norma; Armin; Cori; Maya, and Paolo. Thank you for allowing me to probe your lives, ask infinite questions and tell your stories.

Patrick Walsh plucked this book out of my head and made it real. I couldn't have asked for a more wise, kind and knowledgeable guide to this weird and wonderful world of book publishing. I'm very lucky to have also gained a friend, *consigliere* and cheerleader in the process – thank you.

Heartfelt thanks to Ravi Mirchandani and Tim Duggan – for their wisdom, hard work and skill in shaping this book. Ravi, thank you for seeing the book through my eyes before it was even written. Tim, I'm grateful for your decisiveness and honesty. I'm indebted to Gillian Stern for her empathetic edits, and to Jenn Cheong for her assiduous fact-checking. Philip Gwyn Jones and Grigory Tovbis – thanks for believing in *Code Dependent* from the start.

Thank you to Siobhan Slattery for her boundless enthusiasm, and the wider teams at Picador, Holt and PEW Literary who helped bring this book into the world with such energy, passion and care.

So many people freely shared their expertise as sources, guides and readers for this book. I'll always be grateful for this amazing selflessness. In particular, Mila Miceli, Juan Ortiz Freuler, Carly Kind, Mary Towers, Fieke Jansen, Pete Fussey, James Farrar, Nirit Peled – thank you for the time spent educating and editing me. Thanks to Juanito Vilariño and Paula Cattaneo for helping me navigate Salta – linguistically, geographically and culturally. And huge thanks to Jane Gideon and Christine Spolar for their expert eyes (and pens) that shaped this book into something better.

The Society of Authors' timely grant made much of my travel possible – thank you for allowing me the privilege of reporting this book through my own eyes. And thank you to Helen Mort for allowing me use of her poem from her collection, *The Illustrated Woman*.

I'm lucky to have had the guidance of my writer friends: Oli Franklin-Wallis, who shared all his veteran book-publishing wisdom so freely, Joao Medeiros for helping kick this all off, and to Stephanie Hare for providing feedback on all pages at all stages, and encouraging me to think out loud.

And to friends-like-family: Keya – thank you for reading every word in every version of this book and engaging so deeply with the stories in it. Forever grateful to George, Rati, Nitika, Abha and Darsh for navigating titles, covers, editors and stumbling blocks.

I would not have been able to do this alongside my day job without the encouragement of so many colleagues at the *Financial Times*. My heartfelt thanks to: John Thornhill who read the earliest version of the proposal for this book; Roula Khalaf for the opportunity to lead our coverage of this wild story; India Ross for dozens of WhatsApp brainstorming threads; George Hammond for pointing me to the Heart of Darkness; Matt Vella and Gillian Tett for their advice; my tech team: Murad, Tanya, Tim, Cristina, Sarah, John and Malcolm for all the steadfast support. And to so many others at the *FT* – you know who you are. It's a privilege to work alongside such smart, generous and good humans.

Writing this – or any – book would have been impossible without my family. From my mother, I get my love of stories and of people, which this book is made of. My father's faith in me gifted me self-confidence. My sister is my lifelong soulmate. Thank you for enabling me to juggle writing and parenting, and being my eternal champions. I love you.

To my babies, for magnifying every joy ten-fold and providing perspective.

And finally to David, for the gifts of time, space and unconditional love. For lifting me up, never letting me fall and putting me first always. For you, my words are inadequate.

Endnotes

INTRODUCTION

1 M. Murgia, 'My Identity for Sale', *Wired UK*, October 30, 2014, https://www.wired.co.uk/article/my-identity-for-sale.

2 J. Bridle, 'The Stupidity of AI', *The Guardian*, March 16, 2023, https://www.theguardian.com/technology/2023/mar/16/the-stupidity-of-ai-artificial-intelligence-dall-e-chatgpt#:~:text=They%20enclosed%20our%20imaginations%20in,new%20kinds%20of%20human%20connection.

3 Hanchen Wang et al., 'Scientific Discovery in the Age of Artificial Intelligence', *Nature* 620, no. 7972 (August 3, 2023): 47–60, https://doi.org/10.1038/s41586-023-06221-2.

4 Meredith Whittaker, 'The Steep Cost of Capture', *Interactions* 28, no. 6 (November 10, 2021): 50–55, https://doi.org/10.1145/3488666.

5 V. Eubanks, *Automating Inequality: How High-Tech Tools Profile, Police, and Punish the Poor* (St Martin's Press, 2018).

6 S. Noble, *Algorithms of Oppression: How Search Engines Reinforce Racism* (NYU Press, 2018).

7 Paola Ricaurte, 'Data Epistemologies, The Coloniality of Power, and Resistance', *Television & New Media* 20, no. 4 (May 7, 2019): 350–65, https://doi.org/10.1177/1527476419831640.

8 Michael Roberts et al., 'Common Pitfalls and Recommendations for Using Machine Learning to Detect and Prognosticate for COVID-19 Using Chest Radiographs and CT Scans', *Nature Machine Intelligence* 3, no. 3 (March 15, 2021): 199–217, https://doi.org/10.1038/s42256-021-00307-0.

9 Albert Bandura, 'Toward a Psychology of Human Agency', *Perspectives on*

Psychological Science 1, no. 2 (June 24, 2006): 164–80, https://doi.org/10.1111/j.1745-6916.2006.00011.x.

CHAPTER 1: YOUR LIVELIHOOD

1 Inc. Grand View Research, 'GVR Report Cover Data Collection And Labeling Market Size, Share & Trends Analysis Report By Data Type (Audio, Image/Video, Text), By Vertical (IT, Automotive, Government, Healthcare, BFSI), By Region, And Segment Forecasts, 2023–2030', March 30, 2023, https://www.grandviewresearch.com/industry-analysis/data-collection-labeling-market?utm_source=prnewswire&utm_medium=referral&utm_campaign=ICT_30-March-23&utm_term=data_collection_labeling_market&utm_content=rd1.

2 Karen Hao and Andrea Paola Hernández, 'How the AI Industry Profits from Catastrophe', *MIT Technology Review*, April 20, 2022, https://www.technologyreview.com/2022/04/20/1050392/ai-industry-appen-scale-data-labels/.

3 Madhumita Murgia, 'AI's New Workforce: The Data-Labelling Industry Spreads Globally', *Financial Times*, June 24, 2019, https://www.ft.com/content/56dde36c-aa40-11e9-984c-fac8325aaa04.

4 Mary L. Gray and Siddharth Suri, *Ghost Work: How to Stop Silicon Valley from Building a New Global Underclass* (Houghton Mifflin Harcourt Publishing, 2019).

5 Sama, 'Sama by the Numbers', February 11, 2022, https://www.sama.com/blog/building-an-ethical-supply-chain/.

6 Sama, 'Environmental & Social Impact Report', June 14, 2022, https://etjdg74ic5h.exactdn.com/wp-content/uploads/2023/07/Impact-Report-2023-2.pdf.

7 Ayenat Mersie, 'Court Rules Meta Can Be Sued in Kenya over Alleged Unlawful Redundancies', Reuters, April 20, 2023, https://www.reuters.com/technology/court-rules-meta-can-be-sued-kenya-over-alleged-unlawful-redundancies-2023-04-20/.

8 David Pilling and Madhumita Murgia, '"You Can't Unsee It": The Content Moderators Taking on Facebook', *Financial Times*, May 18, 2023, https://www.ft.com/content/afeb56f2-9ba5-4103-890d-91291aea4caa.

9 Billy Perrigo, 'Inside Facebook's African Sweatshop', *Time*, February 17, 2022, https://time.com/6147458/facebook-africa-content-moderation-employee-treatment/.

10 Milagros Miceli and Julian Posada, 'The Data-Production Dispositif', *CSCW 2022. Forthcoming in the Proceedings of the ACM on Human-Computer Interaction*, May 24, 2022, 1–37.

11 Dave Lee, 'Why Big Tech Pays Poor Kenyans to Teach Self-Driving Cars', BBC News, November 3, 2018, https://www.bbc.co.uk/news/technology-46055595.

CHAPTER 2: YOUR BODY

1 Meredith Somers, 'Deepfakes, Explained', *MIT Sloan Management Review*, July 21, 2020, https://mitsloan.mit.edu/ideas-made-to-matter/deepfakes-explained#:~:text=The%20term%20%E2%80%9Cdeepfake%E2%80%9D%20was%20first,open%20source%20face%2Dswapping%20technology.

2 Karen Hao, 'Deepfake Porn Is Ruining Women's Lives. Now the Law May Finally Ban It', *MIT Technology Review*, February 21, 2021, https://www.technologyreview.com/2021/02/12/1018222/deepfake-revenge-porn-coming-ban/.

3 James Vincent, 'Facebook's Problems Moderating Deepfakes Will Only Get Worse in 2020', *The Verge*, January 15, 2020, https://www.theverge.com/2020/1/15/21067220/deepfake-moderation-apps-tools-2020-facebook-reddit-social-media.

4 Tiffany Hsu, 'As Deepfakes Flourish, Countries Struggle With Response', *The New York Times Magazine*, January 22, 2023, https://www.nytimes.com/2023/01/22/business/media/deepfake-regulation-difficulty.html.

5 Helen Mort, 'This Is Wild', in *Extra Teeth – Issue Four*, ed. Katie Goh (Edinburgh: Extra Teeth, 2021), https://www.extrateeth.co.uk/shop/issuefour.

6 Samantha Cole, 'Creator of DeepNude, App That Undresses Photos of Women, Takes It Offline', *Vice News*, June 29, 2019, https://www.vice.com/en/article/qv7agw/deepnude-app-that-undresses-photos-of-women-takes-it-offline.

7 Matt Burgess, 'The Biggest Deepfake Abuse Site Is Growing in Disturbing Ways', *Wired*, December 15, 2021, https://www.wired.co.uk/article/deepfake-nude-abuse.

8 Ibid.

9 Matt Burgess, 'A Deepfake Porn Bot Is Being Used to Abuse Thousands of Women', *Wired*, October 28, 2020, https://www.wired.co.uk/article/telegram-deepfakes-deepnude-ai.

10 Ibid.
11 Rachel Metz, 'She Thought a Dark Moment in Her Past Was Forgotten. Then She Scanned Her Face Online', *CNN Business*, May 24, 2022, https://edition.cnn.com/2022/05/24/tech/cher-scarlett-facial-recognition-trauma/index.html.
12 Carrie Goldberg, *Nobody's Victim: Fighting Psychos, Stalkers, Pervs, and Trolls* (Little, Brown and Company, 2019).
13 Margaret Talbot, 'The Attorney Fighting Revenge Porn', *The New Yorker*, November 27, 2016, https://www.newyorker.com/magazine/2016/12/05/the-attorney-fighting-revenge-porn.
14 'Section 230', EFF, n.d., https://www.eff.org/issues/cda230.
15 Haleluya Hadero, 'Deepfake Porn Could Be a Growing Problem Amid AI Race', Associated Press News, April 16, 2023, https://apnews.com/article/deepfake-porn-celebrities-dalle-stable-diffusion-midjourney-ai-e7935e9922cda82fbcfb1e1a88d9443a.
16 Ibid.
17 Molly Williams, 'Sheffield Writer Launches Campaign over "Deepfake Porn" after Finding Own Face Used in Violent Sexual Images', *The Star News*, July 21, 2021, https://www.thestar.co.uk/news/politics/sheffield-writer-launches-campaign-over-deepfake-porn-after-finding-own-face-used-in-violent-sexual-images-3295029.
18 'Facts and Figures: Women's Leadership and Political Participation', The United Nations Entity for Gender Equality and the Empowerment of Women, March 7, 2023, https://www.unwomen.org/en/what-we-do/leadership-and-political-participation/facts-and-figures.
19 Jeffery Dastin, 'Amazon Scraps Secret AI Recruiting Tool That Showed Bias against Women', Reuters, October 11, 2018, https://www.reuters.com/article/us-amazon-com-jobs-automation-insight-idUSKCN1MK08G.
20 Mary Ann Sieghart, *The Authority Gap: Why Women Are Still Taken Less Seriously Than Men, and What We Can Do about It* (Transworld, 2021).
21 Steven Feldstein, 'How Artificial Intelligence Systems Could Threaten Democracy', Carnegie Endowment for International Peace, April 24, 2019, https://carnegieendowment.org/2019/04/24/how-artificial-intelligence-systems-could-threaten-democracy-pub-78984.
22 'Deepfakes, Synthetic Media and Generative AI', WITNESS, 2018, https://www.gen-ai.witness.org/.
23 Yinka Bokinni, 'Inside the Metaverse' (United Kingdom: Channel 4, April 25, 2022).

24 Yinka Bokinni, 'A Barrage of Assault, Racism and Rape Jokes: My Nightmare Trip into the Metaverse', *Guardian*, April 25, 2022, https://www.theguardian.com/tv-and-radio/2022/apr/25/a-barrage-of-assault-racism-and-jokes-my-nightmare-trip-into-the-metaverse.

CHAPTER 3: YOUR IDENTITY

1 Nina Dewi Toft Djanegara, 'How 9/11 Sparked the Rise of America's Biometrics Security Empire', *Fast Company*, September 10, 2021, https://www.fastcompany.com/90674661/how-9-11-sparked-the-rise-of-americas-biometrics-security-empire.

2 Kashmir Hill, 'The Secretive Company That Might End Privacy as We Know It', *The New York Times*, January 18, 2020, https://www.nytimes.com/2020/01/18/technology/clearview-privacy-facial-recognition.html.

3 Paul Mozur, 'In Hong Kong Protests, Faces Become Weapons', *The New York Times*, July 26, 2019, https://www.nytimes.com/2019/07/26/technology/hong-kong-protests-facial-recognition-surveillance.html; Stephen Kafeero, 'Uganda Is Using Huawei's Facial Recognition Tech to Crack Down on Dissent after Anti-Government Protests', *Quartz*, November 27, 2020, https://qz.com/africa/1938976/uganda-uses-chinas-huawei-facial-recognition-to-snare-protesters; Alexandra Ulmer and Zeba Siddiqui, 'India's Use of Facial Recognition Tech during Protests Causes Stir', Reuters, February 17, 2020, https://www.reuters.com/article/us-india-citizenship-protests-technology-idUSKBN20B0ZQ.

4 James Vincent, 'FBI Used Facial Recognition to Identify a Capitol Rioter from His Girlfriend's Instagram Posts', *The Verge*, April 21, 2021, https://www.theverge.com/2021/4/21/22395323/fbi-facial-recognition-us-capital-riots-tracked-down-suspect; James Vincent, 'NYPD Used Facial Recognition to Track down Black Lives Matter Activist', *The Verge*, August 18, 2020, https://www.theverge.com/2020/8/18/21373316/nypd-facial-recognition-black-lives-matter-activist-derrick-ingram.

5 Madhumita Murgia, 'How One London Wine Bar Helped Brazil to Cut Crime', *Financial Times*, February 8, 2019, https://www.ft.com/content/605de54a-1e90-11e9-b126-46fc3ad87c65.

6 Johana Bhuiyan, 'Ukraine Uses Facial Recognition Software to Identify Russian Soldiers Killed in Combat', *The Guardian*, March 24, 2022.

7 Joy Buolamwini and Timnit Gebru, 'Gender Shades', MIT Media Lab, 2018, http://gendershades.org/index.html.

8 Kashmir Hill, 'Another Arrest, and Jail Time, Due to a Bad Facial Recognition Match', *The New York Times*, December 29, 2020, https://www.nytimes.com/2020/12/29/technology/facial-recognition-misidentify-jail.html.
9 Kashmir Hill, 'Wrongfully Accused by an Algorithm', *The New York Times*, June 24, 2020, https://www.nytimes.com/2020/06/24/technology/facial-recognition-arrest.html.
10 Antonia Noori Farzan, 'Sri Lankan Police Wrongly Identify Brown University Student as Wanted Suspect in Terror Attack', *The Washington Post*, April 26, 2019, https://www.washingtonpost.com/nation/2019/04/26/sri-lankan-police-wrongly-identify-brown-university-student-wanted-suspect-terror-attack/.
11 Madhumita Venkataramanan, 'The Superpower Police Now Use to Tackle Crime', BBC Online, June 11, 2015, https://www.bbc.com/future/article/20150611-the-superpower-police-now-use-to-tackle-crime.
12 Chris Nuttall, 'London Sets Standard for Surveillance Societies', *Financial Times*, August 1, 2019, https://www.ft.com/content/70b35f8a-b47f-11e9-bec9-fdcab53d6959.
13 Madhumita Murgia, 'London's King's Cross Uses Facial Recognition in Security Cameras', *Financial Times*, August 12, 2019, https://www.ft.com/content/8cbcb3ae-babd-11e9-8a88-aa6628ac896c.
14 ICO, 'Information Commissioner's Opinion: The Use of Live Facial Recognition Technology in Public Places' (London: June 18, 2021).
15 Yuan Yang and Madhumita Murgia, 'Facial recognition: how China cornered the surveillance market', *Financial Times*, December 6, 2019, https://www.ft.com/content/6f1a8f48-1813-11ea-9ee4-11f260415385.
16 Suresh K. Pandey, 'We Are Using the Facial Recognition System and Taking the Help of CCTV and Video Footage to Identify the Accused', said the Delhi Police Commissioner at the Time. 'No Culprit Will Be Spared.' *Outlook India*, January 27, 2021, https://www.outlookindia.com/website/story/india-news-facial-recognition-software-being-used-to-track-those-who-instigated-violence-during-tractor-parade-delhi-police/372380.
17 Hannah Ellis-Petersen and Aakash Hassan, 'Riot Police Attempt to Clear Farmers from Delhi Protest Camp', *The Guardian*, January 29, 2021, https://www.theguardian.com/world/2021/jan/29/riot-police-attempt-to-clear-farmers-from-delhi-protest-camp.
18 Ben Wright, '"It's Game Over": How China Used Its Technotyranny to Crush Dissent', *The Telegraph*, December 4, 2022, https://www.telegraph.

co.uk/business/2022/12/04/how-chinas-technotyranny-has-crushed-lockdown-protests/.

19 Samuel Woodhams, 'Huawei Says Its Surveillance Tech Will Keep African Cities Safe but Activists Worry It'll Be Misused', *Quartz*, March 20, 2020, https://qz.com/africa/1822312/huaweis-surveillance-tech-in-africa-worries-activists.

20 Risdel Kasasira, '45 Dead in Uganda after Arrest of Pop Star Opposition Leader', *Irish Independent*, November 24, 2020, https://www.independent.ie/world-news/45-dead-in-uganda-after-arrest-of-pop-star-opposition-leader/39784406.html.

21 Tambiama Madiega and Hendrik Mildebrath, 'Regulating Facial Recognition in the EU', Publications Office of the European Union, September 2021, https://doi.org/10.2861/140928.

22 Rishabh R. Jain, 'Hyderabad Symbolizes India's Embrace of Surveillance, Facial Recognition Tech', *The Diplomat*, December 20, 2022, https://thediplomat.com/2022/12/hyderabad-symbolizes-indias-embrace-of-surveillance-facial-recognition-tech/.

23 Padma Priya, 'Muslims Falsely Accused in Mecca Masjid Blast Angry, Disappointed After Verdict', *The Wire*, April 17, 2018, https://thewire.in/security/muslims-falsely-accused-in-mecca-masjid-blast-angry-disappointed-after-verdict.

24 Aafaqm Zafar, 'Why India's Privileged Citizens Are Cheerleaders for Surveillance Tech', *Scroll.In*, May 26, 2023, https://scroll.in/article/1049693/why-indias-privileged-citizens-are-cheerleaders-for-surveillance-tech.

25 Jane Croft and Siddharth Venkataramakrishnan, 'Police Use of Facial Recognition Breaches Human Rights Law, London Court Rules', *Financial Times*, August 11, 2020, https://www.ft.com/content/b79e0bee-d32a-4d8e-b9b4-c8ffd3ac23f4.

CHAPTER 4: YOUR HEALTH

1 National Rural Health Mission, 'Seventh Common Review Mission – Maharashtra', February 11, 2014, https://nhm.gov.in/images/pdf/monitoring/crm/7th-crm/report/7th_CRM_Report_Maharashrta.pdf.

2 Albert Bandura, 'Toward a Psychology of Human Agency', *Perspectives on Psychological Science* 1, no. 2 (June 24, 2006): 164–80, https://doi.org/10.1111/j.1745-6916.2006.00011.x.

3 'Qure.ai Appoints Dr. Shibu Vijayan as Medical Director – Global Health', Qure.ai, September 28, 2022, https://www.qure.ai/news_press_coverages/qure-ai-appoints-dr-shibu-vijayan-as-medical-director-global-health.

4 Anjali Singh, 'Qure.ai, PATH India Partner to Provide TB, Covid Screening in Maharashtra', *Business Standard*, September 14, 2023, https://www.business-standard.com/companies/news/qure-ai-path-india-partner-to-provide-tb-covid-screening-in-maharashtra-123091400652_1.html.

5 Kritti Bhalla, 'Qure.ai Raises $40 Million to Expand Its Presence in US and Europe', *Business Insider*, March 29, 2022, https://www.businessinsider.in/business/startups/news/qure-ai-raises-40-million-to-expand-its-presence-in-us-and-europe/articleshow/90514343.cms; Singh, 'Qure.ai, PATH India Partner to Provide TB, Covid Screening in Maharashtra'.

6 'India COVID Death Toll Crosses 400,000 – Half Died in Second Wave', Al Jazeera, July 2, 2021, https://www.aljazeera.com/news/2021/7/2/india-covid-death-toll-400000-black-fungus.

7 V. P. Sharma and Vas Dev, 'Prospects of Malaria Control in Northeastern India with Particular Reference to Assam', January 2006, https://www.nirth.res.in/publications/nsth/4.VP.Sharma.pdf.

8 Atul Gawande, *Complications: A Surgeon's Notes on an Imperfect Science* (Profile Books Ltd, 2002).

9 Sendhil Mullainathan and Ziad Obermeyer, 'Diagnosing Physician Error: A Machine Learning Approach to Low-Value Health Care', *The Quarterly Journal of Economics* 137, no. 2 (April 8, 2022): 679–727, https://doi.org/10.1093/qje/qjab046.

10 '2019 Community Health Needs Assessment – Focus Group Results', n.d., Fort Defiance Indian Hospital Board, Inc., https://www.fdihb.org/documents/FDIHBInc_Community_Health_Needs_Assessment_2021-2022.pdf.

11 Ana M. Cabanas, Pilar Martín-Escudero, and Kirk H. Shelley, 'Improving Pulse Oximetry Accuracy in Dark-Skinned Patients: Technical Aspects and Current Regulations', *British Journal of Anaesthesia* 131, no. 4 (October 2023): 640–44, https://doi.org/10.1016/j.bja.2023.07.005.

12 Michael W. Sjoding et al., 'Racial Bias in Pulse Oximetry Measurement', *New England Journal of Medicine* 383, no. 25 (December 17, 2020): 2477–78, https://doi.org/10.1056/NEJMc2029240.

13 Kari Paul, 'Healthcare Algorithm Used across America Has Dramatic Racial

Biases', *The Guardian*, October 25, 2019, https://www.theguardian.com/society/2019/oct/25/healthcare-algorithm-racial-biases-optum.

14 Ziad Obermeyer et al., 'Dissecting Racial Bias in an Algorithm Used to Manage the Health of Populations', *Science* 366, no. 6464 (October 25, 2019): 447–53, https://doi.org/10.1126/science.aax2342.

15 Jayne Williamson-Lee, 'A.I. Tool Narrows Pain Disparity for Black Patients with Knee Osteoarthritis, Study Finds', *The Science Writer*, July 30, 2021, https://www.thesciencewriter.org/issue-1/ai-tool-narrows-pain-disparity-for-black-patients-with-knee-osteoarthritis-study-finds.

16 Emma Pierson et al., 'An Algorithmic Approach to Reducing Unexplained Pain Disparities in Underserved Populations', *Nature Medicine* 27, no. 1 (January 13, 2021): 136–40, https://doi.org/10.1038/s41591-020-01192-7.

17 ReportLinker, 'The Global Artificial Intelligence (AI) in Medical Diagnostics Market Size Is Expected to Reach $7.3 Billion by 2028, Rising at a Market Growth of 39.6% CAGR during the Forecast Period', *Globe Newswire*, November 23, 2022, https://www.globenewswire.com/news-release/2022/11/23/2561775/0/en/The-Global-Artificial-Intelligence-AI-in-Medical-Diagnostics-Market-size-is-expected-to-reach-7-3-billion-by-2028-rising-at-a-market-growth-of-39-6-CAGR-during-the-forecast-period.html.

18 Kasumi Widner and Sunny Virmani, 'New Milestones in Helping Prevent Eye Disease with Verily', Google, February 25, 2019, https://blog.google/technology/health/new-milestones-helping-prevent-eye-disease-verily/.

19 Wadhwani AI, 'We Are a Google AI Impact Grantee', Wadhwani AI, May 7, 2019, https://www.wadhwaniai.org/2019/05/we-are-a-google-ai-impact-grantee/.

20 Wadhwani AI, 'Laying Data Pipelines to Identify Low Birth Weight Babies', Wadhwani AI, February 1, 2021, https://www.wadhwaniai.org/2021/02/laying-pipelines/.

CHAPTER 5: YOUR FREEDOM

1 Jacqueline Wientjes et al., 'Identifying Potential Offenders on the Basis of Police Records: Development and Validation of the ProKid Risk Assessment Tool', *Journal of Criminological Research, Policy and Practice* 3, no. 4 (December 4, 2017): 249–60, https://doi.org/10.1108/JCRPP-01-2017-0008.

2 Nirit Peled, *MOTHERS* (Netherlands: VRPO, 2022).
3 Ishmael Mugari and Emeka E. Obioha, 'Predictive Policing and Crime Control in The United States of America and Europe: Trends in a Decade of Research and the Future of Predictive Policing', *Social Sciences* 10, no. 6 (June 20, 2021): 234, https://doi.org/10.3390/socsci10060234.
4 Kathleen McKendrick, 'Artificial Intelligence Prediction and Counterterrorism', August 2019, https://www.chathamhouse.org/sites/default/files/2019-08-07-AICounterterrorism.pdf.
5 Julia Angwin et al., 'Machine Bias', *ProPublica*, May 23, 2016, https://www.propublica.org/article/machine-bias-risk-assessments-in-criminal-sentencing.
6 Anouk de Koning, '"Handled with Care": Diffuse Policing and the Production of Inequality in Amsterdam', *Ethnography* 18, no. 4 (December 28, 2017): 535–55, https://doi.org/10.1177/1466138117696107.
7 Ibid.
8 'Automating Injustice: The Use of Artificial Intelligence & Automated Decision-Making Systems in Criminal Justice in Europe', Fair Trials, September 9, 2021, https://www.fairtrials.org/articles/publications/automating-injustice/.
9 Peled.
10 Fieke Jansen, 'Top400: A Top-down Crime Prevention Strategy in Amsterdam' (Amsterdam, November 2022), https://pilpnjcm.nl/wp-content/uploads/2022/11/Top400_topdown-crime-prevention-Amsterdam.pdf.
11 Wientjes et al.
12 Jansen.
13 Peled.
14 Peled.
15 Paul Mutsaers and Tom van Nuenen, 'Predictively Policed: The Dutch CAS Case and Its Forerunners', in *Policing Race, Ethnicity and Culture*, ed. Jan Beek et al. (Manchester University Press, 2023), https://doi.org/10.7765/9781526165596.00010.
16 Sam Corbett-Davies et al., 'A Computer Program Used for Bail and Sentencing Decisions Was Labeled Biased against Blacks. It's Actually Not That Clear', *The Washington Post*, October 17, 2016, https://www.washingtonpost.com/news/monkey-cage/wp/2016/10/17/can-an-algorithm-be-racist-our-analysis-is-more-cautious-than-propublicas/.

17 Reine C. van der Wal, Johan C. Karremans, and Antonius H. N. Cillessen, 'Causes and Consequences of Children's Forgiveness', *Child Development Perspectives* 11, no. 2 (June 2017): 97–101, https://doi.org/10.1111/cdep.12216.

18 Dr Karolina La Fors, 'Legal Remedies For a Forgiving Society: Children's Rights, Data Protection Rights and the Value of Forgiveness in AI-Mediated Risk Profiling of Children by Dutch Authorities', *Computer Law & Security Review* 38, no. 105430 (September 2020): 105430, https://doi.org/10.1016/j.clsr.2020.105430.

CHAPTER 6: YOUR SAFETY NET

1 'INDEC: Poverty Rose in Second Half of 2022, Affecting 39.2% of Argentina's Population', *Buenos Aires Times*, March 30, 2023, https://www.batimes.com.ar/news/argentina/indec-poverty-affected-392-of-argentinas-population-in-second-half-of-2022.phtml.

2 Mariana Sarramea, 'Adolescent Birth Rate in Argentina Has Not Dropped for 20 Years', *Buenos Aires Times*, September 25, 2019, https://www.batimes.com.ar/news/argentina/adolescent-birth-rate-in-argentina-has-not-dropped-for-20-years.phtml#:~:text=The%20situation%20worsens%20in%20terms,10%20and%2019%20years%20old.

3 'Supporting Rural and Indigenous Women in Argentina as Gender-Based Violence Rises during the COVID-19 Pandemic', UN Women, October 15, 2021, https://lac.unwomen.org/en/noticias-y-eventos/articulos/2021/10/apoyo-a-las-mujeres-rurales-e-indigenas-de-argentina.

4 Philip Alston, 'Report of the Special Rapporteur on Extreme Poverty and Human Rights. Promotion and Protection of Human Rights: Human Rights Questions, Including Alternative Approaches for Improving the Effective Enjoyment of Human Rights and Fundamental Freedoms. A/74/48037. Seventy-Fourth Session. Item 72(b) of the Provisional Agenda', United Nations Human Rights Office of the High Commissioner, October 11, 2019, https://www.ohchr.org/en/documents/thematic-reports/a74493-digital-welfare-states-and-human-rights-report-special-rapporteur.

5 Diego Jemio, Alexa Hagerty, and Florencia Aranda, 'The Case of the Creepy Algorithm That "Predicted" Teen Pregnancy', *Wired*, February 16,

2022, https://www.wired.com/story/argentina-algorithms-pregnancy-prediction/.

6 Paz Peña and Joana Varon, 'Decolonising AI: A Transfeminist Approach to Data and Social Justice', Coding Rights, March 3, 2020, https://medium.com/codingrights/decolonising-ai-a-transfeminist-approach-to-data-and-social-justice-a5e52ac72a96.

7 'Sobre La Predicción Automática de Embarazos Adolescentes', Laboratorio de Inteligencia Artificial Aplicada, 2018, https://liaa.dc.uba.ar/es/sobre-la-prediccion-automatica-de-embarazos-adolescentes/.

8 Brad Smith, 'The Need for a Digital Geneva Convention', Microsoft, February 14, 2017; 'Microsoft France Announces $30 Million Commitment towards the Development of Ethical and Trusted Artificial Intelligence', Microsoft, March 29, 2018, https://news.microsoft.com/europe/2018/03/29/microsoft-france-announces-30-million-commitment-towards-the-development-of-ethical-and-trusted-artificial-intelligence/#:~:text=Microsoft%20France%20announces%20%2430%20million,ethical%20and%20trusted%20Artificial%20Intelligence&text=Microsoft%20France%20has%20announced%20a,artificial%20intelligence%20(AI)%20development.

9 Foo Yun Chee, 'Microsoft President Goes to Europe to Shape AI Regulation Debate', Reuters, June 30, 2023, https://www.reuters.com/technology/microsoft-president-goes-europe-shape-ai-regulation-debate-2023-06-29/.

10 Laura Schenquer and Julia Risler, 'Opinion Polls and Surveys in the BANADE Archives: A Productive Use of Governmental Technologies by the Last Military Dictatorship in Argentina (1976–1983)', *Canadian Journal of Latin American and Caribbean Studies* 44, no. 2 (May 4, 2019): 225–42, https://doi.org/10.1080/08263663.2019.1602937.

11 J. Patrice McSherry, 'Tracking the Origins of a State Terror Network: Operation Condor', *Latin American Perspectives* 29, no. 1 (2002): 38–60, http://www.jstor.org/stable/3185071.

CHAPTER 7: YOUR BOSS

1 Troy Griggs and Daisuke Wakabayashi, 'How a Self-Driving Uber Killed a Pedestrian in Arizona', *The New York Times*, March 21, 2018, https://www.nytimes.com/interactive/2018/03/20/us/self-driving-uber-pedestrian-killed.html.

2 Tyler Sonnemaker, 'UberEats Could Be Underpaying Delivery Drivers on 21% of Trips, According to a Programmer Who Reportedly Built a Tool That Found the App Was Lowballing the Miles That Drivers Traveled', *Business Insider*, August 21, 2020, https://www.businessinsider.com/uber-eats-driver-who-scraped-data-alleges-wage-theft-report-2020-8?r=US&IR=T.

3 Matthew Gault, 'Uber Shuts Down App That Told Drivers If Uber Underpaid Them', *Vice News*, February 18, 2021, https://www.vice.com/en/article/wx8yvm/uber-shuts-down-app-that-lets-users-know-how-badly-theyve-been-cheated.

4 Guy Standing, *The Precariat: The New Dangerous Class* (Bloomsbury Publishing, 2011).

5 Heather Stewart, '"Stop or I'll Fire You": The Driver Who Defied Uber's Automated HR', *The Guardian*, April 16, 2023, https://www.theguardian.com/technology/2023/apr/16/stop-or-ill-fire-you-the-driver-who-defied-ubers-automated-hr.

6 Delphine Strauss and Siddharth Venkataramakrishnan, 'Dutch Court Rulings Break New Ground on Gig Worker Data Rights', *Financial Times*, March 12, 2021, https://www.ft.com/content/334d1ca5-26af-40c7-a9c5-c76e3e57fba1.

7 Amanda Sperber and Nichole Sobecki, 'Uber Made Big Promises in Kenya. Drivers Say It's Ruined Their Lives', *Pulitzer Center*, December 1, 2020, https://pulitzercenter.org/stories/uber-made-big-promises-kenya-drivers-say-its-ruined-their-lives.

8 Karen Hao and Nadine Freischlad, 'The Gig Workers Fighting Back against the Algorithms', *MIT Technology Review*, April 21, 2022, https://www.technologyreview.com/2022/04/21/1050381/the-gig-workers-fighting-back-against-the-algorithms/.

9 Ibid.

10 Cosmin Popan, 'Embodied Precariat and Digital Control in the "Gig Economy": The Mobile Labor of Food Delivery Workers', *Journal of Urban Technology*, December 16, 2021, 1–20, https://doi.org/10.1080/10630732.2021.2001714.

11 Zizheng Yu, Emiliano Treré, and Tiziano Bonini, 'The Emergence of Algorithmic Solidarity: Unveiling Mutual Aid Practices and Resistance among Chinese Delivery Workers', *Media International Australia* 183, no. 1 (May 24, 2022): 107–23, https://doi.org/10.1177/1329878X221074793.

12 Popan.
13 Edward Jr Ongweso, 'Organized DoorDash Drivers' #DeclineNow Strategy Is Driving Up Their Pay', *Vice News*, February 21, 2021, https://www.vice.com/en/article/3anwdy/organized-doordash-drivers-declinenow-strategy-is-driving-up-their-pay.
14 Gianluca Iazzolino, '"Going Karura": Colliding Subjectivities and Labour Struggle in Nairobi's Gig Economy', *Environment and Planning A: Economy and Space* 55, no. 5 (August 19, 2023): 1114–30, https://doi.org/10.1177/0308518X211031916.
15 Veena Dubal, 'On Algorithmic Wage Discrimination', *SSRN Electronic Journal* forthcoming (2023), https://doi.org/10.2139/ssrn.4331080.
16 Eloise Barry, 'Uber Drivers Say a "Racist" Algorithm Is Putting Them Out of Work', *Time*, October 12, 2021, https://time.com/6104844/uber-facial-recognition-racist/.
17 Daniel Alan Bey, 'Will "Common Prosperity" Reach China's Takeout Drivers?', *The Diplomat*, March 12, 2022, https://thediplomat.com/2022/03/will-common-prosperity-reach-chinas-takeout-drivers/.
18 Javier Madariaga et al., 'Economía de Plataformas y Empleo ¿Cómo Es Trabajar Para Una App En Argentina?', Centro de Implementación de Políticas Públicas para la Equidad y el Crecimiento (Buenos Aires, May 2019), https://www.cippec.org/wp-content/uploads/ 2019/05/Como-es-trabajar-en-una-app-en-Argentina-CIPPEC-BID-LAB-OIT.pdf.
19 Kate Conger, 'A Worker-Owned Cooperative Tries to Compete With Uber and Lyft', *The New York Times*, May 28, 2021, https://www.nytimes.com/2021/05/28/technology/nyc-uber-lyft-the-drivers-cooperative.html#:~:text=%E2%80%9CThe%20starting%20point%20for%20this,what%20works%20best%20for%20them.%E2%80%9D.
20 Megan Rose Dickey, 'The Drivers Cooperative Thinks Ridehailing Should Be Owned by Drivers, Not Venture Capitalists', *Protocol*, August 20, 2021, https://www.protocol.com/workplace/drivers-cooperative-uber-lyft.
21 Catrin Nye and Sam Bright, 'Altab Ali: The Racist Murder That Mobilised the East End', BBC Online, May 4, 2016, https://www.bbc.co.uk/news/uk-england-london-36191020.
22 Sarah Butler, 'Uber Drivers Entitled to Workers' Rights, UK Supreme Court Rules', *The Guardian*, February 19, 2021, https://www.theguardian.com/technology/2021/feb/19/uber-drivers-workers-uk-

supreme-court-rules-rights#:~:text=It%20ruled%20that%20Uber%20must,challenge%20unfair%20dismissal%2C%20for%20example.

23 'Gig Win: Canada Supreme Court Rules in Favour of UberEats Driver', Al Jazeera, June 26, 2020, https://www.aljazeera.com/economy/2020/6/26/gig-win-canada-supreme-court-rules-in-favour-of-ubereats-driver#:~:text=Canada's%20Supreme%20Court%20on%20Friday,in%20Canada%20as%20company%20employees.; Christoph Stutz and Andreas Becker, 'Switzerland: Uber Drivers Qualify as Gainfully Employed from a Social Security Perspective,' Baker McKenzie, March 29, 2023, https://insightplus.bakermckenzie.com/bm/viewContent.action?key=Ec8teaJ9Var7Qlnw%2Bl5ArV7eOOGbnAEFKCLORG72fHz0%2BNbpi2jDfaB8lgiEyY1JAvAvaah9lF3dzoxprWhI6w%3D%3D&nav=FRbANEucS95NMLRN47z%2BeeOgEFCt8EGQ0qFfoEM4UR4%3D&emailtofriendview=true&freeviewlink=true; Tassilo Hummel, 'French Court Orders Uber to Pay Some $18 Mln to Drivers, Company to Appeal', Reuters, January 20, 2023, https://www.reuters.com/business/autos-transportation/french-court-orders-uber-pay-some-18-mln-drivers-company-appeal-2023-01-20/#:~:text=In%202020%2C%20France's%20top%20court,workers%20such%20as%20paid%20holidays.

24 Peter Guest, '"We're All Fighting the Giant": Gig Workers around the World Are Finally Organizing', *Rest of World*, September 21, 2021, https://restofworld.org/2021/gig-workers-around-the-world-are-finally-organizing/.

25 Guest.

26 Yu, Treré, and Bonini, 'The Emergence of Algorithmic Solidarity: Unveiling Mutual Aid Practices and Resistance among Chinese Delivery Workers'.

27 Lily Kuo, 'Drivers in Kenya Are Protesting against Being "Uber Slaves"', *Quartz*, August 2, 2016, https://qz.com/africa/748149/drivers-in-kenya-are-protesting-against-being-uber-slaves; Meghan Tobin, 'How China's Food Delivery Apps Push Gig Workers to Strike', *Rest of World*, March 23, 2021, https://restofworld.org/2021/china-delivery-apps-strike-labor-meituan/.

CHAPTER 8: YOUR RIGHTS

1 Madhumita Murgia, 'Facebook Content Moderators Required to Sign PTSD Forms', *Financial Times*, January 26, 2020, https://www.ft.com/content/98aad2f0-3ec9-11ea-a01a-bae547046735.

2 Afiq Fitri, 'The UK Has Spent up to £1bn on Drones to Prevent Migrant Crossings', *Tech Monitor*, April 4, 2022, https://techmonitor.ai/government-computing/uk-spent-1bn-drones-prevent-migrant-crossings.

3 Robert Booth, 'UK Warned over Lack of Transparency on Use of AI to Vet Welfare Claims', *The Guardian*, September 3, 2023, https://www.theguardian.com/politics/2023/sep/03/uk-warned-over-lack-transparency-use-ai-vet-welfare-claims#:~:text=The%20DWP%20recently%20expanded%20its,to%20assess%20claimants'%20savings%20declarations.

4 Helen Warrell, 'Home Office under Fire for Using Secretive Visa Algorithm', *Financial Times*, June 9, 2019, https://www.ft.com/content/0206dd56-87b0-11e9-a028-86cea8523dc2.

5 Henry McDonald, 'Home Office to Scrap "Racist Algorithm" for UK Visa Applicants', *The Guardian*, August 4, 2020, https://www.theguardian.com/uk-news/2020/aug/04/home-office-to-scrap-racist-algorithm-for-uk-visa-applicants.

6 Martha Dark, 'UK: Legal Action Threatened over Algorithm Used to Grade Teenagers' Exams', State Watch, August 12, 2020, https://www.statewatch.org/news/2020/august/uk-legal-action-threatened-over-algorithm-used-to-grade-teenagers-exams/.

7 Sally Weale and Heather Stewart, 'A-Level and GCSE Results in England to Be Based on Teacher Assessments in U-Turn', *The Guardian*, August 17, 2020, https://www.theguardian.com/education/2020/aug/17/a-levels-gcse-results-england-based-teacher-assessments-government-u-turn.

8 'Kenya: Meta Sued for 1.6 Billion USD for Fueling Ethiopia Ethnic Violence', Amnesty International, December 14, 2022, https://www.amnesty.org/en/latest/news/2022/12/kenya-meta-sued-for-1-6-billion-usd-for-fueling-ethiopia-ethnic-violence/.

9 Alex Warofka, 'An Independent Assessment of the Human Rights Impact of Facebook in Myanmar', Meta, November 5, 2018, https://about.fb.com/news/2018/11/myanmar-hria/; Sheera Frenkel and Davey Alba, 'In India, Facebook Grapples With an Amplified Version of Its Problems', *The New York Times*, October 23, 2021, https://www.nytimes.com/2021/10/23/technology/facebook-india-misinformation.html.

10 Micah Zenko, 'Obama's Final Drone Strike Data', Council on Foreign Relations, January 20, 2017, https://www.cfr.org/blog/obamas-final-drone-strike-data#:~:text=Less%20than%20two%20weeks%20ago,3%2C797%20people%2C%20including%20324%20civilians.

CHAPTER 9: YOUR FUTURE

1 H. Harding, 'The Impact of Tiananmen on China's Foreign Policy', *The National Bureau of Asian Research* 1, no. 3 (December 1, 1990), https://www.nbr.org/publication/the-impact-of-tiananmen-on-chinas-foreign-policy/.

2 D. Barboza, 'China Surpasses U.S. in Number of Internet Users', *New York Times*, July 26, 2008, https://www.nytimes.com/2008/07/26/business/worldbusiness/26internet.html.

3 Human Rights Watch, 'Human Rights Activism in Post-Tiananmen China', May 30, 2019, https://www.hrw.org/news/2019/05/30/human-rights-activism-post-tiananmen-china.

4 C. Brooker, R. Jones, and M. Schur, 'Nosedive, Season 3 Episode 1', IMDB, October 21, 2016, https://www.imdb.com/title/tt5497778/.

5 L. Maizland, 'China's Repression of Uyghurs in Xinjiang', Council on Foreign Relations, September 22, 2022, https://www.cfr.org/backgrounder/china-xinjiang-uyghurs-muslims-repression-genocide-human-rights#chapter-title-0-1.

6 Maizland.

7 A. Ramzy and C. Buckley, 'The Xinjiang Papers', *The New York Times*, November 16, 2019, https://www.nytimes.com/interactive/2019/11/16/world/asia/china-xinjiang-documents.html.

8 S. Busby, 'Testimony of Deputy Assistant Secretary Scott Busby, Senate Foreign Relations Committee, Subcommittee On East Asia, The Pacific, And International Cybersecurity Policy', https://www.foreign.senate.gov/imo/media/doc/120418_Busby_Testimony.pdf.

9 'The Fight Against Terrorism and Extremism in Xinjiang: Truth and Facts', United Nations Human Rights Office of the High Commissioner, August 2022, https://www.ohchr.org/sites/default/files/documents/countries/2022-08-31/ANNEX_A.pdf.

10 P. Mozur, M. Xiao, and J. Liu, '"An Invisible Cage": How China Is Policing the Future', *The New York Times*, June 25, 2022, https://www.nytimes.com/2022/06/25/technology/china-surveillance-police.html.

11 'Big Data Fuels Crackdown in Minority Region', Humans Rights Watch, February 26, 2018, https://www.hrw.org/news/2018/02/26/china-big-data-fuels-crackdown-minority-region.

12 M. Wang, 'China's Algorithms of Repression', Human Rights Watch, May 2019, https://www.hrw.org/report/2019/05/01/chinas-algorithms-repression/reverse-engineering-xinjiang-police-mass#4458.

13 Human Rights Watch, 'Big Data Program Targets Xinjiang's Muslims', December 9, 2020, https://www.hrw.org/news/2020/12/09/china-big-data-program-targets-xinjiangs-muslims.

14 'Big Data Program Targets Xinjiang's Muslims'.

15 E. Feng, '"Afraid We Will Become The Next Xinjiang": China's Hui Muslims Face Crackdown', *NPR*, September 26, 2019, https://www.npr.org/2019/09/26/763356996/afraid-we-will-become-the-next-xinjiang-chinas-hui-muslims-face-crackdown.

16 Mozur, Xiao, and Liu.

17 A. Mbembe, *Necropolitics* (Duke University Press, 2019).

18 S. Tripathi, 'Abduweli Ayup on Government Use of Facial Recognition Technology', Institute for Human Rights and Business, October 16, 2019, https://voices.ihrb.org/episodes/podcast-abduweli-ayup.

19 P. Mozur, 'In Hong Kong Protests, Faces Become Weapons', *The New York Times*, July 26, 2019, https://www.nytimes.com/2019/07/26/technology/hong-kong-protests-facial-recognition-surveillance.html.

20 S. Bradshaw, 'Influence Operations and Disinformation on Social Media', Centre for International Governance Innovation, 2020, https://www.jstor.org/stable/pdf/resrep27510.9.pdf.

21 Y. Yang and M. Ruehl, 'China's Leading AI Start-Ups Hit by US Blacklisting', *The Financial Times*, October 8, 2019, https://www.ft.com/content/663ab29c-e9bd-11e9-85f4-d00e5018f061.

22 M. Murgia, 'Who's Using Your Face? The Ugly Truth about Facial Recognition', *The Financial Times*, September 18, 2019, https://www.ft.com/content/cf19b956-60a2-11e9-b285-3acd5d43599e.

23 M. Ruehl, P. Riordan, and E. Olcott, 'Can SenseTime Become a Chinese AI Champion?', *The Financial Times*, September 21, 2021, https://www.ft.com/content/c735e0f3-5704-47b5-a76f-7a02d53a1525.

24 J. Pickard and Y. Yang, 'UK Politicians Raise Alarm over Chinese CCTV Providers', *The Financial Times*, July 4, 2022, https://www.ft.com/content/dc74d6ea-8238-456f-9512-931a8cd0656e.

25 Y. Yang, 'UK Limits Use of Chinese-Made Surveillance Systems on Government Sites', *The Financial Times*, November 25, 2022, https://www.ft.com/content/abdc8265-7188-4d59-ab62-596416bc76cb.

26 M. Murgia and C. Shepherd, 'Western AI Researchers Partnered with Chinese Surveillance Firms', *The Financial Times*, April 19, 2019, https://www.ft.com/content/41be9878-61d9-11e9-b285-3acd5d43599e.

27 Y. Yang and M. Murgia, 'Facial Recognition: How China Cornered the Surveillance Market', *The Financial Times*, December 6, 2019, https://www.ft.com/content/6f1a8f48-1813-11ea-9ee4-11f260415385.
28 R. Wu and L. Yuxiu, 'A Law Professor Defends His Rights: The Risks of Facial Recognition Are Greater than You Think', *The Paper, China*, October 21, 2020, https://www.thepaper.cn/newsDetail_forward_9640715.
29 Mozur, Xiao, and Liu.
30 P. Mozur, 'The AI-Surveillance Symbiosis in China: A Big Data China Event', Center for Strategic and International Studies, August 18, 2022, https://www.csis.org/analysis/ai-surveillance-symbiosis-china-big-data-china-event.
31 Y. Yang, 'China's Zero-Covid Protests Create a Rare Nationwide Coalition of Interests', *The Financial Times*, November 28, 2022, https://www.ft.com/content/9fd310a3-cc3f-422a-960c-6a2b63d144dd.
32 P. Mozur, C. Fu, and A. Chang Chien, 'How China's Police Used Phones and Faces to Track Protesters', *The New York Times*, December 4, 2022, https://www.nytimes.com/2022/12/02/business/china-protests-surveillance.html.

CHAPTER 10: YOUR SOCIETY

1 M. Murgia, 'Transformers: The Google Scientists Who Pioneered an AI Revolution', *The Financial Times*, July 23, 2023, https://www.ft.com/content/37bb01af-ee46-4483-982f-ef3921436a50.
2 A. Vaswani et al., 'Attention Is All You Need', *Arxiv*, June 12, 2017, https://arxiv.org/abs/1706.03762.
3 M. Murgia, 'OpenAI's Mira Murati: The Woman Charged with Pushing Generative AI into the Real World', *The Financial Times*, June 18, 2023, https://www.ft.com/content/73f9686e-12cd-47bc-aa6e-52054708b3b3.
4 R. Waters and T. Kinder, 'Microsoft's $10bn Bet on ChatGPT Developer Marks New Era of AI', *The Financial Times*, January 16, 2023, https://www.ft.com/content/a6d71785-b994-48d8-8af2-a07d24f661c5.
5 M. Murgia and Visual Storytelling, 'Generative AI Exists Because of the Transformer', *The Financial Times*, September 12, 2023, https://ig.ft.com/generative-ai/.
6 Murgia and Visual Storytelling.

7 K. Woods, 'GPT Is a Better Therapist than Any Therapist I've Ever Tried', Twitter, April 6, 2023, https://twitter.com/Kat__Woods/status/1644021980948201473.

8 R. Metz, 'AI Therapy Becomes New Use Case for ChatGPT', *Bloomberg Businessweek*, April 18, 2023, https://www.bloomberg.com/news/articles/2023-04-18/ai-therapy-becomes-new-use-case-for-chatgpt?embedded-checkout=true.

9 K. Roose, 'Bing's A.I. Chat: "I Want to Be Alive"', *The New York Times*, February 16, 2023, https://www.nytimes.com/2023/02/16/technology/bing-chatbot-transcript.html.

10 P. Cooper, '#GPT4 Saved My Dog's Life', Twitter, March 25, 2023, https://twitter.com/peakcooper/status/1639716822680236032.

11 M. R. Lee, 'Lawyer Suing Avianca Used ChatGPT Which Invented 6 Cases Now Sanctions Hearing Here', Inner City Press, June 8, 2023, https://www.innercitypress.com/sdny126bcastelaviancachatgpticp060823.html.

12 M. Murgia, 'OpenAI's Red Team: The Experts Hired to "Break" ChatGPT', *The Financial Times*, April 14, 2023, https://www.ft.com/content/0876687a-f8b7-4b39-b513-5fee942831e8.

13 B. Perrigo, S. Shah, and I. Lapowsky, 'TIME 100 AI – Thinkers', *Time*, September 7, 2023, https://time.com/collection/time100-ai/#thinkers.

14 M. Murgia, 'How Actors Are Losing Their Voices to AI', *The Financial Times*, July 1, 2023, https://www.ft.com/content/07d75801-04fd-495c-9a68-310926221554.

15 J. Bridle, 'The Stupidity of AI', *The Guardian*, March 16, 2023, https://www.theguardian.com/technology/2023/mar/16/the-stupidity-of-ai-artificial-intelligence-dall-e-chatgpt#:~:text=They%20enclosed%20our%20imaginations%20in,new%20kinds%20of%20human%20connection.

16 V. Zhou, 'AI Is Already Taking Video Game Illustrators' Jobs in China', *Rest of World*, April 11, 2023, https://restofworld.org/2023/ai-image-china-video-game-layoffs/.

17 Zhou.

18 Spawned, 'We Are Thrilled to Announce That Our Campaign to Gather Artist Opt Outs Has Resulted in 78 Million Artworks Being Opted out of AI Training', Twitter, March 7, 2023, https://twitter.com/spawning_/status/1633196665417920512.

19 T. Chiang, *The Lifecycle of Software Objects* (Subterranean Press, 2010).

20 T. Chiang, 'ChatGPT Is a Blurry JPEG of the Web', *The New Yorker*,

February 9, 2023, https://www.newyorker.com/tech/annals-of-technology/chatgpt-is-a-blurry-jpeg-of-the-web.

21 E. M. Forster, 'The Machine Stops', *Oxford and Cambridge Review*, November 1909.

EPILOGUE

1 M. Murgia and A. Raval, 'AI in Recruitment: The Death Knell of the CV?', *The Financial Times*, June 18, 2023, https://www.ft.com/content/98e5f47a-7d0d-4e63-9a63-ff36d62782b8.

2 A. Glaese et al., 'Improving Alignment of Dialogue Agents via Targeted Human Judgements', *Arxiv*, September 28, 2022, https://doi.org/10.48550/arXiv.2209.14375.

3 Anthropic, 'Claude's Constitution', May 9, 2023, https://www.anthropic.com/index/claudes-constitution.

4 Anthropic.

5 'The Rome Call for AI Ethics', RenAIssance Foundation, February 28, 2020, https://www.romecall.org/the-call/.

6 M. Murgia, 'The Vatican and the Moral Conundrums of AI', *Financial Times*, February 15, 2023, https://www.ft.com/content/40ba0b91-7e72-415b-8ac6-4031252576cc.

7 L. Nicoletti and D. Bass, 'Humans Are Biased. Generative AI Is Even Worse', Bloomberg, June 9, 2023, https://www.bloomberg.com/graphics/2023-generative-ai-bias/.

8 'Microsoft Responsible AI Standard', Microsoft, June 2022.

Index

INDEX

Madhumita Murgia is the first Artificial Intelligence Editor of the *Financial Times* and has been writing about AI and the social impacts of technology, for *Wired* and the *FT*, for over a decade. Born and raised in India, she was educated as an immunologist in the UK. She lives in London.